Praise for *Handle with CARE*

You won't get far into this book without realizing an overwhelming sense of responsibility for your employees because so much employee turnover is caused by the relationship with their supervisor. Just a little further into the book you no longer feel overwhelmed, but excited about all the ways you as a leader can make a difference. I enjoyed the book from cover to cover, but it could also serve as a quick reference for those times we as leaders need to get out of the box to make our companies great places to work.

—Joy Flora, President, Merry Maids

People want to do good work—if they know their manager cares. This book shows managers how to care.

—Jim Cathcart, author,
The Acorn Principle and *Relationship Selling*

Barbara Glanz has figured it out! Have you? The deepest need in human existence is to know that we are loved, accepted, and engaged in work that matters—and this doesn't change just because we walk through the front doors of the office. Address this need in your employees and you will inspire a level of commitment and dedication that the competition finds incredibly hard to replicate! Barbara builds the business case for creating a sense of joy and aliveness among your employees and then offers hundreds of creative ways to get there.

—Kevin Freiberg, co-author of the best-selling
*NUTS! Southwest Airlines' Crazy Recipe for
Business and Personal Success*

Through a unique combination of research, personal experience, and inspirational passion, Barbara shares hundreds of practical, creative ideas for anyone wanting to keep their best and brightest employees.

—Tom Heetderks, Senior Director,
People Development, KFC

Do you want to bring some heart, soul, and humanity back into your workplace? Read this awesome book! Barbara Glanz has compiled joyful, touching tips that will help you to unleash the power of positive energy in your organization and keep your team happy, strong, and invested in their work.

—Patti Rager, R.N., President and Publisher,
Nursing Spectrum

This book challenges all of us who lead to spend more time on our most important asset—people. Don't just read this book—practice it!

—DeBorah Lenchard, Professional Development
and Education, Chicago Mercantile Exchange

Leaders: learn from this book and CARE for your people if you want a stable, productive workforce in this turbulent decade.

—Roger E. Herman, CSP, CMC, FIMC, author,
*Keeping Good People, How to Become an
Employer of Choice* and *Impending Crisis*

Your success as a manager or supervisor depends on the performance of your people. This book will help you get the very best they are capable of giving.

—Mike Stewart, CSP, author, *Close More Sales!
Persuasion Skills That Boost Your Selling Power*

So many people rarely hear a sincere word of appreciation, that when they do, it really brightens their day—and they often tell others about it. I love handling people with CARE!

—Jim Gwinn, CEO, CRISTA

Barbara Glanz has written a thoughtful, provocative book for business managers and leaders who want to create ideal workplaces that foster creativity, motivation, and loyalty. Through research studies and vivid examples, she proves that relationships and sense of purpose are paramount to ideal work, and then offers meaty stories from real-world examples to show how organizations are striving to offer joy and meaning to employees.

—Catherine D. Fyock, CSP, SPHR,
author, *Get the Best*

Anyone who supervisors or manages others needs to read this book. Handle with CARE *is filled with dozens of examples of what top companies are doing to recognize, reward, and rev up their employees. Using research results, case studies, and immediately implementable action ideas, Barbara Glanz is a master at showing us how to CARE for our employees.*

—Joan Brannick, Ph.D., author,
Hiring@NetSpeed, and co-author,
Finding and Keeping Great Employees

HANDLE WITH CARE: MOTIVATING AND RETAINING YOUR EMPLOYEES

Barbara A. Glanz, CSP

McGraw-Hill

New York Chicago San Francisco Lisbon London
Madrid Mexico City Milan New Delhi San Juan
Seoul Singapore Sydney Toronto

McGraw-Hill

A Division of The McGraw·Hill Companies

The sponsoring editor for this book was Richard Narramore. Design, production, and editorial services provided by CWL Publishing Enterprises, Inc., Madison, Wisconsin, www.cwlpub.com. Editing by Robert Magnan.

Printed and bound by Quebecor World Martinsburg.

This publication is designed to provide accurate and authoritative information in regard to the subject matter covered. It is sold with the understanding that neither the author nor the publisher is engaged in rendering legal, accounting, or other professional service. If legal advice or other expert assistance is required, the services of a competent professional person should be sought.
—*From a Declaration of Principles jointly adopted by a Committee of the American Bar Association and a Committee of Publishers*

This book is printed on recycled, acid-free paper containing a minimum of 50% recycled de-inked fiber.

Contents

Dedication

To my God, who has blessed me with the awesome
privilege of being His messenger in a hurting world.

To my husband in Heaven, without whose love
and support I could never have become the person I am.

And to all the supervisors and managers out there who are
already CARE-ing for their precious employees.

The author has donated 10% of all royalties from this book to CARE
International Relief and Development Agency.

Foreword

I t is often said that the little things make the biggest difference. This is particularly true when energizing and engaging employees in the workplace.

If every leader read this book and adopted a few of the simple to implement ideas presented by Barbara Glanz, the workplace would be a warm and friendly place. And there would never be another discussion about employee retention.

As an HR leader, I am dismayed to find that business leaders often fail to pay attention to the little things that make the biggest difference in the lives of their team members. A pat on the back, a high five, or a simple "thank you" can be more effective than a raise or a bonus if it comes from the heart.

This book provides simple, yet effective ideas from real life leaders and organizations that can be implemented in any work environment with wonderful results.

Barbara Glanz has presented practical and useful suggestions to help business leaders retain the best talent. This book should be part of every manager's toolkit. It is full of ideas that work in any environment to engage the hearts and minds of employees.

—Libby Sartain
Senior Vice President
and Chief People Yahoo,
Yahoo! Inc.

Preface

This book has come out of my deep passion to help organizations create workplaces that are more caring, creative, and fun. It is my belief that the place where one works should be a place of *joy*. We spend more hours of our lives in that place than in any other, and the good news is that it is not hard for this spirit to happen and it doesn't have to cost a lot of money. As you will see, that spirit of joy can begin with just a single person anywhere in an organization and it can spread throughout a workplace in ways that are almost miraculous.

This book is a testimonial to those individuals and organizations that have made a commitment to creating a workplace that is more than just about the bottom line. We have spent so much time in the past decade focusing on systems and processes that we have forgotten about human beings. And now, with the advent of technology that goes beyond our wildest dreams, it is even more critical for organizations to focus on their people.

All the research shows that what people really want much more than money is a feeling that their work is important and appreciated and that they are respected and valued as human beings and partners in whatever work they have chosen. We interviewed over 1,200 non-management workers in preparing this manuscript, and we found some interesting things:

- ▶ People do not quit organizations. They quit bosses.
- ▶ People are searching for a sense of purpose and meaning in their work, no matter what that work is.
- ▶ People want to be respected as whole human beings with a life outside of work.
- ▶ People will do almost anything for a supervisor or manager who respects and appreciates them.

We know that the average cost of replacing an employee is approximately $50,000, and the current labor pool is shrinking. So, retention is a critical issue for nearly every organization in business today. As I have interviewed people across the country, I have asked them the question, "Why did you leave your last job?" Amazingly, 7% said they left their last job *because their supervisor or manager did not say "good morning" to them*. Keeping good people can be as simple as treating people with common courtesy!

Over and over, as I speak and consult with organizations, I am finding that many supervisors and managers exemplify what the decades-old Peter Principle suggests: people are promoted to their level of incompetency. What I find is that very often supervisors or managers have been promoted because they were great at a frontline or lower-level job; yet most of the time they are given little, if any, training for this new position. It is just assumed that because they were great at a lower-level job, they will be good at this one.

Understandably, these bosses are often insecure and fearful in their roles, and they simply do not understand what their employees really want. Instead, they try to find ways to give them more money or benefits, and spend little or no time on building relationships. This book is all about the importance of relationships and recognizing workers as human beings. When supervisors and managers *really internalize* the principles in this book and then have lots of choices of ideas to make these principles come alive in their workplace, I guarantee that turnover will go down, productivity will go up, and people will begin to truly enjoy their work experience.

This book is divided into four parts:

Part 1. The Research. The first section will be a discussion of the purpose of the book and some foundational concepts and models, other current research, the process of our research, and the research results directly from frontline workers.

Part 2. Ideas and Stories from Managers, Employees, and Organizations Who CARE. This section will focus on the results of the research from the perspective of an actual manager's experience with frontline workers and professional staff.

Part 3. How to CARE: Dozens of Action Ideas. The third section is a resource of dozens of immediately applicable action ideas to support the research results. These ideas are organized according to the acronym "CARE," representing the elements of a joyful workplace: C = Creative Communication; A = Atmosphere and Appreciation for All; R = Respect and Reason for Being; E = Empathy and Enthusiasm.

Appendices. This part of the book contains exercises and tools for managers and supervisors to use with their employees on an ongoing basis to determine their progress in creating a "CARE-ing" environment as well as a bibliography.

This book is intended primarily for supervisors and managers and those who would like to be one someday. Since they receive the least amount of training in most organizations and the research has shown them to be the *most critical link* to employee motivation and retention, their behavior will, to a large extent, determine whether or not employees are happy and productive. I would like to help them become leaders who affirm, support, develop, and coach their employees instead of bosses who criticize, demand, and intimidate them.

Use this book as a resource and guide to help supervisors and managers in any organization to

- ▸ understand what their employees *really* want,
- ▸ "whack" their thinking with dozens of simple, low-cost, creative ideas that they, too, can implement in their workplaces, and
- ▸ use tools to measure how they are doing in their desire to motivate and retain their employees.

It is my belief that after reading this book, supervisors and managers should be held personally accountable for the turnover in their departments. As they learn to build relationships on the human level and to create an environment of trust, respect, and joy, their employees will choose to do their best work, and everyone will win.

In the fourth annual *United States @ Work® Study 2000*, Aon Consulting's Loyalty Institute found that "Management's ability to create a 'sense of pride and spirit' in an organization is the most effective way to recruit, retain, and motivate a high-performance work force." Please share your ideas with me as you find ways to bring more joy to your places of work. Together we can help to make this world a kinder, gentler place for all of us to live and work.

Barbara A. Glanz, CSP
Barbara Glanz Communications, Inc.
E-mail: bglanz@barbaraglanz.com
Web site: www.barbaraglanz.com

Acknowledgments

I want to thank **Anita Vigil** of the Shedd Aquarium for all her help on this book. She is one of the best managers I have ever met in all my work with organizations. She is compassionate and caring as well as tough when it comes to quality work, integrity, and high standards. Thank you, Anita, for your reality checks and especially for your friendship!

To **John McPherson**, my friend and creator of "Close to Home" for generously letting me use so many of his precious cartoons. John, you always make me smile and sometimes even laugh out loud.

To **Mike Chiodo** of Domino's Franchise Association for his help on the original questionnaire.

To **Antonette Addante** and **Matt Glenn** for inputting all the data.

To **Mike and John Morey** of Morey & Associates for analysis of the data.

To **Mary Schulz** for help with research.

To **Shannon Johnston**, a dear friend and mentor for many years, who gave me computer help as well as honest advice on the instruments I created as a result of our research.

To my special friend, **Mike Stewart**, who listened, advised, encouraged, and made me laugh during long hours of writing and editing.

To my assistant, **Norma O'Day**, for keeping the office going when I was off in Florida writing, for help in getting all the permissions, and especially for the long hours preparing the notes. She even worked on her birthday!

To **Larry Emond**, Chief Marketing Officer at The Gallup Oganization, who shared with me much valuable information.

To **all the writers and researchers** who gave me permission to use their work.

To **all my client friends** who contributed ideas, encouragement, and faith in this project.

A special thank-you goes to all the staff at Horizons West on Siesta Key in Sarasota, Florida—**Pat, Lorrie, Jeff, Jeff, Steve, Bonnie,** and **Cathy**. Most of this book was written while I was at our little villa there, and these are the folks who helped me survive without my wonderful husband. They took care of my car, did small jobs around the house, helped with cleaning when company came so I could write, and generally took care of me when I was alone and newly widowed. They have all become my friends.

Introduction

Did you know?

- Between the ages of 21 and 65 we spend roughly 11,000 days of our lives in the workplace.

Did you know?

- 46% of employees leaving a company do so because they feel unappreciated.
- 61% said their bosses don't place much importance on them as people.
- 88% said they do not receive acknowledgment for the work they do.

Did you know?

According to a February 2001 study by Development Dimensions International titled *Retaining Talent: A Benchmarking Study*, almost one-third of all employees surveyed expect to leave for another job within the next year. About 20% estimate their chances of leaving to be greater than 50%.[1]

Keeping good people as they're being offered more money, bigger perks, and better benefits is harder than ever. And it's going to get tougher. By the year 2008, there will be an estimated 161 million jobs for 155 million workers. So it's important to know that, to a large extent, employees stay because their managers create a place where they want to be. In their fourth annual *United States @ Work® Study 2000*, Aon Consulting found that "Management's ability to create a 'sense of pride and spirit' in an organization is the most effective way to recruit, retain, and motivate a high-performance work force."[2]

Marcus Buckingham, a senior vice president at The Gallup Organization, based in Princeton, New Jersey, has polled more than two million employees at 700 companies worldwide for an ongoing workplace-trends project over a 25-year period. He found that immediate supervisors are the single largest influence on an employee's decision to quit. "People leave managers, not companies," Buckingham says in an article titled "Best Bosses Tell All" by Margaret Littman in *Working Woman*, October 2000.[3]

This was the conclusion of the Gallup study: "The length of an employee's stay in an organization is largely determined by his relationship with his immediate supervisor." And Development Dimensions International in Pittsburgh, Pennsylvania, found that the major attractions employees look for in an organization are work/life balance, meaningful work, trust, and a better relationship with their bosses:

> An employee's relationship with his or her supervisor or manager and work-life balance are the most important determinants for staying with an organization.
>
> Motivational fit and cooperation and trust play a large role in determining employee retention. Employees want to work in a supportive environment that gives them an opportunity to make meaningful contributions. The top five factors affecting an employee's decision to stay or leave are listed below. The percentage of employees who rated the factor as *very important for retention* is listed in parentheses.

- Quality of relationship with supervisor or manager (78%)
- Ability to balance work and home life (78%)
- Amount of meaningful work—the feeling of making a difference (76%)
- Level of cooperation with co-workers (74%)
- Level of trust in the workplace (71%)

This same study found that rather than going away, job turnover is going into overdrive. The DDI surveys show that 31% of employees are dissatisfied or neutral about their jobs. Also, 42% of HR professionals reported higher turnover this year than last. 43% expect it to continue at that high level next year, and 31% expect turnover to increase even more. *98% of HR professionals admitted their organizations need to do better at employee retention.*[4]

USA Today on September 2, 1998, featured a Dun & Bradstreet study that reported, "Small-business owners and managers expect retaining good workers to become their biggest problem in the coming year."

It has long been a concern of management to determine what motivates frontline and hourly workers and keeps them committed to the job. Today, however, an even newer problem exists—for the first time ever, there is a dearth of workers to fill all the frontline positions available. Turnover is at its highest ever, and organizations are scrambling to attract and retain the few workers who are left.

Not only has the overall work ethic and long-term loyalty to an organization significantly declined for this employment level, but also frontline and hourly workers now have more choices than ever, so the norm has become bouncing from job to job.

Our belief is that in order for organizations which rely on frontline and hourly workers to survive, they must learn more about this vitally important sector of the workforce and their unique needs—and they need to learn from the workers themselves!

Since supervisors and lower level managers receive the least amount of training in most organizations and our research has shown them to be the *most critical link* to employee retention, this book is specifically designed for them.

Notes

1. Development Dimensions International. 2001. *Retaining Talent: A Benchmarking Study*.

2. Editor. 2000. "New Perks Won't Solve All Your Retention Problems." *HR Magazine*, July, p. 10. (Aon Consulting, *Fourth Annual United States @ Work® Study 2000*.)

3. Littman, Margaret. 2000. "Best Bosses Tell All." *Working Woman*, October.

4. The Recognition Practice, 3033 W. 109th Place, Westminster, CO 80031-6825.

PART 1

THE RESEARCH IS IN—
UNDERSTANDING WHAT
MOTIVATES EMPLOYEES

Chapter 1

What the Research on Employee Motivation Shows

Insofar as employee commitment exists, it is to the boss, to the team, and to the project. That's different from loyalty, which previously was to the name on the building or to the brand. Therefore, any retention strategy must be driven by individual managers and supervisors, not just the folks in human resources.

—President, Aon Consulting

As reported in *The New York Times* from the U.S. Conference of Mayors, the projected number of low-skill workers for each available job in 2003:

- ▸ Detroit: 24
- ▸ Newark: 12
- ▸ New York: 6
- ▸ Chicago: 5

▶ Washington: 2
▶ Los Angeles/Long Beach: 2
▶ Miami: 1[1]

Study after study has been done to determine what frontline and professional staff really want, and the results have been nearly the same for years. However, many supervisors and managers seem to have discounted these results as "soft" and have not really listened to what their employees are saying. In fact, they often blame organizational policy or pay scale for the loss of employees when the exciting news is that they have more power than anyone else to keep good employees in their organization.

In a study conducted in 1946, 1981, and 1995, 1,000 employees

Employees	Supervisors
1. Interesting work	1. Good wages
2. Full appreciation of work done	2. Job security
3. Feeling of being in on things	3. Promotion and growth in the org.
4. Job security	4. Good working conditions
5. Good wages	5. Interesting work
6. Promotion and growth in the org.	6. Personal loyalty to employees
7. Good working conditions	7. Tactful discipline
8. Personal loyalty to employees	8. Full appreciation of work done
9. Tactful discipline	9. Sympathetic help with personal problems
10. Sympathetic help with problems	10. Feeling of being in on things

Figure 1-1. The difference between what employees think is important and what supervisors think is important. From Kovach, Kenneth A. 1995. "Employee Motivation: Addressing a Crucial Factor in Your Organization's Performance." *Employment Relations Today*, Vol. 22, No. 2. New York: John Wiley & Sons, Inc.

were asked to rank-order 10 rewards in terms of motivational value. Immediately afterward, the employees' supervisors were asked to rank the rewards as they thought the employees would.

What is most interesting to me about this study is:

1. How little supervisors and managers *really* understand their employees.
2. How little actual control they have over the things they *think* their employees want (good wages, job security, promotion and growth in the organization).
3. How *much* control they have over the things employees actually want (interesting work, full appreciation of work done, and a feeling of being in on things).
4. Even though the study was first done 55 years ago, employees still want many of the same things from their jobs.

In their book, *Love 'Em or Lose 'Em: Getting Good People to Stay* (San Francisco: Berrett-Koehler Publishers, Inc., 1999, 2nd edition, 2002), Beverly Kaye and Sharon Jordan-Evans share their research on the most common reasons people stay with an organization, listed in order of popularity and frequency. They also point out that 90% of the respondents listed at least one of the first three items among the top three or four reasons they stayed:

- ▶ Career growth, learning and development
- ▶ Exciting work and challenge
- ▶ Meaningful work, making a difference and a contribution
- ▶ Great people
- ▶ Being part of a team
- ▶ Good boss
- ▶ Recognition for work well done
- ▶ Fun on the job
- ▶ Autonomy, sense of control over my work
- ▶ Flexibility—for example, in work hours and dress code

- Fair pay and benefits
- Inspiring leadership
- Pride in organization, its mission, and quality of product
- Great work environment
- Location
- Job security
- Family-friendly
- Cutting-edge technology[2]

(Reprinted with permission from Beverly Kaye and Sharon Jordan-Evans)

Which of these are important to your employees and which ones are in your control as a supervisor or manager?

The Gallup Organization has also studied the effect of how workers' attitudes, emotions, and behaviors impacted the bottom line in a workplace. They conducted hundreds of focus groups and thousands of worker interviews in all kinds of organizations, at all levels, in most industries and in many countries. From this input, researchers identified the major satisfaction generators, the key elements that supervisors might significantly influence and control, as opposed to those they might be powerless to do anything about, such as rates of pay and hours of work.

The elements of worker engagement they found most powerfully linked to improved business outcomes such as growth, productivity, and loyalty were such things as clear expectations from management, being able to do what they do best, having proper materials and equipment, receiving immediate recognition, being cared about as a human being, being asked their opinions, feeling a sense of mission about their jobs, having a friend to talk to at work, and having opportunities for growth and development.

Their conclusion was that degrees of engagement vary in departments throughout the organization, so employee satisfaction is more dependent on the local atmosphere than on that of the whole corporation. This supports our finding that people do not quit organizations.

They quit bosses.

In a survey for Kepner-Tregoe management consultants, Yankelovich Partners found:

▶ Workers don't like their companies. There is a really alienated workforce.

▶ 60% of workers say they are not rewarded or recognized for good job performance, while 63% believe poor job performance receives immediate attention.

▶ 63% of workers say their supervisors don't know what motivates them to do their best.

▶ Empowerment is a joke in many companies. Workers still feel their input is not valued. 33% say their employers never value their ideas.

▶ 41% of workers feel their team assignments are unrealistic or unfair; 80% of their managers disagree.[3]

In their never-ending quest to cut overhead, many companies are turning to new micro-cubicles.

Close to Home by John McPherson/Dist by Universal Press Syndicate

All of these issues revolve around the relationship between management and staff, but ironically, managers are usually not chosen for their interpersonal skills but rather for their ability to achieve financial objectives. It is our mission in this book to help supervisors and managers understand that in order to achieve the highest financial objectives, they must first respect and value their employees.

The Inventure Group, Eden Prairie, Minnesota, interviewed 5,000 employees from a variety of organizations to discover how connected people were with their jobs. They found that only 10 to 15% of the workforce is truly "engaged" in their work, giving their very best to their jobs. 8 to 10% are "burned out," suffering from over-engagement. They are disoriented and are experiencing a loss of passion and an overwhelming sense of tiredness.

This leaves 75 to 80% of our workforce that is "rusted out"— doing the bare minimum. They are disengaged, using their time to avoid committing more than absolutely necessary. They want to keep their job but are not doing it to the best of their ability. I call these folks "slot-fillers" and, according to the experts, they make up the majority of today's workforce. The Inventure Group's conclusion: "Doing enough to get by might well become America's new work ethic!"[4]

Baxter International did an 18-month study with their employees worldwide and found that what their employees globally valued most was *being respected as whole human beings with a life beyond work.*[5] Aon Consulting's *America @ Work®* *Study 1998* found that of 17 factors that correlate significantly to workforce commitment, salary did not make the top 10. The top thing employees said affected their commitment to their employer was "an employer's recognition of the importance of personal and family time."[6]

The Hay Group, in a three-year survey of employee attitudes in which satisfaction with more than 50 factors was analyzed, reported that 69% of "committed" employees—workers planning to stay with their employers for more than five years—found their greatest satis-faction in "respectful treatment."[7]

In the *Fortune* article, "The 100 Best Companies to Work for in America" (January 12, 1998), Anne Fisher writes,

> A formal retention program, which often includes enticements like big cash bonuses for longevity, is better than nothing. But it probably won't help much if a company hasn't already created a culture that makes people want to stick around. Make no mistake; it's commitment that creates meaning in their work and it's meaningful work that moti-

vates Southwest employees to be the most productive workforce in the U.S. airline industry.[8]

Supervisors and managers, in their day-to-day interaction with employees, help create the culture of an organization, and it is often their individual behavior that either results in committed, loyal, motivated employees or causes employees to leave the organization. A study by the Saratoga Institute found that the 10 issues most related to work satisfaction and the intention to stay or to leave are more influenced by an employee's immediate supervisor than by any other organizational position or person.[9]

Sharon Jordan-Evans, the co-author of *Love 'Em or Lose 'Em: Getting Good People to Stay*, says emphatically, "People don't quit companies. They quit bosses." Ruth Roth, Director of HR Policies for the Charles Schwab Corporation, says, "Everything we learn about retention always leads us back to managers."[10] It is my experience that, as supervisors and managers begin to relate to rtheir employeees on a more human level, retention and motivation will no longer be such critical issues.

The ideas in this book will help supervisors and managers create a new relatonship of trust, appreciation, and respect with their employees, resulting in happier workers, higher productivity, and a workplace of CARE-ing and joy.

Notes

1. "The Welfare Challenge in America's Cities." Survey by the U.S. Conference of Mayors. 202-293-7330.
2. Kaye, Beverly, and Jordan-Evans, Sharon. 1999. *Love 'Em or Lose 'Em: Getting Good People to Stay*. San Francisco, CA: Berrett-Koehler Publishers, Inc., p. 6.
3. Yankelovich Partners, 20 Glover Avenue, Norwalk CT 06850, 203-846-0100, www.yankelovich.com.
4. Association for Quality and Participation. 1997. "The Death of

Ambition—Only 10% of Workers Are Engaged." Excerpted from *News for a Change,* November, p. 4.

5. Editor. 1998. "Work/Life Study = Respect." *Employee Services Management (ESM) Magazine,* March, p. 6.

6. Aon Consulting. *America @ Work® Study 1998.* 800-438-6487. www.aon.com.

7. Editor. 1997. "Getting Personal." *Entrepreneur,* December, p. 120.

8. Fisher, Anne. 1998. "The 100 Best Companies to Work for in America." *Fortune.* January 12, pp. 68-70.

9. Saratoga Institute. 2001. *Summary of Employee Retention Findings.* www.saratoga-institute.com.

10. Kaye, Beverly, and Jordan-Evans, Sharon. 1999. *Love 'Em or Lose 'Em: Getting Good People to Stay.* San Francisco, CA: Berrett-Koehler Publishers, Inc.

Chapter 2

Our Study

Background of the Study

My associates and I designed a questionnaire that covers what we feel are the essential elements in understanding the motivation of frontline workers. The questionnaire (a description of which is included in Appendix D) contains a combination of qualitative and quantitative questions and is simply and clearly written. Above all, it is actionable and results in actual implementable information. The ultimate question is *What do these frontline workers REALLY want from their managers and from their jobs?*

We defined our target group as any workers who were non-management, including frontline, hourly, and professional staff. We obtained over 1,200 responses to the questionnaire from a large variety of industries that depend on frontline workers, including organizations in both the profit and non-profit sectors. Some of these organizations, both large and small, are:

- Domino's Pizza
- Boeing
- Robins & Morton Group (construction)
- Great Clips
- APAC TeleServices
- Priority Health Services
- Deloitte & Touche
- Downriver Guidance Clinic, Southgate, MI
- New York Aquarium
- Aquarium of the Americas, New Orleans
- Holiday Inns
- The Field Museum, Chicago
- Zondervan Publishing
- Round Table Pizza
- Hyatt Hotels
- Stiles Machinery, Inc.
- Trinity Towers of Coastal Bend, Corpus Christi, TX
- Hoops Drive-In, Blytheville, AR
- Central Avenue Grill Los Alamos, NM
- CGH Medical Center, Sterling, IL
- Brooks Construction Co.

- KFC (Tricon)
- Family Christian Stores
- Embassy Suites Hotels
- State of Idaho
- Hilton Hotels
- Strong Mutual Funds
- Development Centers
- The John G. Shedd Aquarium
- Hilltop Diner
- National Aquarium, Baltimore
- The Adler Planetarium, Chicago
- State of Wyoming
- Lufkin National Bank Co., TX
- 7-Eleven, Inc.
- School District 96, IL
- Savings Bank of Rockville, IL
- Wetherill Associates, Inc.
- Ticketmaster
- Wood Lane Residential Services, Bowling Green, OH
- Monroe County Sheriff's Office

The Results

In this chapter I will highlight the results that we thought were significant.

Respondent Data

Wages
- 6% Earned $4-$6
- 31% Earned $8-$12
- 24% Earned $6-$8
- 16% Earned $12 or More

Education
- 6% Still in High School
- 11% In College
- 22% Finished College
- 18% Finished High School
- 40% Some College
- 4 % Post-Graduate Work

First Job
- 4% Yes
- 96% No

Number of Prior Jobs
- 4% One
- 15% Three
- 15% Five
- 7% Two
- 18% Four
- 42% Six or More

Age
- 7% 15-20
- 11% 25-30
- 50% Over 40
- 10% 20-25
- 21% 30-40

How Affect Life if Lose Job
- 62% Horrible
- 32% Not matter
- 5% Blessing

Plan on Staying with Organization
- 67% Not Very Long
- 33% A Long Time

Summary of Respondent Data. Over half the respondents earned $8 to $12 an hour, were over 40, had had some college, and had had five to six prior jobs. Two thirds of them thought it would be awful if they lost their jobs and that same number said they did not plan on staying with their organization very long.

Factors That Encourage You to Do Your Very Best

We asked respondents to rate these factors as "None," "Very Little," "Some," "Quite a Bit," or "A Whole Lot." Then we added the percentages of "Quite a Bit" and "A Whole Lot" to rank-order the items in terms of how respondents viewed them as motivators. These are the results (percentage of respondents who said "Quite a Bit" or "A Whole Lot"):

- ▶ Being Trusted 91%
- ▶ Doing Meaningful Work 88%
- ▶ Feeling Appreciated 88%
- ▶ Better Training 86%
- ▶ Being Treated Fairly 86%
- ▶ Doing Interesting Work 85%
- ▶ Being Respected 83%
- ▶ Having the Right Tools for the Job 78%
- ▶ Opportunity for Advancement 74%
- ▶ Freedom to Make Decisions 72%
- ▶ Knowing What Is Going on in the Company 70%
- ▶ Great Benefits 70%
- ▶ Involvement in Decision Making 66%
- ▶ Being Evaluated Regularly 58%
- ▶ Flexible Hours 57%
- ▶ Getting More Money 56%

Summary: Employee retention is not about money! Retention is about the human level, how employees are treated as people. As we look at this data as well as many other studies that have been done, we see that what employees want most is to be respected and treated as valuable human beings.

The most important information that comes from this study is that if supervisors and managers meet the human needs of these employees, they *will* stay, reducing turnover and creating commitment to the organization. The rest of this book will give you ideas about how you can do that.

Other Interesting Findings

When we asked employees if their job was fun, we received the following information:

- 33% Almost always
- 63% Sometimes
- 4% Never

When we asked if pay was enough to keep them if their job was *not* fun, we received these results:

- 36% Yes
- 64% No

Two thirds of our respondents said money would not keep them in an organization that did not create an environment of joy. Several other responses were interesting:

Are you treated fairly?

- 54% Almost always
- 42% Sometimes
- 4% Never

This means that over 400 of our respondents feel that they are only treated fairly part of the time and 40 of them feel that they are never treated fairly.

Do you feel listened to?

- Enough
- 40% Not enough
- 6% Not at all

Over 400 respondents do not feel they are listened to enough and 60 of them feel they are not listened to at all.

Are you recognized for extra effort?

- 58% Yes
- 42% No

Over 400 respondents out of 1,200 do not feel they have been recognized appropriately. However, when we asked if not being recognized for extra effort affected their treatment of customers, 86% said it did *not* affect how they treated customers, which indicates a sense of personal pride in their work.

When asked if their pay was fair, 44% responded "yes" and 56% responded "no," indicating a concern about reimbursement.

When we asked them about customer service, we received some interesting answers:

What kind of service does your organization give?
- 50% Great
- 49% O.K.
- 1% Bad

What kind of service do you give?
- 74% Great
- 26% O.K.

75% said it was important to give great service. The interesting thing here is the difference between what kind of service they feel they give and what kind of service their whole organization gives. Could this be a difference between perception and reality ?

We also found some concerns with communication:

Does your manager give clear instructions?
- 41% Always
- 46% Occasionally
- 12% Not usually
- 1% Never

Are you given clear priorities?
- 53% Yes
- 17% No
- 30% Occasionally

Do you agree with the priorities?
- 18% Always
- 81% Sometimes
- 1% Never

The lack of agreement on priorities suggests a difference in perspective. So often the frontline workers know much more than management about what is *really* going on and what is *really* important. If we think about the question on listening and the fact that over 400 respondents did not feel listened to enough, it probably means that management has not taken time to ask the employees for input or, if they've asked, perhaps they haven't really listened.

In general we found that most of these respondents were quite satisfied with their job conditions:

- ▶ 81% said they had enough of the right tools to do their job.
- ▶ 73% were evaluated regularly.
- ▶ 82% felt the evaluation process was fair.
- ▶ 91% had an opportunity to give input during their evaluations.
- ▶ 92% are proud of where they work.
- ▶ 79% felt they had a boss who cared about them, although 21% (200+ respondents) did not.
- ▶ 76% felt they were respected.
- ▶ 79% respected their manager.
- ▶ 89% knew what was expected of them.
- ▶ 77% said their company has a mission statement and 74% of them knew it. However, only 51% felt it helped them to do a better job.
- ▶ 88% felt their job was "very important" to the success of their organization.

Open-Ended Questions

Many of the answers to these open-ended questions were very poignant. I have included the most frequent answers as well as some of the most touching comments. What was very interesting is that in these questions, "money" as an answer was ranked higher than in the responses to what motivated them in the earlier, more objective part of the survey, where money was ranked the lowest. My suspicion is that, when asked what they need, employees often say "money" because it is easier and more acceptable to express than their deepest feelings and needs.

What has kept you from looking for another job?

The most often mentioned answers were:

- Love Their Work
- People
- Interesting Work
- Positive Atmosphere
- Benefits
- Flexible Hours

What would make you leave your job?

The most often mentioned answers were:

- Lack of Trust/Respect
- More Money
- Bad Management/Boss
- No Advancement

If you could select one thing management could do to make coming to work more enjoyable, what would it be?

The most often mentioned answers were:

- Fair treatment
- Appreciation
- Relaxed Atmosphere/Fun
- Clear Communication
- Freedom to Do Work
- Trust/Respect
- Positive Attitude

Some of the most powerful comments were:

- Treat people like human beings, don't be so obsessed with errors.
- Make everyone feel that they are important to this institution.
- A more relaxed atmosphere, less suspicion, less animosity.
- Sincerity and positive attitude by management.
- Take time to greet and visit with each employee, even if only for a minute.
- Positive co-workers—shelve the nasty gossip, get in, sit down, hold on, and shut up.
- Don't hover over us like a vacuum.
- Our supervisor already does this. When we turn in our time sheets, we get treats. She sends birthday cards and once a month carry-ins. She really boosts morale and brings us closer.
- No temper tantrums.

- Notice Me!
- Have more faith in me.
- Smile/Good Morning.
- Let us know what is going on.
- Treat everyone equally.
- Get rid of the negativity.
- Trust me.
- Being included.
- Fewer Meetings.
- Let me go to class.
- Have confidence in my abilities.
- Be more open.
- Make a hard job more fun.
- Less bickering.
- Be at work and take care of problems.
- Less bureaucracy.
- Focus on your own department.
- No guilt trips.
- Lighten up!
- Be more approachable.
- Support me in conflicts.
- Listen to my ideas.
- Recognize the good.
- Fire negative co-workers.
- Emphasize family more.
- Get to know me personally.
- Atmosphere of hope.
- Stop jumping to conclusions.
- Voice to speak/Space to breathe.
- Be yourself.
- Treat me like a human.
- More compassion.

Besides money, what would you like for rewards and recognition?

The most often mentioned answers were:

- Appreciation—Words
- Time off
- Trust/Respect
- Freedom
- Training

Is there anything else you want to say?

- This survey was so timely—just today after being treated coldly by a disgruntled boss who had had a bad weekend, I once again wondered why I stay. Fortunately, others I work with and for make a big difference. Money is fine, but the biggest thing to me is respect.
- I had a supervisor that would pick a different office person a day and tell them how inept or incompetent we were. Not a good situation.
- I love working with my co-workers and clients. But we need more communication and recognition is very poor.
- I am not appreciated for what I do as a person.
- I'm more motivated in the workplace when I'm respected and trusted.
- I have a great situation. My boss always encourages me, makes me feel important. That makes me want to do my best.
- Management doesn't understand.
- *Listen* to workers!
- I hope my comments count.
- I used to work where I never heard "thank you" and now I hear it all the time.
- The frontline gets a bum rap.
- I would appreciate being treated as an adult.
- Recognize our gifts.
- Guest service is thankless.
- Coming to work should not be a drag.

- Management lowers morale.
- A lot of people don't get credit.
- I *do* make a difference!
- There is so little recognition of spirit.
- Work should be more fun.
- Together, we can do anything.
- So glad you're doing this survey.
- Pay is not the only thing that is important.
- Managers have separated themselves.
- My boss is not positive.
- Everyone is valuable.
- This boosts my faith.
- What happened to the team?
- Upper management forgets little people.
- If things don't change, a lot of people will leave.

Chapter 3

Two Models for
Understanding Your Employees

One of the models I use as the foundation for all my work is the Human-Business Model (Figure 3-1). It is a visual representation of every interaction we have with anyone. In each interaction there are two levels: the *business* level, meeting whatever the person's external needs are, and the *human* level, which is all about how the person feels during that interaction.

All over the world I ask two questions of my audiences:

▸ Have you ever been to a doctor who treated you only on the business level? How did that make you feel?

▸ Have you ever worked for a manager who interacted with you only on the business level? Did you do your best work for that person?

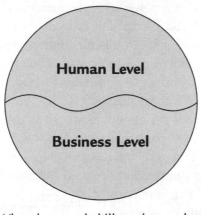

When love and skill work together,
expect a masterpiece.   —Charles Reade

Figure 3-1. Human-Business Model—in any interaction, two sides, personal and financial
Reprinted with permission from *CARE Packages for the Workplace: Dozens of Little Things You Can Do to Regenerate Spirit at Work* (McGraw-Hill, 1996), p. 12.

As a supervisor or manager, you probably spend most of your time in the bottom half of the Human-Business Model. But do you have a relationship with each of your direct reports on the human level? Do you know something about their family situation? Do you know the passion of each one of your employees (what really excites them, where they spend their free time)? Do you find ways to remember personal things about them and to comment on them or ask questions, to share interesting ideas, articles, or materials that relate to their passionate interest?

By taking the time to remember something personal about an employee, a manager shows how important each individual is to the organization, and that is the beginning of a relationship. Human beings worldwide are crying out to be recognized as valuable human beings, not simply workers, objects, or numbers.

This model is also a powerful representation of what it means to coach an employee. The information or feedback communicated is the business level, but *how* it is given is the human level. I often ask, "Has anyone ever given you painful information but in a kind and caring way?" That is a perfect example of the Human-Business Model in action.

My definition of a great manager is "A Developer of People." A manager who coaches an employee on both the business and the human levels and gives constructive feedback will help the employee develop into a better person and a better employee. Employees rarely leave managers and supervisors who treat them with care and respect!

Another model that is important in understanding interactions is the Choice Model. It basically says that in any interaction we have with anyone, we have three choices: We can either discount that person by making him or her feel less important than us or the organization (-), we can just take care of the person's business need (0), or we can create a human-level connection (+). The "slot filler," who does just enough to get by, becomes simply a transaction giver. But when one creates a human-level connection, he or she is building a relationship, a skill that supervisors and managers need to cultivate in order to retain their employees and likewise employees need to learn to retain their customers.

> You were given a lot of wonderful powers. You have the power to think, to love, to create, to imagine, to plan. The greatest power you have is the power to choose. Wherever you are today, you are there because you chose to be there.
> —Lou Holtz

Some time ago I spoke at the Hyatt Regency Hotel in downtown Chicago, and my husband and I stayed afterwards to have lunch in their garden restaurant. Our waiter, Mario, was being very attentive. About the second or third time he came to our table, I said "Mario, you're doing a great job, and I really like your smile."

He began to beam, stood up very tall, and replied, "You can just call me 'Super Mario!'" The touching result was that for the rest of the

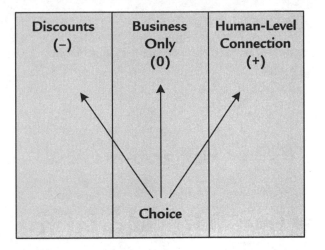

Discounts (–)	Business Only (0)	Human-Level Connection (+)

Choice

The choice we offer people is what creates accountability. —Peter Block, *Stewardship*

Figure 3-2. A choice in any interaction
Reprinted with permission from *CARE Packages for the Workplace: Dozens of Little Things You Can Do to Regenerate Spirit at Work* (McGraw-Hill, 1996), p. 11.

hour we were there, he *was* "super Mario." I took the time to recognize him as a person and to thank him for his good work, and he simply blossomed.

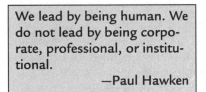

> We lead by being human. We do not lead by being corporate, professional, or institutional.
>
> —Paul Hawken

By creating that human level connection and going beyond just getting the business done, each supervisor and manager can give this precious gift to each employee every single day, a gift which says, "I see you as a valuable, unique, important contributor to our organization." Use these two models to help visualize the kinds of interaction that you would like to have with your employees.

Chapter 4

The CARE Model for Motivating and Retaining Your Employees

Today's new worker demands to be treated as an individual and not as a number.... Unfortunately, though management is often good at giving kudos to other managers and to those in the important and visible professional ranks—the "heroes" and the "champions"—it is often woefully inept when it comes to saluting the troops. Respect for the individual and recognition of the contributions that a person is able to make within the confines of his job are of paramount importance in keeping the best.[1]

—Martin John Yate, *Keeping the Best and Other Thoughts on Building a Super Competitive Workforce*

As I have studied the issues of motivation and retention over the years, I have found that a shorthand way to remember the elements of a joyful workplace is to think of the acronym CARE.

C = Creative Communication
A = Atmosphere and Appreciation for All
R = Respect and Reason for Being
E = Empathy and Enthusiasm

C = Creative Communication

Effective communication is a large part of what contributes to a healthy, cooperative work environment. Organizations must be open and honest in their communications with employees. Employees can take bad news; what they can't live with is the fear that they're being kept in the dark. Be open, be honest, be up-front, be creative, be real. In order to establish this environment, organizations need to communicate well by holding frequent "townhall" meetings to dispel rumors, keep any promises they have made, and clearly articulate the company's progress.

Runzheimer International, a consulting firm, has found that the average manager spends 80% of his or her time communicating: 10% writing, 15% reading, 25% listening, and 30% speaking. Some tips they suggest to improve communication with employees are:

- ▶ Talk the language of the troops in the trenches, not that of the crowd in the ivory tower.
- ▶ Be clear and consistent.
- ▶ Don't rely on one avenue of communication; use everything from e-mail to videotapes.[2]

A manager who is compassionate yet honest with employees is one who will be difficult to leave.

A new survey by Pitney Bowes reports that U. S. workers handle an average of 204 messages a day, counting all calls, voice mails, e-

> The leader needs to be in touch with the employees and communicate with them on a daily basis.
> —Donald Petersen, former CEO, Ford Motor Company

> True communicating is not just taking turns talking; it's about the transfer of meaning with understanding and without judgment.
> —Nancy Stern, President and Owner, Communication Plus

mails, postal mail, and even Post-it® notes.[3] With this daily deluge of communications, we need to do something extra, something that surprises people, to get their attention for our most important communications to be heard and heeded.

Here are three questions to ask whenever you have an important message to communicate:

1. **Does it get the information across clearly and accurately?** This is the business level of the communication, and while it is of the utmost importance, many messages are ignored, dumped, or deleted when only this level is dealt with because they are so boring. Think about most of the communications you get from the government, for example.

2. **How does it make the receiver feel?** This is the human level of the communication. The look of the message, the tone, and word choice all can have an impact on whether the communication is effective. If we are trying to "sell" someone on something, we need to create a rapport, a relationship of trust, to get them on our side. Think about marketing materials that have impacted you to make a buying decision, for example. Another example is when you are doing exit interviews. Change the question "Why are you leaving?" to "Why aren't you staying?" Just this slight difference in wording will help focus the employee's answers differently.

3. **Does it surprise the receiver or get his/her attention?** This is most important with a critical communication because it ensures that the receiver *will* get the message. Certainly we can't do this with every communication; however, whenever you communicate in a creative way, people will remember it.

For example, aren't there certain television commercials that you will never forget because they got your attention?

Here's a summary of our findings about *communicating creatively*:

▶ Provide creative recruitment ads and hiring procedures.

▶ Share important information frequently and honestly through open forums and "state of the organization" meetings.

▶ Provide formal, informal, vertical, and horizontal channels of communication.

▶ Keep in touch with employees at all levels through face-to-face interactions.

▶ Offer constant informal feedback.

▶ Make expectations clear.

▶ Involve all employees in decision making.

▶ Promote creative, positive meetings.

You will find many more creative communication ideas in Part 3 of this book.

A = Atmosphere

A person moved into a new town and asked one of the residents, "What are the people in this town like?" The resident asked, "What were the people like in the town you just left?" The new person answered, "They were unfriendly and nasty." And the town resident said, "I think you'll find the people here are just about the same."

Later, the same resident was approached by another new arrival, who asked the same question. Again, the resident asked, "What were the people like in the town you

> Employees need to feel they play an important part in a team effort. Leaders recognize that others work with them, not for them, and they encourage teamwork by creating an open and inclusive atmosphere.
> —William Bickham,
> *Liberating the Human Spirit in the Workplace*

> The very best working environment is one in which people can work hard and disagree openly about professional issues without taking things personally, all the while caring about each other very much as human beings.
> —Bob Wall,
> *Working Relationships*

just left?" The answer was "The people were warm and friendly." And the resident answered, "I think you'll find the people here are just about the same."

A *Workforce Magazine* study asked the question, "What are you most likely to find in your workplace?" 47% of the respondents said "Gossip and backbiting."[4] This kind of atmosphere is all too prevalent in the autocratic and fear-based atmosphere of many organizations today.

Charles A. O'Reilly III and Jeffrey Pfeffer, in their book, *Hidden Value: How Great Companies Achieve Extraordinary Results with Ordinary People*, present case studies that demonstrate that a company's culture and environment are the best predictors of an employee's success and are far better recruiting tools than starting salaries or stock options. These predictors include such questions as:

- Are you having fun on your job?
- Does your company empower its people?
- Are employees treated fairly, with respect?
- Does rank have very little meaning?
- Is HR a source of "no" or "yes"?
- What kind of atmosphere are you creating in your work area?[5]

Here's a summary of our findings about how to create a positive work *atmosphere*:

- Encourage fun in the workplace.
- Create a good physical place to work, including needed resources to do the job right.
- Establish a mentoring program.
- Actively promote positive relations among co-workers.

- ▶ Support frequent contests, celebrations, and team-building activities.
- ▶ Build an atmosphere of trust and fairness.
- ▶ Make employees an essential part of the company's community—an inclusive, extended-family relationship.

You will find many immediately applicable ideas to help you create a more caring atmosphere in Part 3.

> Every organization has an atmosphere, an energy that is immediately palpable; (anyone entering it can discern) whether it's the kind of organization that is open, dynamic, and respectful of the individual, or uncaring.
> —Alex Pattakos, consultant and former president of Renaissance Business Associates

A = Appreciation for All

In all the current research on what keeps employees motivated and productive, appreciation is always one of the top three desires. Mark Twain once said that he could go for a month on one good compliment.

Over and over again I have found that supervisors and managers who truly appreciate their employees and show it in small but powerful ways have the lowest turnover and the highest commitment from their employees. Most of us would do just about anything for a manager who appreciates us and our work. If you are not normally an appreciative person, make it your business to learn from someone who is, like from Arte Nathan, formerly Vice President of Human Resources at the Bellagio Resort in Las Vegas.

"We spend our time catching people doing things right, not doing things wrong. All you look for on

> Three billion people on the face of the earth go to bed hungry every night, but four billion people go to bed every night hungry for a simple word of encouragement and recognition.
> —Cavett Robert, founder, National Speakers Association

> Recognition is so easy to do and so inexpensive to distribute that there is simply no excuse for not doing it.
> —Rosabeth Moss Kanter

your job, all anyone looks for, is a pat on the back," says Nathan, who gives positive reinforcement credit for the casino and hotel's mere 12% annual turnover rate for hourly employees. In comparison, the national rate for the lodging industry is 52%, according to the American Hotel & Motel Association.[6] This is a concrete, bottom-line, business example of what happens when employees feel appreciated.

Here's a summary of our findings about how to create *appreciation for all* in your workplace:

- ▶ Get to know employees as individuals (personalization of appreciation, rewards, and recognition). What is their passion?
- ▶ Find out what is satisfying and dissatisfying to each employee.
- ▶ Make rewards and recognition constantly changing.
- ▶ Delegate responsibility for programs of rewards and recognition so employees at all levels are involved.
- ▶ Make appreciation a part of daily management routine.

> You never know when a moment and a few sincere words can have an impact on a life.
> —Zig Ziglar

You will find many immediately applicable ideas to appreciate your employees in Part 3.

R = Respect

People in good companies throughout the world treat each other with dignity, respect, and fairness—that's practically the definition of a good company. We want to earn competitive advantage over the good companies, so we have to do more. We want to go beyond tolerance and try to find the richness in each individual.
—Dick Agnich, Senior Vice President,
Texas Instruments

Tom Chappell, the co-founder of Tom's of Maine with his wife Kate, has built his company around treating customers and employees as real people with family histories and futures, not as abstract categories or statistics.

> Treat people as though they were what they ought to be and you help them become what they are capable of being.
>
> —Goethe

They believe in the following principles:

- ▶ Build "I–thou," not "I–it" relationships, respecting the dignity of persons versus their utility.
- ▶ Give away power and creativity flourishes. Employees who have a stake in the company's power are the most passionate and creative workers you will ever find.
- ▶ Make room for the complex beauty of diversity.[7]

When we focus on employees as individuals and not numbers, we are treating them with respect. Part of this respect is learning about employees and encouraging and valuing their strengths. Unless employers are able to engage the whole person, they are not even coming close to capturing the potential contribution of each employee.

Marcus Buckingham, a senior vice president at The Gallup Organization in Princeton, New Jersey, has polled more than two million employees at 700 companies worldwide for an ongoing workplace-trends project over 25 years. In

> All organizations need to adapt to changing conditions, but if they lose sight of the need to treat people humanely and respectfully, they will forget that it is not just organizations and programs that need to change, but the people who make them happen.
>
> —Kenneth Cloke and Joan Goldsmith, *Thank God It's Monday*

his polling, just 15% of American workers said they had the opportunity to use their strengths every day. 69% said they didn't even get to use them once a week. He adds that the most successful managers are those who work hard to motivate and develop employees without pigeonholing them. Managers should focus on the individual strengths, not weaknesses, of each worker, and then find the right fit for the blend of individual talents and capabilities.[8]

In their *1999 National Business Ethics Study*, fewer than half (47%) of more than 2,300 employees questioned by Hudson and Walker Information, Inc., a Washington, D.C. policy research organization, consider their senior leaders "people of high integrity," and even fewer feel a strong sense of personal attachment to their workplace or believe their employer deserves their loyalty. Only four out of 10 of these workers say their companies show real concern for employees.

The Hudson and Walker study went on to cite six management qualities that are most important to instilling a commitment from employees:

- ▶ Fairness (including fair pay)
- ▶ Care and concern for employees
- ▶ Workers' satisfaction with routine job activities
- ▶ Trust in employees
- ▶ The reputation of the organization
- ▶ Work and job resources[9]

Of these six qualities, four are based on respect for the individual. The direct relationship between personal attachment to the workplace and mutual respect between managers and employees can't be more clear.

To increase *respect* for its employees, organizations must:

- ▶ Foster flexibility in every area—hours, benefits, tasks.
- ▶ Provide ongoing training and personal development—growth opportunities.
- ▶ Develop an organization-wide code of ethics and cascade that process down to each team—agreement on behaviors they will use with one another in daily interactions.

▶ Give employees freedom whenever possible to choose projects and find challenging work according to their interests, skills, and passion.

▶ Provide internal promotion and transfer opportunities.

▶ Focus on giving up power, *not accumulating it. Adopt "servant leadership" as a guiding principle.*

> Organizations need to understand that such things as employee loyalty and morale are quite relevant to their success. They must learn to value people in new ways—to allow them to connect their dreams and desires with what they do at work.
>
> —David Trickett, Chairperson, The New Academy of Business

You will find many immediately applicable ideas to foster more respect in your workplace in Part 3.

R = Reason for Being

> When people feel they are being of service to something larger than themselves, then something happens—an alchemy—that transcends logical thought and possibilities; the undoable gets done, the impossible is possible. People now want to find purpose to their lives in general and their work in particular, and there is a growing awareness that what we do all day has some bearing on ourselves as individuals, on our communities, and on the world.
>
> —Craig Neal, founder and President, The Heartland Institute

People are desperately seeking meaning in their work. Look at all the current writing about spirituality in the workplace. David Whyte, a poet who is now reading his poetry in corporate boardrooms, says, "We're all desperate to belong to something larger than ourselves. 'Soulful work' is where you feel you belong."[10] And Allan Cox, the author of *Redefining Corporate Soul,* says, "People are returning to the idea that putting our heart into things, not depending solely on rationality, is the way to go. Unleashing the talent and creativity that has been

> A company that lives its values, knows its purpose, and follows a mission can become an incubator for a caring, ethical future generation of business people and citizens.
>
> —Allan Cox,
> *Redefining Corporate Soul*

latent in employees will lead to better communication, more effective teamwork, greater trust, and ultimately higher profits."[11]

In their book, *Hidden Value: How Great Companies Achieve Extraordinary Results with Ordinary People*, Charles A. O'Reilly III and Jeffrey Pfeffer state, "To the extent that any organization can truly unleash the hidden value in its people, it will increase its chance of success. Employees are smart, trustworthy people who have the ability and desire to do the right thing for the company."[12]

Alan Briskin, the author of *The Stirring of Soul in the Workplace*, says, "The soul of many corporate workers is dormant. It's as if a part of ourselves were asleep. For organizations to be successful, they need the imagination and vitality of all their workers. People who are sleeping cannot work collaboratively."[13] Finding a sense of purpose in one's work, a reason for being, then, becomes a way to reawaken employees' spirits.

Tim Webster, the CEO of American Italian Pasta Company, the largest producers and marketers of dry pasta in North America, says,[14]

> I think that it is the essence of the ultimate leader's responsibility to create a clearly understood reason for being for the company and to pursue that reason for being with passion and tenacity.... I believe that people's motivation will be greater and more sustainable if it comes from the heart and the stomach than purely from an intellectual belief. I think you have to stir them from the inside.

I ask my audiences to think of their work as a calling, something much more than simply a job. I ask them to think about the question, "How is what I do every day making someone's life better?" No matter whether you clean the toilets or run the company, you can find a way that your work makes someone's life better. And that adds a new purpose and pride to that very important work.

One of the most important things a supervisor or manager can do is to help employees make this connection—that their work, whatever that work may be, is making a difference in someone's life.

To give their employees a *reason for being*, organizations must:

- ▶ Emphasize the deeper, broader purpose of each person's work— How is what they do every day making someone's life better?
- ▶ Engender pride and commitment through the organization's culture and brand—How are we special?
- ▶ Help employees to understand the organization's mission statement, vision, and values, and how these apply to their day-to-day working.
- ▶ Encourage employees to write their own personal mission statements.
- ▶ Support character development and integrity training.
- ▶ Promote a spirit of family in the organization.

You will find many immediately applicable ideas in Part 3 to help employees find a deeper sense of purpose and mission in their work.

E = Empathy

The moral is simple: If you satisfy their deep wants, employees become more cognitively and emotionally engaged and will perform better. And this is so across national and corporate cultures, in all occupations, regardless of rates of pay, because the underlying needs are universal.

—James K. Harter,
"Taking Feedback to the Bottom Line,"
Gallup Management Journal, Spring 2001

The March 1, 2001, edition of *USA Today* featured a Hilton Generational Time Survey of 1,220 adults in January of 2001. When asked how they felt about their lives, Americans gave these answers:[15]

Need more fun	68%
Need a long vacation	67%
Often feel stressed	66%
Feel time is crunched	60%
Want less work, more play	51%
Feel pressured to succeed	49%
Feel overwhelmed	48%

When we consider these statistics, it becomes even clearer how important it is for organizations to care more about their employees as human beings. When organizations listen to employees' personal needs and help to provide resources to fill those needs such as daycare, elder care, financial and personal help, and other ways to make their *whole* lives easier, they will be creating loyal, motivated employees in the process.[16]

> I believe that man will not merely endure: he will prevail. He is immortal, not because he alone among creatures has an inexhaustible voice, but because he has a soul, a spirit capable of compassion and sacrifice and endurance.
> —William Faulkner

Another need people have is to be of service to others. Organizations that encourage and support employees in community service projects will win the commitment and loyalty that is missing in many workplaces today, and they will be making this world a better place at the same time.

Most of all, supervisors and managers need to be human beings themselves, filled with a passion for the importance of the work they are doing. In their book, *True Leaders,* Bette Price and George Ritcheske tell about their interview with Jack Kahl, the founder of Manco, Inc.:[17]

> As the founder of Manco, Inc., Kahl is invited to speak to a lot of business groups. The title of one of his favorite speeches is, "Don't Park your Heart at the Curb." The premise of the speech, Kahl says, is, "Don't leave your heart just for your family. Bring it inside and take a

risk because that shows that you're going to show people that you are 100 percent involved in the business, and you want them to be 100 percent involved." Kahl says many leaders fail to develop themselves from a human perspective. "That's a very serious thing I am saying," Kahl emphasizes. "Leaders don't like to share their humanity. Many have a hard time letting their souls out."

> It is not how much you do but how much love you put into the doing and sharing with others that is important.
> —Mother Teresa

It's one of the biggest things he sees lacking in leaders. Kahl says too many tend to be afraid to inject their heartfelt emotions into the business so that their people can sense that "this is a human being, not just a bottom line person." Kahl doesn't understand the fear and points out, "The greatest corporations in the world and the greatest passionate military or spiritual leaders are people that touch your soul, not just your head."

In order to *empathize* with their employees, organizations must:

▶ Support work/life programs.
▶ Foster understanding of personal concerns/problems/needs.
▶ Encourage job shadowing and exchanges.
▶ Provide monthly and yearly social welfare opportunities, encouraging employees to give back and care about the world outside their own doors.

You will find many immediately applicable ideas to create empathy in Part 3.

E = Enthusiasm

Nothing great was ever achieved without enthusiasm.
—Ralph Waldo Emerson

Cultivate the ability to love living. Love people. Love the sky under which you live, love beauty, love God. The person who loves becomes enthusiastic, filled with the sparkle and joy of life. And then he goes on to fill it full of meaning.
—Norman Vincent Peale

My personal motto is "Spreading Contagious Enthusiasm™." I believe that when someone is enthusiastic about their work and about life, they are a joy to be around, and they lift the spirits of others. I took this motto for my life from a quotation by a man who was a legend in the management field, Francis Likert. He said, "If a high level of performance is to be achieved, it appears to be necessary for a supervisor to have high performance goals and a contagious enthusiasm as to the importance of these goals."

Are you, as a supervisor or manager, "contagiously enthusiastic" about the importance of the work you and your employees are doing? If you are not enthusiastic, how can you expect your employees to be?

> I would rather be ashes than dust. I would rather that my spark should burn out in a brilliant blaze than it should be stifled by dry-rot. I would rather be a superb meteor, every atom of me in magnificent glow, than a sleepy and permanent planet. The proper function of man is to live, not to exist.
>
> —Jack London

The root words of the word "enthusiasm" are "en theos" which mean "of or from God." No matter what your belief system is, creating and encouraging a feeling that one is doing something of value and of high calling adds a sense of joy and celebration to any workplace. We all need to celebrate more in our lives. So often we focus on what is going wrong instead of what is going right. As you begin to create a feeling of enthusiasm for your very important work, you will find loyalty and productivity blossoming!

To spread *contagious enthusiasm* among employees, organizations must:

- ▶ Celebrate what is going *right* on a frequent basis.
- ▶ Hold "guerilla" or spontaneous celebrations often.
- ▶ Encourage positive work relations through team-building and training.

▶ Get employees at all levels involved in planning and executing celebrations of all kinds.

You will find many more immediately applicable ideas for creating enthusiasm in Part 3.

> Apathy can only be overcome by enthusiasm, and enthusiasm can only be aroused by two things: first, an ideal which takes the imagination by storm, and second, a definite intelligible plan for carrying that ideal into practice.
> —Arnold Toynbee

Notes

1. Yate, Martin John. 1991. *Keeping the Best and Other Thoughts on Building a Super Competitive Workforce.* Holbrook, MA: Bob Adams, Inc., p. 34.

2. Editor. 1996. "Work Hard at Communication." *Chicago Tribune*, Business Section, April 15.

3. Dauten, Dale. 2000. "Giving Workers Freedom to Be Productive Provides Incentive to Stay." *Chicago Tribune*, October 22, Section 5, p. 8.

4. Study for *Workforce Magazine.* www.workforce.com.

5. Auerbach, Carol. 2000. "Unleashing the Potential of Every Employee." *HR Magazine,* December, p. 175.

6. Littman, Margaret. 2000. "Best Bosses Tell All." *Working Woman*, October, p. 55.

7. Chappell, Tom. 1994. "The Soul of a Business." *Executive Female*, January/February, p. 40.

8. Littman, Margaret. 2000. "Best Bosses Tell All." *Working Woman*, October, p. 51.

9. Hudson Institute. 1999. *National Business Ethics Study.* 1015 18th Street, NW, Suite 300, Washington DC 20036, 202-223-7770.

10. Stern, Gary M. 1996. "Soul at Work." *New Age,* November/December, p. 73. Adapted from *The Heart Aroused* by David Whyte, New York, NY: Bantam Doubleday Dell 1994, 1996.

11. Cox, Allan. 1996. *Redefining Corporate Soul.* New York, NY: McGraw-Hill.

12. O'Reilly, Charles A., and Jeffrey Pfeffer. 2000. *Hidden Value: How Great Companies Achieve Extraordinary Results with Ordinary People.* Boston, MA: Harvard Business School Press.

13. Briskin, Alan. 1996. *The Stirring of Soul in the Workplace*. San Francisco, CA: Jossey-Bass.

14. Price, Bette, and Ritcheske, George. 2001. *True Leaders: How Exceptional CEOs and Presidents Make a Difference by Building People and Profits*. Chicago, IL: Dearborn Trade, pp. 30-31.

15. Joseph, Lori, and Laird, Bob. 2001. "Snapshots." *USA Today*, March 1, p. 1.

16. Editor. 1998. "Work/Life Study = Respect." *Employee Services Management (ESM) Magazine*. March, p. 6.

17. Price, Bette, and Ritcheske, George. 2001. *True Leaders: How Exceptional CEOs and Presidents Make a Difference by Building People and Profits*. Chicago, IL: Dearborn Trade, p. 28.

PART 2

IDEAS AND STORIES FROM MANAGERS, EMPLOYEES, AND ORGANIZATIONS WHO CARE

Chapter 5

A Manager
Who CAREs

S everal years ago, I received a call from Anita Vigil, a manager at the John G. Shedd Aquarium in Chicago, IL, who said she had read an article in which I had been quoted, and she felt they could use some help in their organization to boost morale. As I worked with Anita over the next six months, I became more and more impressed with her ability as a manager of frontline and hourly workers. She possessed both the business knowledge to do her job as well as the compassion and "street smarts" necessary to manage this difficult group on the human level. Here, she writes about CARE in her own words.

A Manager's Perspective on CARE

By Anita Vigil, Director of Sales Operations,
The John G. Shedd Aquarium,
Chicago, Illinois

When I first read one of Barbara Glanz's articles in a business publication, I knew that she was the management guru for whom I was searching. She wrote about her belief that you can't pay, perk, plead, or threaten people enough to motivate them to give great, consistent customer service. Her philosophy was that they have to want to give it. It must be from the heart.

Barbara and I both believe that it is the supervisory/management level that is most critical in creating a positive, motivated staff. If you look around any organization, you will see that there are many people who get promoted to positions of management when they have no idea how to manage. For example, I know managers at many organizations who get things done by being demeaning, manipulating, and basically quite nasty. They behave as if the staff that reports to them are the enemy. They lie to employees and think nothing of taking advantage of them.

Yes, they sometimes get things done, but they don't create anything positive. There are no relationships built, and very few people feel good about who they are or the job they are doing. These managers can tell people what to do, but they have no idea how to lead. If you can lead, you can help your team accomplish great things, with a lot less work and personal stress, more fun, and the possibility to learn and grow together with your staff. Talk about a win/win opportunity!

Thankfully, we've all encountered employees who demonstrate great customer service and behave with integrity in the worst possible environments. These people are not your average employees, however. The reality is that most people do not respond well to negative treatment. They should still be expected to do their jobs, but they should also be able to expect that they will be treated decently. I'm sure your mother told you that you can catch more flies with honey than you can with vinegar. We need to use the same concept with employees.

Anita's Story

I came to the Shedd Aquarium in Chicago, Illinois, in October of 1996. I began as the Admissions Coordinator, managing the ticket sellers and supervisors. Soon I was promoted to Sales Operations Manager, in charge of the Admissions and Group Reservations area. After a year or so at this position, I became Assistant Director of Sales, in charge of the Admissions ticket sellers and the Merchandising area. After our Director of Sales left the Shedd, I became the Director of Sales Operations. I now have one manager, an asset protection employee (whom I added once I took over in Merchandising), and nine supervisors as my direct area of responsibility. These are all guest-interactive staff. Together we generate over 60% of the operating capital for the aquarium and are responsible for the tracking and movement of approximately two million guests per year.

The staff that I manage is typical of most restaurant and retail operations. The majority of them are not with us for a career. It can be a very transient group with little buy-in to the organization. On the other hand, the animal care and interpretive areas of the aquarium usually attract staff with college degrees and/or folks who are interested and involved with our mission, so we have a wide variety of career expectations and commitment to our organization.

Because of our location (downtown major metropolitan area), we are pulling in a very diverse group, many of whom live in the inner city areas. We are mixing a number of different groups and classes from many different backgrounds. This can create problems, but it can also create phenomenal opportunities for growth and change, both personally and professionally. It's an exciting time, and I feel very fortunate to be a part of things to come!

When I met Barbara, I learned the CARE acronym she uses to explain the elements of a spirited workplace, Creative Communication, Atmosphere, Respect, Reason for Being, Empathy, and Enthusiasm. In my jobs, in my businesses, and with my children, I've tried to implement these same concepts. By using these ideas in my work each day, I believe that I have made a difference in the lives of many of the staff that I have managed. I know that many of them have made a difference in mine.

Creative Communication

The main organizational structure of the aquarium begins with the Management Council. It consists of a group of approximately 25 directors from every department of the aquarium. We handle operational issues and help each other get our jobs done. Sometimes we present problems and task forces (temporary) are formed to investigate possibilities and report back to the group. If the issues presented involve philosophical or organizational changes, they are presented to Leadership Council (made up of seven VPs). Together with the President, this team makes all major decisions involving the aquarium.

While there is excellent communication at this level, a few years ago it became very apparent to me that the supervisory level was being left out of any type of feedback loop in the aquarium. They were told about procedures from the Management Council, but didn't have any cohesiveness or input when it came to questioning a process. It also became evident to me at a Customer Service Team meeting that some of the supervisors didn't even know one another.

As a result, I proposed a Supervisors Forum at the aquarium to bring together all guest-interactive department supervisors once a week. Currently, there are about 20 people who meet regularly. They request guest trainers, they discuss issues involving guests and staff, and they get to know each other. As they become more familiar with procedures and one another, the entire operation of the aquarium runs more smoothly. These are the people who are doing the daily work of the building, and it is essential that they should be comfortable enough with one another to pick up the phone or the radio and ask for backup.

Since the inception of the Forum, the departments have been calling on each other and asking for help much more often. They also have a better understanding of what the other supervisors' jobs are. We spent our first meeting going around the room and explaining how we arrived at this particular job. Each person got to hear backgrounds and past jobs and a little about one another's personal lives. They related on a much more human level than they ever had in the past. Instead of competing against each other, they felt comfortable actually helping each other and offering advice.

We have many teams at the aquarium that actually assist in the day-to-day management of the building. These teams create a sense of involvement, commitment to the organization, and a feeling of being in on things. I personally sit on an Internal Customer Service team (Team Spirit), an External Customer Service team (the X-team!), a Customer Service Training team, an Employee Benefits team, the Diversity team, and the Management Council, and I help out with the Supervisors Forum. We have many animal-oriented teams and a Conservation team as well as a "Green Team" that looks at our in-house practices on recycling and environmental issues.

The aquarium now has an Intranet page with any "late-breaking news." When you turn your computer on in the morning, this page pops up first. It gives you up-to-date animal information, as well as any procedural changes that might take place. All of these teams and means of communication inform each employee, from the President down to the ticket taker of what is going on at the aquarium.

Atmosphere

When I started four years ago at the Shedd, there were many personal and operational issues that needed to be addressed in the Admissions area. There was a high level of paranoia in the department, it was not a very positive place to work, and turnover was high. The first thing I did was to take a few months to work with the staff, learn the issues, and develop trust.

I had to fire a few people who were dishonest and pulling the morale down with them. Then I initiated one-on-one meetings with each employee. I continued with these individual meetings about every six months. I would put up a sign-up sheet in the office with one hour blocked out for each employee. Staff would sign up and we would meet. To open up the communication, I had a list of prepared questions for them to answer. Here is what I used to get the conversation going:

- Why did you want to work in the Admissions department at Shedd Aquarium?
- What position do you like to work in the most and least? Why?
- What sort of training would you like to receive?
- What tools do you need to better perform your job? (for example: training manual, new ticket printers, etc.)
- What is the most asked question from our guests when they approach the ticket counter?
- Where do you see yourself in five years? What can we do to support you?
- What type of training would help you to better serve our guests?
- If you could change one process, what would it be? Why? (for example: cashing out)
- What would make your job more fun?
- Any other topic you would like to ask about or discuss?

It took about a year and a half of this interaction to uncover the real issues. Building trust and open communication was one important way in which I was able to turn a very fearful group into a group that comes into my office (or calls me or e-mails me from home) when there is something going on that they don't like.

I have always had an open door policy. That goes for my direct reports as well as *their* direct reports. I have always been open to listening to anyone's concerns. I do my best to take care of issues that the group brings to me. I believe that I behave in a very fair manner towards everyone. My belief is to "seek first to understand and then make sure that you are understood" philosophy. The people whom I work with know that I will stand behind my words. And they know that I expect them to do the same.

I recently put some ground rules together for the frontline staff to follow. These were not unusual ground rules (we all knew they were in existence; they just weren't being enforced as they should have been), but they were unpopular. There would be no reading, writing, eating, or drinking at any of the posts in the public areas. Who wants to go to a museum and see the person in the main entry areas reading a book or eating a donut?

I knew the staff was not happy about this because we had a drawer full of books, magazines, and food that was taken away from them throughout the day. The supervisors were taking any of the offending items and holding them for the sales staff as they went on break or lunch. Unreasonable? I didn't think so. One of the sales staff decided to write an anonymous letter to me listing all of the reasons why the "new" policy was a bad idea. This person didn't have the courage to sign her name but chose to sign off with the department name as if her department had elected her their spokesperson.

The following is the letter that I received in my mailbox:

To Anita,
How in the world are you going to say we can't read at our posts? If there are no customers coming and we are just sitting there, why can't we read or do homework? It won't affect us taking tickets or

selling tickets because we are going to stop what we are doing and help the customer. If we can't talk to someone, then what are we going to do? Also why can't we drink at our posts? If we have a spill-proof cup, it shouldn't matter. We think it's bull----.

—Admissions Staff

The next morning, at the department meeting, I passed out 20 copies of the letter so that everyone could see what they had unwittingly signed their collective name to. Everyone seemed to recognize who the author was. One of our longtime employees said that she knew that the staff was writing up a petition to express concerns about the policy. She named who was in charge of typing this petition up and told me that I would have it by the next week. Not a problem! I am happy to listen to concerns ("seek first to understand") and I am also bound to respond within my capacity as a manager. I never received the petition and the staff is complying with the basic rules.

Appreciation for All

Summer is always the busiest time at the aquarium. During my first summer there, I initiated a monthly dinner meeting for all my staff to show our appreciation of their hard work. We order pizza, salad, and soda, and encourage the employees to vent frustrations, ask questions, and give suggestions. This was one of the first occasions that employees had the opportunity to speak directly to management. The first meeting went for about two and a half hours and was charged with emotion. By the end of it, however, we were relating much more openly and honestly.

From my very first day at the aquarium I always say "thank you" to everyone when they leave for the day. Whether or not I liked their behavior that day or whether or not they did something incorrectly, they always receive a "thank you." My behavior was noticed right away by a couple of the supervisors. After four years, I now hear most of the supervisors in the department saying "thank you" as their staff leaves for the day. It's a simple thing to do that goes a long way.

Thanksgiving weekend has also always been a very busy time for us at the aquarium. Any staff who work on Thanksgiving day receive a turkey dinner in our restaurant. However, the two days following Thanksgiving are extremely hectic for staff as well. Since some of them get only 30 minutes for lunch, and since the lines in our cafeteria are quite lengthy, we take over a conference room for those two days and bring in food and drinks for our frontline workers. In years past, we have brought in a TV and VCR, as well as candy and chips. The room becomes a haven for staff who are deluged by the crowds of visitors in the building. It has now become a standing tradition, with other frontline departments asking to have their staff included.

Another great idea is our new secret shopper program. We are just beginning to organize this program now. We select a few people from the frontline departments each month who have demonstrated great customer service. As a reward, they receive a day out on the aquarium! We equip them with a Palm Pilot that has a survey loaded into it. This survey addresses the ticket-buying process, the store (merchandising) experience, the food-buying experience, lines, exhibits, etc.

The employee can take their family with them on their outing. They spend the day at one of the other cooperative

Inspired by a children's book he'd seen, Todd incorporated sound buttons into his resume.

museums in the program. They purchase tickets, food, and an item from the gift shop. They are then reimbursed by that museum for their ticket, their lunch, and up to $10 in merchandise. For this, the museum receives a comprehensive secret shopper analysis completed by folks who know what type of service they should be receiving—all for less than it would cost to have a secret shopper service come in. The museum receives valuable feedback on its services and the employees are "perked" for the day. This lets them know that they are valued as employees and that their input counts. It also serves to make them more aware of good and bad customer service!

Respect

Within the supervisory team, we have created a "Code of Ethics," a list of behaviors that we have all agreed we will use in our interactions with one another. We have put it in writing, and everyone on the team has signed it. It is in a frame in each supervisory team member's office. This helps us all to remember promises that we have made to each other.

Rather than confronting someone on an issue that we believe they have fallen down on, we can just say, "Remember the Code," and it forces us to look it over again and see where we were out of alignment … where we behaved without integrity.

Our Code

- ▶ We will not gossip about team members (other supervisors/ managers) in the presence of staff.
- ▶ Information shared in supervisors' meetings is absolutely confidential. Topics of discussion should not be shared with staff.
- ▶ We will treat all staff with the same amount of respect that we want to receive.
- ▶ If someone on our team upsets us, we will be proactive about finding a way to respectfully resolve it.
- ▶ We will make it our personal responsibility to make all new staff members feel welcome.

When I first started at the aquarium, I remember having a confrontation with one of the cashiers. I had only been there for about four or five weeks and after a Saturday morning meeting before one of our busiest days, I found a tray of dirty dishes and glassware on a shelf in our coat check room off the main entrance. Since we were just breaking up from the meeting, I handed the tray to Mary and asked her to take it down to the kitchen. She nodded affirmatively and then proceeded to walk out the door *without the tray*!

I immediately went after her with the tray because I felt that, especially as a new manager to the company, I had to stand my ground and not back down. I had the tray in my hand and told Mary that I guessed she must have forgotten that I asked her to take this tray downstairs. She said that she hadn't forgotten but was too busy getting ready for the doors to open to our guests to take the time to take it downstairs at that moment. Her attitude was pretty confrontational at this point.

With some of the staff watching to see how I would handle her behavior (I had heard stories of her previous bad behavior), I made a quick decision to not force this small issue to start our working relationship. Instead, I told Mary that she should go on and get set up to sell tickets, that I didn't realize how late it was getting. I told her that I would be glad to take the tray down for her this time, since I was not expected to be at a specific post in a few minutes as she was. She seemed rather surprised but said nothing.

After this episode, however, I never had any problems with her fulfilling a request that I made. We had many discussions after that, even to the point of putting her on a final notice for a number of issues, and, ultimately, she did quit. But the entire time she was at the Shedd, we had a very open, honest working relationship. And based on some of the discussions that we had while she was being counseled for unprofessional behavior, she decided to change her major in college and go into Business. This happened, in large part, she says, because of the coaching that I gave her regarding her leadership and people skills.

When Mary finally received the respect that she craved, she changed her life. She still calls me from time to time and has come by a few times to show off her baby boy. I consider her a friend. It took a while, and a lot of patience, but I ended up with a win/win! (Mary's real name is used with her full permission.)

One of the staff members that I "inherited' when I started this job was Deneen. Deneen is a very bright, street-smart woman. She is also very opinionated and can be very intimidating. She has an air about her that says, "Don't mess with me!" She and I went head-to-head many times for the first year that I worked at the Shedd. Her customer service skills range from horrible to excellent, depending upon her mood. Her consistency left a great deal to be desired. She, too, was on a final notice for unacceptable customer service.

Gradually, employees at Milnard Industries began to abuse the company's casual-dress policy.

I wanted to work with Deneen because, even with all of her issues with other staff members and her shaky customer service, I knew that she was honest. When you're a cashier handling upwards of $5,000 per day, honesty is a valuable asset to have. Managing a large department of cashiers, one tries to find a balance. Not everyone can be everything. So you find key people for different reasons.

When a supervisor's position became available, however, Deneen turned it down. It seemed that she liked to tell people what to do but not on a regular basis and not when she had to be held accountable for outcomes. Sometimes I think that she enjoyed the challenge of leading other staff without ever being sanctioned a "leader." At any rate, I knew that she was valuable—I just didn't know if I could hold out long enough to find out what the extent of her value actually was. By creating a relationship of respect between us, using lots and lots of hard work and patience, Deneen and I created a good working relationship even though I knew she had not reached her full potential.

Reason for Being

About a year and a half ago, I took on the management of an additional department, our two museum stores. At that time, we had an overabundance of staff and supervisors, many of whom we knew were stealing merchandise, money, or time.

We had an average of 130 hours of overtime per pay period. One of the first things I did was to restructure the staff and reduce overtime to zero hours. I was able to terminate the employment of at least six staff who were dragging the entire department down.

The energy in the department almost immediately changed from negative and highly inflammatory to an air of excitement and possibilities! The department began showing a profit as theft decreased and morale increased. We still, however, had a ways to go. There were still a few holdouts who were creating a lot of problems. At about this time, a Director of Merchandising (Deb) was hired to manage our warehouse operation. Deb had far more experience than I did when it came to retail operations. She suggested that I establish a new position that would report directly to me. This person could maintain an eye on external and internal theft issues and report any opportunities for dishonest behavior.

I decided that, since our own Security department wasn't really able to assist us in any way because they had the entire building to contend with, I would take one of my full-time positions and create a brand new position. I called this position "Asset Protection." What I needed was a person who was extremely honest, street-smart, not easily intimidated, and, if they saw something that wasn't right, would have the courage to report it to me quickly so that we could act on it. When I described the qualifications needed for this position to Jewel, our Operations Manager, her response was "You're going to take Deneen, aren't you?" Out of the 50 or so staff that I had, one person immediately came to mind—Deneen!

Since her appointment to this position one year ago, she has been instrumental in identifying employee theft issues and guest theft issues. I have her going over paperwork for both our Admissions department and our Merchandising department. Her customer service skills have increased, and I have witnessed more positive changes about her. She always knew that she could be more of an asset. We just needed to identify her talent and give her a deeper sense of purpose within a position description. She is someone on my team that I rely upon for her honesty and her fearlessness when it comes to identifying theft. Her loyalty to her manager and the Shedd Aquarium has become her reason for being!

A few months ago, I organized a breakfast meeting for both our Admissions and Merchandising staffs. All of the supervisors and sales associates were in attendance. After we went over some changes in procedure, I printed out for them a list of the aquarium's strategic goals for the coming year. We talked about all areas and department contributions.

Then I pulled out the goal that was more specific to our departments—increasing internal and external customer service. I listed ways that this directly included them. I wanted them to understand that they are an integral part of this goal. Then I proceeded to diagram their connection to other departments. I believe that a team that really understands what part they play and how they contribute is going to give more. It becomes a matter of personal pride and sense of purpose, as opposed to a way to simply "make money."

Empathy

I recently had a cashier who had been exhibiting poor customer service, was late a few times in a row, and missed some evening meetings that she had made a commitment to attend. I was hurt that she missed these meetings and upset about her poor customer service. I asked her if she would meet me for a few minutes when she went on break. Instead of meeting in my office (which is very much *my* territory), I asked her to meet me in an empty lunch area.

When she arrived, we talked for a few minutes about family, and then I asked her if she was OK. I told her that some of the supervisors expressed concern that she didn't seem herself and that she missed some of the meetings that she said she would attend. These questions opened up a floodgate of personal issues that the supervisors were not aware of. This girl is barely 20 years old and has two small children. She lives with her boyfriend and children in a two-bedroom apartment. She had recently taken in her aunt (with her teenage son) because they lost their apartment. Her boyfriend's brother was also living with them, as he had suffered multiple gunshot wounds at the hand of a robber.

Without getting into the medical details, suffice it to say that when she got home each day, she was faced with two small children, difficult houseguests, and a gunshot victim. This would have been a huge burden for someone of my age with teenagers and some experience. But for this child, it was overwhelming!

Now that I understood what *her* issues were, I could easily prioritize what the aquarium (and I) needed from her. I told her that we would help her by letting up on our restrictions *temporarily*, because we were not in an extremely busy period. Her tardies would not count against her for the next 30 days while she tried to cope with her personal life. And, obviously, I did not require her to attend any of our evening meetings. She has since been relieved of both of her house-guests and is back to her original responsibilities. Because of my personal, caring approach through her time of crisis, she did not add a job loss to her problems, and the Shedd did not lose a valued employee.

Staff turnover is very expensive. It doesn't matter what your actual business is—if you have a lot of frontline (guest-interactive) staff, you are dealing with a pretty transient group. You don't always have folks who are really committed to your business. They don't ordinarily get paid a great deal of money, and they have little decision-making power. What you do have to offer them is respect and a concern for their situation.

For example, most of our staff is female. We have some who are single mothers and some who are students (and some who are both!). We try to schedule around their lives as often as possible. We try to hire staff who are in school because they have goals. It has been my experience that it is easier to manage someone who has some goals and direction in their life. Single moms bring some scheduling challenges but make up for it in many ways, not the least of which is an employee who wants to do a good job and who is not necessarily interested in job-hopping every other month.

Enthusiasm

In a bid to add some creativity and something fun and different to our environment, I found a pianist and voice teacher to work with the staff for four nights in November, rehearsing Christmas music. The week before Christmas the teacher came in to the Shedd and played a baby grand piano that we had rented for the occasion. Three times per day, the cashiers from Admissions and Merchandising who were not busy came out into the main foyer and sang Christmas songs.

We also put out a call to all other departments to join us, if they were so inclined. We had staff from Education, Human Resources, Maintenance, Food Service, Visitor Service, Aquarists, and Membership/Development join us at various times. I had staff come to me from other departments to let me know that they play an instrument and would like to get involved.

Now, we are considering purchasing the piano and actually creating a musical ensemble that would perform one or two afternoons per week. This would involve the entire building. Staff from all over the building have called and e-mailed me to say how great their day went when they spent a few minutes out of each afternoon singing! It was not unusual to hear staff in offices and on the front line singing to themselves after the performances were over. It's true that it's very difficult to be in a bad mood when you're singing! It was not only great for the staff, but the recipients of those great moods were the guests visiting the aquarium.

I manage the staff and operations of our Admissions cashiers and our Merchandising cashiers (we have two stores in the building). One of my peers, Deb Stambler, the Merchandising Director, shares my budget in Merchandising and some of the daily problems that we encounter trying to run the stores. We decided that, since it had been a rough year for the frontline staff, we would take them out to a local restaurant for the holidays.

Since there are approximately 50 staff between the two departments, we worked out a partial trade with one of the local restaurants (tickets for meals) and worked with one of our vendors to put together a nice little gift package for each staff person. For about $7.00 per person, we were able to have a bright red T-shirt made with a small logo on the corner of the shirt that said "SHEDD VIP" with a dolphin underneath it. We also had a commuter mug made up with the same "SHEDD VIP" on the front and a motivational quote on the back. We added some milk chocolate fish candy and put them all in a little gift bag. The response was great! I still have people calling to thank me (even the people who didn't show up for the dinner, since we gave the gift bags to everyone whether they showed up or not).

Some of the supervisors have organized a few potluck lunches for staff. In our business, Saturday is our busiest day. The supervisors thought that it would be nice to give the staff something to look forward to at their lunch break on those days. Everyone brings in something to eat and share with the rest of the staff.

About three years ago, a project was initiated at the Shedd to give a Christmas celebration and some gifts to young kids from the inner city. We titled it "Project Angelfish." Many frontline staff are heavily involved with this project. We identify a different neighborhood each year, with the help of our Educational Outreach staff, and bring them in to the aquarium for a light breakfast, games, gifts, and a dolphin presentation. This is a chance for the kids to feel honored and an opportunity for staff to volunteer some of their time to a cause.

I have recently taken all of the supervisors in my departments offsite for a retreat. We borrowed another museum's conference room nearby with a beautiful view of the Chicago skyline. We appointed a couple of trusted employees on staff as team leaders. They were paid a higher wage for the day, and they took care of the departments while the rest of us were gone. It was a time for all of us to work on personal and professional goal setting, as well as discuss changes that were to come in the departments. I had breakfast and lunch catered in, and we took the day to recharge.

Summary

As a CARE-ing manager, these are my seven guiding philosophies:

1. If there is someone on my staff or another manager that I have to deal with that I really do not like, I take some time to talk

with them until I find something to like and respect about them. I don't do this exclusively for them. I do it for me, so that I can experience less stress when I am around them. The funny thing is that it works for them, as well.

2. It's OK if I don't like someone whom I manage. We can still get the job done and work together.

3. I strive to understand first ... but then I make darn sure that I am understood. Asking questions does not make me weak.

4. I am not afraid to have someone on my staff who disagrees with me, even if they consistently do so. It's like being in sales—objections are gifts to better communication. Everything on this planet is alive because of positive and negative charges.

5. I don't try to gather a staff who are all alike.

6. I don't just manage my staff—I always try to make a difference in their lives! They're human beings first and then employees. I help them try to look for "the lesson" when a concern needs to be addressed. We set personal and professional goals and try to help each other stay true to them. Even when I have to let someone go, I always try to leave them with their self-respect.

7. A sense of humor is mandatory! I try not to take myself too seriously. Humor can come in handy in tense situations. If one of the supervisors is having a hard time talking with me or letting me know what is upsetting them, I will often threaten to sing to pass the time. I tell them I can do show tunes or Top 40. I try to make light of my own insecurities and weaknesses so that the supervisors and staff have an easier time looking at theirs.

All in all, I have witnessed a great deal of growth in much of the staff who have stayed at the Shedd over the last six years. As we have employed the concepts and ideas of the CARE acronym, we have made great strides in creating a fun, creative, caring, and productive place to work.

But even as positions are terminated, I attempt to make employees understand that this doesn't mean that they're bad or stupid because they couldn't keep this particular job. I let them know (many times before the actual termination) that this was a choice that they made. They actually chose to be fired by the behavior that they exhibited or by the rules that they chose not to follow. This takes things out of the personal arena and lets them walk out with dignity. I believe that differences are made when humans really relate to humans. If you work from the heart level in your communication, you are responded to from that very same level, so even if the relationship ends, it doesn't demoralize or destroy anyone. And the bottom line is that these former employees have learned a valuable life lesson. When they are allowed to leave with dignity, it also impacts the employees who stay. They know this is still a good place to work!

> —Anita Vigil,
> The John G. Shedd Aquarium,
> Chicago, Illinois

Chapter 6

Reward and Respect: Suggestions from Employees

Throughout the past few years, I have conducted brainstorming sessions with a number of groups of employees across the country to have them share ideas that would make their workplaces more positive and caring. Some of the groups were composed of managers, some of frontline employees, and some were mixed. Regardless of their level, I asked them to think of things that would make their workplaces more enjoyable places to work.

In the following pages you will find ideas from several sources, both public and private: Ameriking, the parent company of Burger King, a well-known retail chain; the Chicago Mercantile Exchange, a group that deals in futures and options in an environment similar to the stock market; the San Francisco Management Association, an association of Social Security managers from the Western states; the Midwest Practice Management Conference sponsored by the Ohio,

Indiana, and Kentucky CPA Societies; the Pacific Northwest Division of Nationwide Insurance Company; and Bay Alarm Company of Walnut Creek, California. You will be amazed at the similarity of these lists. Employees across the country, across job levels, and across industries really want the same things!

Don't be overwhelmed by all the ideas on these lists. No one is expecting managers to implement all of these suggestions. Supervisors and managers can start by picking one idea from this list to put into action each month. Map out a plan for all 12 months of the year.

- Let employees be boss for the day
- Let employees choose their own schedule for one week
- Christmas parties
- Pizza parties
- Gift certificates
- Halloween costume contest
- Limousine trips
- Sleigh rides
- Movie passes
- Bowling nights
- Points for good job—have auction for prizes
- Gold star
- New name tag (i.e., big badge)
- Bake a cake
- Three minutes of positive thoughts
- Connect with crew member, focus on value of crew member
- Praise
- What can I do for you?
- Respect them
- Remember that they are humans, not robots
- Day off with pay
- Poster with name

- Special hat
- No uniform for a day
- Have appreciation party; give each employee a certificate
- Help employee hardship cases, e.g., buy them a turkey
- Employee group pictures
- Meeting night
- Positive corrective criticism
- Thanks
- Focus on teamwork
- Give encouragement
- Give responsibility
- Exchange food with pizza shop for special treat for crew
- Paid 15-minute break
- Potluck on holidays—added incentive to work
- Dress-up days
- One week off a year with pay
- Full-page ad in employee newsletter
- Ideal parking space
- Buy them a pager
- Buy a birthday flag for the flagpole
- Have an employee night
- Date of hire anniversary
- Praise them in front of others/customers
- Wash their car
- Bouquet of flowers to crew
- Bring in desserts
- Going-away party
- Welcome committee
- Birthday card with key chain
- Cake for graduates
- Let employees vote on things
- Participate in softball games

- Allow radio for special occasion
- Gift exchange
- Pick up employees if they have car problems
- Decorate break room—make more enjoyable
- Make a flamboyant and colorful badge and wear to recognize outstanding performance
- Make a special song for your crew
- Soda
- Pokemon toys
- $25 gift certificate for favorite restaurant
- Tickets to theme park
- Compliment them on paper (write up!)
- Remember their birthdays
- Flowers
- Fun day at work
- Contests
- Don't order; ask!
- Respect their ideas
- Give them a chance to speak
- Put up a banner with their names
- Change their station for a day
- Pokemon characters look-alike contest
- "Box o' Goodies"—candy, stress toys, instant lottery tickets, food coupons
- Put a piece of candy on work station
- Smiley face card on work station
- Flower on shirt for the day
- "How is your day going?"
- Newsletter
- Special photos
- Break the rules

- Find their passion
- Show concern
- Ask about their home life
- Help them out if task is difficult
- Treat them as individuals
- Open doors to great conversation
- Be kind
- Radio announcement
- Karaoke night
- Street clothes day
- Have special button to wear saying, "You are Special"
- Recognition poster: Thank you for a great _____!
- Balloon or something similar as reward that brings attention in the person's work area for performing a task especially well
- Use individual mail grams to employee
- Praise employees on report shared with peers—write on it
- Get business cards for staff
- Interview an employee and tell staff his/her story
- Name office appliances after employees
- Make breakfast for staff
- "Gag" award ceremony
- Give out Kudos candy bars
- Get a recipe book compiled of employees' recipes
- Gifts from the community for employee appreciation week
- Take your unit to lunch/breakfast
- Let someone off for two hours administrative leave
- Certificate "good for one interview"
- Chocolate
- Thank-you gram
- Recognition at meeting
- Send a joke on e-mail

- Let them do a task they enjoy doing
- Statuette for passing on
- Give help with tasks
- "Employee of the Month" parking space
- Offer to do unpleasant task for them
- Get details from client when they send a thank-you note; talk about it in meeting
- Put stickers on the statistical reports
- Buy special pens: the kind they prefer
- Give holiday gifts
- Contests to reinforce awareness of a problem area
- Take best performer in an area of work out to lunch with the management team
- Picnics
- Softball games
- Ice cream social
- Parking lot barbecue
- Funny video
- Fitness week—extra time at lunch for walking
- Bring in an outside speaker
- Popcorn for mandated video viewing
- Voucher for car wash
- Decorate their station
- Random act of kindness for each other
- Say "I'm glad you are in this office"
- "CARE packages"
- Have regular staff meetings
- Clean-up project in the office
- Give them an ice cream cone
- Have jar of trinket prizes
- Pass the puppy (stuffed animal)
- Raffle/drawing

- Send recognition memos to the boss with a copy to the employee
- Recognition buttons
- Call their mother
- Off-site meetings
- Fill surgical gloves with goodies with a note that says, "Thanks for working hand in hand"
- Emotional Bank Account: Deposits and Withdrawals
- One hour off their regular job
- Solicit input from staff re: who did a good thing
- Positive observation—put in file
- Joke board
- Neck rubs
- Give space for lateness
- Show cartoons
- Decorate for holidays
- Scavenger hunt
- After-work activities: bowling, happy hours, picnics
- Funny toys that represent something you've done
- Decorate each person's desk or office for birthday
- Give hugs or pat on the back
- Smile
- Use first name
- Read jokes from *Reader's Digest* at staff meetings
- Ask for suggestions and use them
- A "nut" of the month
- Schedule fire drills at 4:15 p.m.
- On-the-spot awards
- Celebrate small successes
- Empower them—let them make own decisions
- Acknowledge busy days
- Write a poem
- Discuss strengths of the office

- Assign an off-site project
- Pocket planner
- Makeover
- Fill in for your staff; assist with duties
- Open forum
- Promote somebody
- Send to seminar
- Comp time
- Collect promos from seminars
- Game/destress room
- Summer concert at lunch
- Magazine subscription
- Positive phrases
- Quiet corner
- Good chair for the day
- "Word of the day" treat for whoever has the best word
- Anniversary awards—buy carnation for the lapel
- Create a wish bowl, have them put their appreciation wishes on paper in the bowl, and grant the wish weekly
- Let them in on what's going on in the company
- Lift the veil of secrecy
- Let them out early once in a while
- Have a candy dish
- Apologize when wrong
- Be fair to everyone, not just certain people
- Kid day
- Pet day
- Department outing
- Mental health day
- E-mail thanks
- Make good things public
- Job clarification

- Uplifting office music
- Subsidize commuting
- Free parking
- Give them your office for a day
- Warm hats
- Contests
- Laugh at their jokes
- Bring in watermelon in the summer
- Memo to file about good things too! Send to Human Resources also
- Raffles
- Employee bingo for half day off
- Golf outing
- Free video rentals
- Agreement to do nice things with understanding that recipient will pass them on
- Let them chair meeting
- Daily thank-you award
- "Get out of jail free" cards
- Family tree—nicknames, etc.
- Schedule time away from work
- Listen closely
- Show respect
- Show compassion
- Be a peacemaker
- Recognition for attendance
- Better explanations for why certain things happen
- If the performance evaluation doesn't dramatically change from job description, then we don't need it
- Recognition for loyalty and number of years working
- More communication with the departments and directors
- Smile at people

- To actually see department heads/head of company (at least once a month) walking around
- Be more personal
- Write letter to employee's boss
- Laugh more
- Speak to more people
- Give better stipends
- Employee of the month
- Parking spot
- Take doors off all offices
- Fix elevators
- Nap rooms
- Couches in bathrooms
- Better coffee, like Starbucks
- Sensitivity training
- Consistent policy
- Cross training—learning about each other
- Spotlight on Customer Service—at each of your team meetings have a spotlight on customer service where team members can catch each other doing something right
- Recognize another team—plan a special recognition celebration for another team in your organization
- Team Member Recognition Week—set aside a week dedicated to encouraging team members to recognize one another
- The "Noticer"—select a team member to serve as "Noticer," to actively notice the good work of the team
- Coupon Recognition System—give each employee 10 or 20 coupons to distribute to a co-worker for doing something extraordinary, redeem them for a prize at the end of the year.
- Visibility to senior managers—make it a point to introduce employees who have done an excellent job to senior managers.

- Behind the Scenes Award—Develop a "Behind the Scenes" award specifically for those whose actions are not usually in the spotlight.
- Gossip about the Good Things!—When you hear a positive remark about one of your employees, pass it on to them (in person if possible) ASAP.
- Showcase Their Talents—Seek out assignments that showcase an employee's unique and special skills, talents, and abilities.
- Look Under your Chair—At team meetings, randomly tape a few gift certificates to the bottom of the chairs. Don't tell anyone—let this be a complete surprise!
- Food for Thought—Purchase from Successories some posters and other materials to serve as food for thought and give them to the team when they need it the most.
- Capture the Moment—Bring a Polaroid camera to work, take condid photos of employees, and post the photos.
- Team Camera—Purchase a disposable camera that the entire team can use to take spontaneous photos.
- Create a "Team Space"—Establish a place to display memos, posters, photos, etc., recognizing progress toward goals and thanking individual employees for their help. Use color and lots of white space for visual impact. Choose a spot that is visible and gets lots of traffic.
- Capture the Energy—Make a photo collage from a recent staff meeting or team-building exercise. Try to capture as many candid photos of the team as you can. Let the team create the collage.
- Five-minute vacation
- Christmas bonus
- Day off on birthday
- Brainstorming

- Flag football league
- Halloween candy
- Flextime
- Name something after them
- Time off in summer
- Warm up their car in winter
- Scavenger hunt for new employees
- Casual day
- "No shoes" day—leave them at the door
- In-house miniature golf
- Baby picture day
- A rose for each employee
- "No e-mail" day
- Have everyone do the Hokey Pokey at break
- Invite spouses for lunch
- Superman T-shirts

As you can see, even the smallest things, like saying hello in the morning or walking someone to their car at night, can have a profound impact on individual employees. Almost all of these ideas are within every manager's budget. Which ones jumped out at you?

Chapter 7

Ideas and Tools from World-Class Organizations

From Nationwide Insurance, Portland, Oregon

Use the following as a guide to gather "personal preferences" for each of your team members. This will help you build your "people level" database. Feel free to adjust the template to suit your needs and the environment. You can use this as a survey or as a guide during a one-on-one discussion. Be sure to reveal your preferences to the team as well.

Team Member's Name _____

Birthdate _____

- ▶ How do you prefer to receive recognition, i.e., publicly, privately, both?
- ▶ What tangible rewards motivate you most, e.g., money, gift certificates, food, etc.?

- ▶ What intangible rewards motivate you most, e.g., personal thank-you from my manager, thank-you from my team member, etc.?
- ▶ What should your teammates and I *never* do when recognizing you?
- ▶ What special skills, talents, or abilities would you like to share at work that your current job doesn't provide you the opportunity to showcase?
- ▶ Favorite color
- ▶ Favorite food
- ▶ Favorite candy/snack
- ▶ Favorite type of music
- ▶ Favorite singer/band
- ▶ Favorite album, CD, or cassette
- ▶ Favorite vacation spot
- ▶ Favorite book
- ▶ Hobbies
- ▶ Unique fact or characteristic about yourself

(Reprinted with permission from Nationwide Insurance, Portland, Oregon)

A Sample Employee Rewards Survey

We know that every individual has different dreams and desires. In order to make our incentives more meaningful and personal to you, we would like to know your top preferences in each of the following categories. (Note: You may fill in your own ideas here.)

Under $50:

- ▶ Restaurant coupons
- ▶ Phone cards
- ▶ Grocery coupons
- ▶ Gasoline cards
- ▶ Magazine subscriptions

- Gift certificate to a bookstore
- Other_____

$50-$100

- Theme park passes
- Theater/arts tickets
- Massages
- Gourmet dinners
- Other_____

$100-$200

- House cleaning
- Day spa visit
- Flowers for a month
- A one-day seminar
- Department store gift certificate
- Other_____

$200-$400

- Catered party
- Champagne balloon ride
- Retail gift certificates
- Weekend in a hotel
- Other_____

$400-$700

- Association membership
- Ski weekend
- One-year tennis club membership
- Weekend in a fancy hotel
- Airline tickets
- Other_____

$700-$1000

- ▶ Caribbean cruise
- ▶ Limo/dinner/symphony evening
- ▶ Super Bowl or Olympics tickets
- ▶ Other_____

$1000-$2000

- ▶ Box seats/season tickets
- ▶ Golf or health club membership
- ▶ Special vacation
- ▶ Other_____

Walk-on-Water Wishes

- ▶ Porsche 911 year lease
- ▶ Beach house summer lease
- ▶ International adventure travel
- ▶ Trip to a spa retreat
- ▶ Other_____

*(Reprinted with permission from Gail Howerton, MA, CLP, CLL, CEO [Chief Energizing Officer™] of Fun*cilitators™, Fredricksburg, Virginia)*

Regular Team Meetings

The ratio of "we's" to "I's" is the best indicator of the development of a team.

—Lewis W. Eigen

Regular communication with your team is essential to achieving success. The following expectations have been developed to assist you in holding monthly team meetings.

Minimum agenda items for a meaningful team meeting:

- ▶ Recognition
- ▶ Team-building exercise

▶ Share monthly team results
▶ Dissemination of important information
▶ Solicit feedback/ideas on any timely information, issues, or changes

(Reprinted with permission from Nationwide Insurance, Portland, Oregon)

Ideas I will implement:

PART

3

HOW TO CARE:
DOZENS OF ACTION IDEAS

Chapter 8

C = Creative Communication

The key to success is to get out into the store and listen to what the associates have to say. It's terribly important for everyone to get involved. Our best ideas come from clerks and stockboys.
—Sam Walton

Our Gallup research showed that employees like e-mail and voice-mail, but only as a back-up to face-to-face communication. We learned that employees like to get communications from their immediate supervisor.
—Hillary Johnson,
Director of Organization
Performance, AstraZeneca U.S.

In his article titled "Good Communication, Bad Morale" in *IABC Communication World*, John Gerstner, CEO (Communicator/Educator/Organizer), Davenport, Iowa, describes good communication:

Good communication is the glue that can bind an organization together in its quest to be the best. Good communication is the fiber optics cable that shines critical light throughout the organization and lets everyone know how the battle is going. Good communication prepares and helps employees change. Good communication recognizes excellence and promotes it. Good communication eases the disappointment of scarce promotion and career opportunities....Good communication creates a sense of unity and pride. Good communication, finally, helps employees buy into the new business reality with trust, loyalty, and enthusiasm. Good communicators, then, have the single greatest opportunity to make an impact on their organizations.[1]

Here are his five ways to structure communication to boost morale, especially when you are communicating difficult news:

▶ **Be up-front.** Be forthright about the competitive climate your company faces. Communicate as clearly and regularly and as far in advance as you can about what your company is going through and the strategy it is pursuing. Add that all-important perspective from your chief officers on why the changes are necessary, and what they are intended to bring about. Employees should be told what skills will be essential to the business in the future.

▶ **Be honest.** How you say it is as important as what you say. Lay the bad news on the line with as little spin as possible. Fight for communication that rings with a tone of honesty and forthrightness. If you can't be frank, avoid the subject.

▶ **Be human.** Managers should not simply reel off numbers but give sound, candid explanations in a way that recognizes and respects the feelings of both the affected and unaffected employees. All comments about difficult decisions should be prefaced with sincere, from-the-heart pronouncements about the pain that went into making these difficult decisions.

▶ **Be reassuring.** Management must convey a realistic and persuasive case for optimism. Employees must get a sense that they are part of a new organization that is moving aggressively ahead.

▶ **Be real.** Communicators must be real about their role in the organization. And to do that requires a 100% fired up attitude that what you're doing is damned important and is crucial to the success of your organization.

The following pages cover hundreds of ways to improve communication creatively in your workplace. Read how your colleagues from companies all over the United States have adopted creative ways to hold meetings, send messages, talk to their employees, and improve the way business is conducted.

The Idea: Encourage Creative Meetings

Did you know? These meeting facts are reported from the 3M Meeting Management Institute:

▶ The average time spent in meetings is 1.7 hours per day per professional employee.

▶ Executives spend at least 50% of their time in meetings.

▶ On an average day, more than 17 million meetings are held.

▶ Meetings with fewer than 10 participants make up 88% of meetings.

▶ The most productive meetings last under an hour, but the average meeting length is about two hours.[2]

Bob Greene, a syndicated columnist, humorously suggests: "Give corporate America tax breaks for getting rid of meetings and watch our economy soar, and the mood of the workplace broaden into a half-remembered grin."

Making meetings creative, innovative, productive, and positive is one of the ways managers and supervisors can raise morale and keep employees feeling good about their workplace.

Tips for Implementation

A creative communication idea for meetings that I've been sharing with my audiences is to begin every meeting they attend, whether it is in their workplace, their school, their church, or their community, with *three minutes of "good news."* Just ask anyone in the meeting to share any good thing that has happened to them—on the job, in their family, in their community.

My clients are telling me that the results are dramatic. Not only are their meetings more positive and productive, but they are shorter, people are coming on time because they don't want to miss the good news, and they are learning things about one another they never knew before.

Since most meetings focus on what is going wrong, what a joy it is to begin with what is going *right*! We all need to be more positive people in our workplaces and focus on the good we have done.

If you are uncomfortable with the "good news" idea, try starting every meeting with some short sharing time on the human level (five to 10 minutes):

> ▶ Have people share something they love—a hobby, a collection, a pastime.
> ▶ Have all attendees tell one thing about their families.
> ▶ Have each person share the greatest way he or she can think of to spend a birthday.
> ▶ Have participants share what they would do with a thousand dollars if they could not save or invest it but had to spend it on something.
> ▶ Have each person share a favorite vacation spot.
> ▶ Have each person share where he or she grew up.

When people share something that is important or unique to them, it creates relationships and team-building as well as adding some light-hearted fun. You will see a difference in the amount of cooperation and sharing in your meetings.

The Idea in Action

Stan Richards, the founder of **The Richards Group**, an ad agency in Dallas, Texas, came up with an innovative plan for his company's meetings. When the company grew to take up a second floor, he worried that communication would become more formal and less effective. So, he began holding regular meetings in a stairwell that connected the two floors. The idea was to gather everyone so they could hear news straight from the founder.

Even though the company employs more than 400 people today and is one of the largest individually owned ad agencies in the U.S., the Stairwell Meetings continue. They are part of a strategy to maintain the spirit of small-company communication inside a fast-growing outfit.

Richards says in an article in the April 1999 issue of *Fast Company* magazine, "Being together is the key—all of us hearing something at exactly the same time. The event that brings us together varies. Another key point: Meeting in the staircase lets us be a little theatrical. Once, when we were courting an airline client, we even dropped oxygen masks from the fourth floor.... I'll call a meeting within 15 minutes of receiving information. People should hear good news— or bad news—right away.... If I call a meeting, we announce it over the loudspeaker, and people gather in the stairwell. I usually stand on the second level, so everyone can hear me. We try to keep it short: I announce the news and offer a brief

Management unveils its new formula for determining comp time.

explanation. Then I might answer a question or two.... But this is not an occasion for group analysis or deep discussion. It's all about communication, pure and simple."[3]

When they designed their new space, they made sure the stairwell extended to every floor and was right in the center of the office. They say it has become the focal point of their workplace. Does your organization have a special "meeting place" for everyone to hear news straight from the founder? With teleconferencing and other technology, even employees off-site can be included with a little planning.

Tom's of Maine holds business meetings in a circle. In many Native American cultures, the circle is the basis for ritual gatherings, representing the idea that everything is connected to everything else. At Tom's they use the circle to make it easier for them to listen to each other, no matter how diverse they, or their views, may be.

The co-founder of the company, Tom Chappell, believes that a company should be an interdependent body where every part from the CEO to the production line can contribute to the creative process. The circle is egalitarian and suggests wholeness or completeness. In his book, *The Soul of a Business,* he says,

> The power of the circle is in its openness; it is the place where you are willing to "open up" and listen. And when you listen, you learn, you affirm, you support. The circle can take the idea of one person and turn it into the idea of the group. A spark of an idea is raised, discussed, argued; some disagree with it, some applaud it, others add to it, and the original idea gets better, more complex, yet more formed. One person's idea has now become everyone's idea.[4]

At 9 a.m. every morning, the executives of the **Ritz-Carlton Hotel** meet in the hallway outside the president's office for a 10-minute stand-up meeting. The unusual meeting is run by a volunteer facilitator and has three parts. Part One is the topic of the week, which is e-mailed to every hotel around the world so that all employees everywhere are focusing on just one issue each week. Part 2 is a review of one of their "customer service basics," and Part 3 is focused on operational issues that are specific to each department.[5]

Because employees often associate regular meeting rooms with wasted time, boring speeches, and irrelevant information, when you have an important topic to discuss, hold the meeting in an unusual location. *The Motivational Manager* newsletter tells that the chairman of **Campbell Soup** held a board meeting in the back room of a supermarket. After the meeting, the participants roamed the aisles looking for comments about their products.[6]

A *Newsweek* article titled "Mired in Meetings" shares that the average manager spends one and a half days a week in meetings. A single meeting in a big company costs around $15,000. To combat this waste of time and money, some companies have declared "Meetingless Fridays." William Pagonis of **Sears** has the best idea—everyone must stand at meetings because sit-down meetings take 34% longer. He carries out his rapid-fire, vertical briefings in 15 minutes or less![7]

At the end of a regular meeting, dedicate the last five to 10 minutes to asking participants to share concerns and ideas regarding some aspect of your workplace that was not a part of the meeting agenda. This reinforces that you care about what they think, and it provides you a good chance to listen to their ideas.[8]

In his book, *101 Ways to Make Meetings Active,* **Mel Silberman** advocates that meetings need to be *unusual* to achieve results since usual meetings are plagued by unequal participation, strong egos, tangents, communication that is not open and honest, and a dull and deadly climate. He shares several ways to make your meetings unusual:

1. **Give them something to do before the meeting.** Ask them to read something, interview someone, collect data, etc., so that they come vested in the outcome.

2. **Set up the room to encourage participation.** More participation occurs if people are in face-to-face proximity to each other. If the room is not set up that way, move the furniture!

3. **Equalize participation by:**
   ▶ Going around the group or establishing a rule that no one speak twice until everyone who wants has spoken.
   ▶ Having the participants call on each other rather than everything going through the leader.
   ▶ Providing time for people on one side of the meeting table to discuss an issue and then move to a different side … or designate sections of the room.
   ▶ Having other roles besides leader, such as recorder, timekeeper, summarizer, reporter, and follow-up coordinator.

4. **Limit endless participation by:**
   ▶ Adhering to time limits.
   ▶ Stating how many people can talk in a given period of time.
   ▶ Establishing a "parking lot" to place ideas that can be taken up at a later time.

5. **Begin the meeting "at the end."** When participants express their vision of what the group might accomplish, they create a climate of excitement and expectation. Ask participants to imagine that the meeting is over and the meeting was successful and productive. Ask, "What was the most important thing we accomplished today?"

6. **Involve everyone in disseminating information** by dividing it up and asking different people to present what they have been assigned. Give them any reports, charts, graphs, or other documents they may need in their presentation.

7. **Stimulate creative thinking by using lots of brainstorming.** If the issue is too big to handle, break it down into smaller parts before getting creative. It's easier to come up with idea that way. For example, a creative marketing plan can be subdivid-

ed into categories such as message, graphic appeal, target audience, medium, etc.

8. **Manage conflict by stopping a tense meeting** and asking participants to spend ten minutes taking on the viewpoints of people they disagree with. You'll get lots of laughs and some needed clarity of what people are actually saying.

9. **Create consensus in small groups** before trying to achieve it with the entire group. It is often easier to achieve agreement this way.[9]

(Reprinted with permission from Mel Silberman)

The Idea: Find Creative Ways to Keep in Touch

The Idea in Action

Sinara Stull O'Donnell, in her article, "Random Acts of Service—Why Do We Keep Going Back?" writes about a creative way for an agent to keep in touch with her clients:

> Betsy Bogue is a life insurance agent for The Guardian in Los Angeles and a member of the Million-Dollar Round Table. She is also a poet. Every year, she writes a special poem for her policyholders and sends it as a Thanksgiving card. The theme has many subjects, but revolves around celebration of life and thankfulness. Her poems appear on refrigerators and bulletin boards and send a message, "I'm thinking of you."[10]

This is something any supervisor or manager could do for his/her employees.

Send cards to employees on all kinds of occasions—Flag Day, Bald Eagle Appreciation Days, International Pickle Week, National Day of Compassion, a new local area code, the semiannual time change. CardSenders and Cards in the Mail will create them for you and, with a sample of your handwriting, they can add a personalized handwritten note and signature inside. Hallmark has a new line of cards with friendly messages for the workplace such as "Congratulations! The spotlight becomes you" and "Sorry I went into orbit." Called "Out of the Blue," these cards strive to facilitate communication, says Hallmark. In this electronic age of hastily written e-mails and impersonal faxes, a greeting card stands out.[11]

"Talking" billboards are one of the newest and most creative ways to advertise or communicate. Through the use of text, these billboards direct commuters to tune into a specific frequency on their radio. Generally effective within a one-mile radius, the FCC-approved frequency plays a message 30 seconds to a few minutes in length. Think of creative ways you could use these billboards to celebrate employees, send a message about your company's values, or thank both employees and customers.[12]

Madelyn the Microwave sent this memo to her friends at the **Council of Logistics Management** in Oak Brook, Illinois:

> I was so ashamed! Although it was not my fault, I was only doing what I was supposed to do—what I was designed to do. But I fell victim to neglect and abuse.
>
> I was dirty and smelly. Your lunches were on my sides, on my top, on my front, and, if you'll pardon the expression, on my bottom! Bits and pieces of months of lunches, tiny morsels of spattered food, meat and sauces and veggies clung to me.
>
> I would never find myself in this embarrassing situation if you would just take a moment and be sure there is a clean paper towel on my

bottom, and if you would cover your dishes with a paper towel before "turning me on." Is that too much to ask for all the service I give to you? I think not! I'll bet the people at C.H. Green would love to have me come and stay with them. I'll bet they would treat me with the respect I deserve. Rodney Dangerfield gets more respect than I do. And you know how much respect he gets. So how about it?

I'm nice and clean and sweet smelling this morning. Please help me to stay this way.

At **Nationwide Insurance** in Columbus, Ohio, the Office of Procurement was behind locked doors and accessible only by calling the person they need to see and asking them to allow their entrance. Just outside their area, but not behind locked doors, was the VP of Corporate Facilities and his secretary, who are always interrupted by someone wanting into procurement. To limit interruptions, they put up a large sign that says:

Welcome to Our Neighborhood

Corporate Facilities Occupants:
Kathy Holland, Craig Thomas

(Sorry, we cannot help you with access to our neighbors, Procurement/ACM. You may gain access to them via the telephone provided.)

BUT, IF YOUR TOILET BACKS UP, YOU'VE COME TO THE RIGHT PLACE!

This certainly gave everyone on the floor a chuckle!

In an Editor's Note in *Training* magazine, we read how they handled an error in one of the articles they printed:

Harless' fifth principle is to use self-paced instruction whenever possible. We inadvertently lost it during the editing process. The responsible parties have been digitized and deleted.[13]

Everyone loves a sense of humor!

The Idea: Talk to Employees

If a supervisor or manager wants to improve communication and morale, they must be visible and available to talk with employees.

The Idea in Action

At **Armstrong Machine Works**, a division of Armstrong International, either the general manager or the controller hands out employee's paychecks every week, whether they work in the office or in the shop. To do this, the GM or controller must know all the names of over 300 employees. Why do they do this? In his book, *Managing by Storying Around*, David Armstrong says,

> We want everybody to have a chance to be heard. While we have an open door policy, not everybody feels comfortable walking into the corner office. By having an officer of the company hand out paychecks, everyone is assured that at least once a week, he'll have a chance to ask a question, voice a concern, or suggest an idea to one of the people in charge.[14]

Several organizations I have worked with have what they call "grapevine sessions" to stop the flow of the rumor mill and to help create more open communication throughout the organization. The company-wide understanding is that any employee can call a grapevine session at any time that he or she feels there are too many rumblings, rumors, and concerns going on, simply by going to the president or another officer of the company and requesting it. On that same day, all employees who are able are asked to gather in a large area of the company, and the president or whatever company officer is available addresses their questions and concerns in an informal way. Some organizations schedule these informal communication meetings on a regular basis. Often they are followed by a relaxing, social time sponsored by the company, with the group sharing snacks and a soft drink, and the discussion continues in a more relaxed setting.

One of the keys to these sessions working is the commitment by the company officers to be completely open and honest. Even when they can't give specific information, they *can* honestly explain why and when they will be able to share certain information. Another issue of vital importance in larger organizations is to include off-site personnel by either audiotaping or videotaping these sessions and then sending out tapes within 24 hours. It is best to set limits to these meetings—no more than 45 minutes to one hour, and to determine an organizational code of conduct as to what behaviors are acceptable in these meetings. These grapevine sessions can be implemented in departments or divisions or throughout the whole organization.

Several organizations use breakfasts or lunches as special times for senior management and employees to get to know one another better. Sharing a meal creates an atmosphere that encourages openness and bonding. **Iowa Electric Light and Power** has a program called "Lunch with Management." At least twice a month officers of the company are available at different locations, such as the general office, operations locations, and the power plants, and employees can sign up to share that time with them. At **Greenville Utilities Commission** employees can fill out a coupon and then they are randomly selected for an informal breakfast or lunch with general management. These informal meetings allow a new level of understanding and communication to permeate the organization.

Kenneth Smith, the General Manager of the **O'Hare Hilton Hotel** in Chicago, Illinois, has a "Meet the Manager" meeting once a month. These informal meetings are held in a neutral room at different times, and he encourages open, off-the-record discussions of whatever the employees would like to talk about. Ken always shares his philosophy that the *employee* has the most important job in the company, and his job is least important. This level of communication and respect has won his hotel the award for the outstanding airport hotel in the country! Ken also sends a birthday card to each employee on his or her special day.

To better improve communication between his senior management and his employees, a senior manager decided to give each of his direct reports five paper silhouettes of his hand for Christmas each year. Each paper "Helping Hand" represents one hour of his time which the employees can choose to use any way they want during the year. Not only do they have lots of fun teasing him about baby-sitting, mowing their lawns, or walking their dogs, but as the manager he actually does the tasks the employees choose, such as sorting and delivering mail, answering telephones, entering data, and covering the front desk. He not only learns more about them and their work, but he also creates a new spirit of teamwork and communication.

 The **Gymboree Corp.** in Burlingame, California, each year surveys all 7000 employees. They ask how they feel about working there and what they can do to make work a better experience. To make sure that they get at what's really going on, they ask questions in many different ways. Then they assemble a team to work on what they've learned. Many changes have occurred as a result of these surveys. Gary White, the CEO, says that keeping employees happy is the key to long-term success. That means keeping the channels of communication open—measuring satisfaction through surveys as well as just by walking around and checking in with people.[15]

In their book, *True Leaders,* Bette Price and George Ritcheske share how Jim Nicholson, President and CEO of **PVS Chemicals, Inc.**, Lou Smith, President and CEO of the **Ewing Marion Kauffman Foundation**, and Garrett Boone, the Chairman and co-founder of **The Container Store**, creatively communicate with their employees:

> ▶ **"Call Jim Day."** PVS Chemicals' Jim Nicholson picks one day a quarter and designates it as "Call Jim Day." "You can call up, you don't have to identify yourself, it's just an open direct access for

folks to call up and vent or praise or complain," Nicholson explains. It's open to employees, their spouses, even their kids—anyone who wants to call. And there are no filters—no secretary who screens the call and says that Nicholson is not available.[16]

▶ **Chats with Lou.** Five times a year Lou Smith convenes a group of 30 to 50 associates so he can spend time listening to their ideas, their suggestions, and just about anything they want to talk about. To create an environment conducive to listening, they have built a special room modeled after an Indian Kiva, where tiered seating in a circular design allows everyone to see Smith when he sits on a stool in the middle and also allows him to see each participant. He gives each associate a chance to talk with him, and he is quick to point out that there are audiovisual gadgets in the room—no microphones, no speakers, no projectors, no screens—nothing to distract from the important ability to fully listen. He says, "Create an environment wherein you can hear what is being said and therefore you can be in a position to provide some vision, some leadership, some direction, some substance to what you've heard."[17]

▶ **Sharing Information.** Talking to people and letting them know what is going on is deeply important to Garrett Boone of The Container Store. Boone says,

We have staff meetings which are anywhere from two to four times a year with everybody from store managers to sales managers from all of the stores, and sometimes (other) people that the store manager wants to send. Everybody in the corporate office is invited. All the distribution managers and supervisors attend. So, you have this company-wide meeting where everybody talks about everything we are doing—the past, the present, the future—the goals, whether we hit them, what our financial performance is. Then all the information discussed is made up into this magazine and everybody in the company gets a copy of it—part-time people, seasonal people, anybody who is working for us at the time.

Additionally, every store, every day, gets sales reports that show all 22 stores—not just their store, but every store in the company, every single day. "I think that creates trust," Boone says. "In most retail organizations, even the store manager probably doesn't get information about other stores' sales—maybe the district or something—but not the whole company. Most companies are stingier than heck when it comes to praising people and getting our information," Boone says. Not The Container Store![18]

Another example of the importance of talking with employees is also shared in *True Leaders* when David Novak wanted the job as CEO of **Pepsi-Cola Company** even though he knew nothing about operations. The way he made up for his lack of knowledge was that he went to the people:

> I went to the front line. I went out and met with the sales people, the people in the warehouse, people on the (production) line, and I asked them, "What should we do?" So, I learned from the people who really knew the business what we should do and then I could use my power, my leverage in the organization, to go back and work on the processes and the tools that would help us to get things done. It was amazing.

Armed with this firsthand information, Novak said he could be in a market for one day, sit down at the end of the day, and rattle off four or five things that needed to be worked out.[19]

Michael Bonsignore, chairman and CEO of **Honeywell International**, known for his ability to mix freely with employees at all levels of the company and elicit their ideas, spends two days a week traveling to Honeywell plants and offices in the U.S. and abroad to meet staff. The trips are time-consuming and often exhausting but are a critical way to keep employees motivated, he believes. When he visited a plant in Freeport, Illinois, he held a general town meeting and then met with 20 "high-potential" employees, asking questions and listening to their thoughts. In an article in the *Chicago Tribune*, he says, "Since no other executive but me is present at those small meetings, there's an atmosphere of candor, and a chance to get a unique perspective I would never get if I stayed in my office."[20]

The Idea: Creative Newsletters

In her book *CARE Packages for the Workplace*, Barbara Glanz says, "When each of us fully understands the choices we have to make a difference ... we can leave with a new sense of purpose and commitment to one another and to our very important jobs." I see our newsletter as an opportunity for each of us to make a *choice* to share our happiness and pride with one another, and thus make a difference!

The Idea in Action

APAC Customer Services, Inc., a firm headquartered in Deerfield, Illinois, with call centers throughout the country, had a creative idea for a newsletter. The story—"We Want the 'Scoop'!"—was printed in their monthly newsletter.

We Want the "Scoop"!

Have you ever wanted to be a reporter? Here's your chance! We want you to "scoop" us on the *great things happening in your center or department*. Submit a story and/or photograph (preferably black and white) with a caption for the newsletter. If your article/photo is printed, not only will you have the byline, but you will also be awarded with a certificate of recognition and a gift. Even if your story is not printed, you will still receive a certificate of recognition for your contribution. There is no limit to the number of stories you can submit, so put your press hat on and sharpen your pencils. The presses are ready to roll!

During acquisitions and mergers, one organization created a newsletter that is printed on an as-needed but at least weekly basis called "The Rumor Buster." Ruth Bramson, senior vice president of HR at

Shaw's Supermarkets of New England, which recently acquired another company, and who started the newsletter, says, "Communication is the major stumbling block to a successful merger. 'The Rumor Buster' addressed whatever horrendous rumors were going around at the moment. We found it to be an incredibly useful tool." This kind of newsletter, I think, may be appropriate in any large company![21]

The Idea: Creative Fundraising

The Idea in Action

The **Salesian Sisters** of North Haledon, New Jersey, have come up with a creative way to raise funds for their order. They have begun an "Adopt a Sister" program. For $200 a year, donors can "adopt" an elderly nun to pray for them. The sisters have attracted thousands of donors from all over the world. Apparently, lots of people believe it's good to have friends with friends in high places! "One-to-One with a Nazareth Nun" is a similar program begun by the **Sisters of the Holy Family of Nazareth** in Philadelphia.[22] Corporate marketers can learn a lot from these creative nuns!

Think of creative ways you could use employees to raise funds for special parties or charitable projects.

The Idea: Creative Recruitment Ideas

The Idea in Action

In a time of tough competition for employees, many organizations are finding creative ways to communicate their need to hire.

American Express looks for applicants by advertising on the back of grocery store cash register receipts in North Carolina.[23]

Ohio employers needing workers put printed sticky-backed announcements of job opportunities on car windows in the high school parking lots during commencement ceremonies.[24]

To energize employee referral programs, **MasterCard** in St. Louis sends fliers with paychecks as a reminder of their referral rewards. They also send promotional letters to employees' homes. The idea is to get spouses involved in helping refer job candidates. With this and other creative referral boosters, MasterCard fills 40% of its open positions.[25]

These organizations certainly are finding unusual ways to get the attention of prospective workers!

Other creative recruitment ideas are shared by Andy Chan, President and CEO of **eProNet**, an online recruiting and career management network in San Mateo, California, in an interview with *Success in Recruiting and Retaining* newsletter:

▶ **Treat them like royalty.** One service organization pursuing a golden candidate on the opposite coast had its chairman of the board make the first call to the candidate. The candidate was flown first class to New York City for the interview. He took the job. Two weeks earlier, he didn't even know he was a prospect.

▶ **Sell the dream.** What is your company's vision? How is your company going to change the world? Why would great people want to work there? You have to sell the dream and show your own passion. "Golden Needle candidates"—hot prospects who are currently employed—"want to live the dream," Chan says.

▶ **Find that special perk.** Come up with something out of the ordinary your company can offer and target it to the applicant's interest. One recruiter got tickets to the U.S. Open tournament for a job candidate who loved golf—and closed the deal just as Tiger Woods sank a putt on the 14th hole![26]

▶ **Help transferees overcome cold feet.** Tactics like job-hunting help for the candidate's spouse, regional photo albums, and videotapes help recruit both husband and wife. "We engage the spouse early on," says Sam Gassett, president of **Primus Associates LC**, an executive search firm in Austin, Texas. "We contact the spouse at home 'by accident' when we know the candidate will not be there, because it's important to understand the spouse's informal attitude to moving and living here."[27]

To recruit software engineers, **Softricity, Inc.**, a Boston-based software developer, rents an orange van with promotional advertising on the outside and a flashing light on top that revolves when the vehicle is standing. Called "Recruiting on Wheels," the van hits the streets during lunch and rush hours. Employees hand out pens and cookies with the company logo. Everywhere the van stops, employees encourage taxi drivers to let them put cookies in their cabs, persuade bus drivers to look the other way while they put cookies on the seats, and even cajole shoeshine workers into helping pass out the pens. Everyone from the vice presidents to the sales representatives get involved in the recruiting process. After just eight days the HR Director says that the number of applications and interviews shot up dramatically![28]

Texas Instruments has added a raffle for a chance to win a $52,000 Ford, Lincoln, or Mercury vehicle to its employee referral program, which used to give employees a $1500 bonus if they recommended a successful job applicant. Since the raffle was added, the number of referrals has tripled.[29]

At **BabyCenter**, an online site for new parents in San Francisco, employees who refer new hires receive $2000 cash, a bottle of Dom Perignon, flowers, and balloons. About half of all new employees are referrals.[30]

IKEA, a Swedish furniture manufacturer, posts job openings in a handwritten, graffiti-like manner, in men's and women's bathrooms at several upscale restaurants. They received four times the number of applications in 60 days![31]

Kelly Services based in Troy, Michigan, ran ads on video monitors in 7-Eleven convenience stores in the Baltimore area to recruit workers for a distribution company. They also plan to use the monitors at Subway sandwich shops and Shell gas stations.[32]

Manpower, Inc., based in Milwaukee, Wisconsin, has recruited the help of about 275 churches around the country to search for workers. For every prospect referred to Manpower the churches get a $50 bonus.[33]

A recent **Booz Allen Hamilton Inc.** recruitment ad pictured paper clips, a diaper pin, and text about the firm's "human side" to push its family-friendliness.[34]

Seen on the employment site of **Thinksource Inc.**,: "Does the majority of stuff on the Web make you puke? Work at Thinksource and make it better. It would be cool if you have an extensive collection of T-shirts and enjoy loud music."[35]

The Idea: Boosting Everyone's Creativity

The Idea in Action

Chris Baum, the vice president of sales and marketing for **Sonesta Hotels & Resorts**, uses some interesting techniques to tap the creativity of his sales force in his national sales meetings. One of the things he does is to have everyone check their cell phones at the door. A "telehost" is assigned to collect the phones, answer any calls during the meeting, and keep track of messages.

He also has the meeting revolve around an activity. One such activity is a cooking class. Groups of two or three people each prepare a part of a meal that everyone gets to eat. This gets the group away from the routine, creates trust and team-building, and can promote "out of the box" ideas. Another interesting activity was a sand-castle-building contest to promote networking opportunities across sales regions. They were given an hour to create everything a city would need to survive. Not only did they have a wonderful time, but they got to know one another well in the process. Communicating in ways that are different from one's usual routine "whack" the thinking and stimulate new ideas.[36]

The Idea: Improving Communication

People work better and suffer less stress and fewer complications when they are well informed. At the same time, information attracts information. Managers who are generous with what they know seem to get as much as they give. The ability to attract, create, and disseminate information can become an immense managerial asset, a self-perpetuating information network and a means of creating the trust that the upward flow of candid information depends on.

The Idea in Action

Lois P. Frankel, President of **Corporate Coaching International** in Pasadena, California, believes that all work is social, and that involves communication. In an article in *Fast Company*, May 1999, she says, "Establishing good working relationships can help us secure the cooperation of the people we need to accomplish our tasks." Here are some of her favorite techniques:

- ▶ Once a day, drop into someone's office for a 10-minute talk.
- ▶ When people talk to you, listen.
- ▶ When you need help, ask for it.
- ▶ Begin conversations with small talk. "If you always talk about work, people will think that you only care about work—and that you don't care about them."
- ▶ Don't let your desire to be liked keep you from being straightforward.

▶ Do favors for others—even when you can't anticipate that a favor will be returned.[37]

Symmetrix, Inc., a Lexington, Massachusetts-based consulting group, has Friday Forums to encourage debate and discussion. Every Friday morning all employees gather in the company's amphitheater for a no-holds-barred session in which ideas are exchanged, challenged, and talked through as they discuss technical aspects of projects they're working on, batting around ideas for solving stumbling blocks and problems. Departmental reports are also given. On the fourth Friday of the month the financial books are presented so everyone knows exactly where the company stands. Every week changes are made, both internally and externally, because of the ideas generated at these forums.[38]

Todd's relationship with management improved dramatically once he started bringing his new pet to work.

Close to Home by John McPherson/Dist by Universal Press Syndicate

The Idea: Creative Voice Mail

The Idea in Action

Many people agree with the national columnist who has called voice mail "a poisonous moat barring humanity from the gates of intercourse." In fact, according to TARP in Arlington, Virginia, 70% of people want to talk to a person rather than a machine.[39]

Voice mail can be one of the most frustrating technological developments for anyone in sales because it is almost impossible to get a real person on the phone. Orvel Ray Wilson, co-author of *Guerrilla TeleSelling,* shares some creative messages that can help you get your calls returned:

▶ **The insomnia message.** Because most voice mail has a time stamp, you can leave a messages at odd hours to make a strong impression: "Hi, it's 3:30 in the morning and I was just thinking about your account with us, and I couldn't sleep, so I decided to send you this message..."

▶ **The mile-high message.** Next time you're on a plane, use the onboard phone to call people you wish to reach: "Hi, I'm calling from 37,000 feet on my way to Chicago. I was thinking about you and just had to call."

▶ **The stockholder's message.** Buy a few shares of your prospect's stock. Then leave a message introducing yourself as a concerned stockholder.

▶ **The "who you're not" message.** "Hi. I'm not with the IRS. I'm not selling insurance. I'm not looking for a job or a donation. I don't want to borrow money, but I do want to talk to you about... "

▶ **The "file a missing person" message.** "Hello. Your staff doesn't seem to know where you are, and frankly, I'm concerned. I just wanted to let you know that I've filed a missing person report.

▶ **The persistent or pest message.** Larry Winget, a motivational speaker from Tulsa, Oklahoma, uses this one: "There is a fine line between being persistent and being a pest. I want to serve you well, yet never be a pest. Will you please call and tell me how best to serve you?"

And for those clients or prospects who have a really good sense of humor:

▶ **The kiddy call message.** Have your kids make a call: "My daddy is going crazy waiting for you to call him back. Would you please call? As soon as you do, he can take me for ice cream."[40] (*Reprinted with permission from Orvel Ray Wilson from* Guerrilla Teleselling)

Although these ideas were suggested for salespeople calling customers, why not use the same creativity in leaving voice mail messages internally, especially if you want to get a response.

Many people have begun to personalize their voice mail messages, which makes them much more interesting. I, for example, always leave my travel schedule as well as a short "thought for the day" on my voice mail. Hardly a week ever goes by that I don't get a message saying, "I got the wrong number, but I *love* your voice mail message!"

Carol Dennis at **Farmland Insurance** in Des Moines, Iowa, leaves this message: "Hello. This is Carol Dennis at Farmland Insurance. It is a rainy Thursday, April 3. But remember ... April showers bring May flowers. Please leave your name..."

The Idea: Using Stories to Communicate

The Idea in Action

Anita Ward, a vice president of **Cambridge Technology Partners**, uses campfire stories as a means to build morale, increase commitment, and help employees buy into change. Change is emotionally difficult for most people, and unless they can make it personal and meaningful, change initiatives will die. Campfire stories, according to Ward, encourage change by making it more human. They turn experiences into narratives, people into heroes, and new ideas into enduring traditions.

Her process:

> Typically I invite people to sit down with me in a safe, comfortable setting. I get them to talk about the themes, emotions, and sensibilities that surround change. For example, when I helped launch a diversity

initiative, I encouraged people to talk about their early experiences. What was it like to grow up in a Chinese-American family? Then, after I talk with people, I retell their stories to the rest of the organization. I start out by publishing each campfire story in as many formats as possible: e-mail, a newsletter, photos, a collaborative database. I also tap into an informal social network by enlisting people whom I call "tribal elders." These are people who have strong social bonds—like all of the smokers out on a street corner. Tribal elders can help champion and perpetuate a story. All of a sudden, change is no longer an abstract business mandate—it's a message embodied in a hero. So the adoption rate goes up, because people like to follow heroes.[41]

Tip

I often suggest to my clients that they start a collection of company legends in both audio and written form. Some of them have even videotaped employees telling about favorite management gaffs, great customer service stories, legendary sales meetings, etc. Just as we love to retell favorite family stories, employees love to retell experiences that have been memorable for them. These collections of stories build pride and help to capture a culture. They are particularly valuable for new employees to learn the "human" history of an organization.

The Idea: Designing Anonymous Forms of Communication

Often employees do not feel secure enough to share deep concerns or hard truths with their managers, so one of the ways to get this information—while you are working on building a relationship of trust so they will feel comfortable to tell you—is to design anonymous forms of communication—such vehicles as suggestion boxes, questionnaires, and performance appraisals. Here are some other creative ways to do this.

One manager took advantage of an odd condition in his office space. Their offices were on the 9th and 10th floors of the building and had two elevators which every employee rode several times a day. The boss put a bulletin board in each of them and posted frequent notices, including a weekly newsletter about office activities, personnel changes, etc.

He then let it be known informally that the bulletin boards were open to everyone—no approvals required—and when the first employee notices appeared, he made a point to keep them there for a full week. There were only two rules. No clippings from newspapers and magazines—contributions had to be original. And nothing tasteless or abusive—but complaints and bellyaching were OK.

The bulletin boards flourished, partly because most people had at least an occasional chance to ride alone and post their own views in private. For a while there was even an anonymous weekly newspaper that handed out praise and criticism pretty freely and irreverently. It made some people uncomfortable, but it had no more avid reader than the boss, who learned volumes.[42]

The Idea in Action

"I give everybody my e-mail address" and roughly twice a week a staffer sends an unsigned message, reports the CEO at **Eastman Kodak**. He pays extra attention to messages that repeat the same theme, and major changes have been instituted as a result of these communications.[43]

At **Browning-Ferris Industries, Inc.** (now part of Allied Waste Industries), anonymous complaints are aired in open electronic forums. The CEO invites employees to send him unsigned, critical questions via an e-mail system that disguises the writer's identity, and posts daily replies on an electronic bulletin board. Executives screen questions and remove redundant or slanderous messages before posting. Again major changes have occurred since this system was begun.[44]

The CEO of **Rite Aid** installed InTouch, an outside voice-mail service. At any hour staffers may call a toll-free service and leave messages. InTouch prepares verbatim transcripts for its clients, who never hear callers' voices. The CEO says he reads the transcript every morning and takes each one seriously.[45]

Dedicate an e-mail address to *employee retention*. Be sure it is set up so that employees can send anonymous messages. Let everyone know you are looking for causes of turnover, reasons employees leave the company. This is a good way to find out about potential problems.

The Idea: Using E-Mail Carefully

The Idea in Action

Jane Ranshaw, a communications consultant from Chicago, IL, in an article titled "Surviving E-Mail—Road Rage on the Information Superhighway" in *Training Today* (July/August 1999), writes about some important strategies to use when you are communicating with your employees by e-mail:

► The first step is to determine whether e-mail is the best method for communicating. If there is a chance for misunderstanding, a face-to-face meeting may be the better choice. According to Nigel Nicholson, professor of organizational behavior at the London Business School, people have a tendency to "hear bad news first and loudest." In other words, employees often look for bad news even if the sender did not intend it. A message that appears slightly challenging or ironic to the sender often strikes the recipient as hostile or sarcastic.

► Watch your tone. What seems brisk and businesslike to you may set off a reaction in the receiver. To check for a possibly hostile tone, print e-mail and read it aloud before sending it. Should you receive an e-mail that irritates you, avoid responding in kind.

► When you're emotional, wait to respond. Type the message if you must, but leave the recipient line blank. That way, the message can't be sent accidentally when you sign on.

▸ Send copies only to those who really need to receive a copy.

▸ Avoid all capitals—they're like shouting and make an innocuous message sound harsh.

▸ Ask permission to forward e-mail.

▸ Use meaningful subject lines.

▸ Limit length of the e-mail. Most recipients read only one screen of information, so longer messages are less likely to be read.

▸ Avoid all lower case.

▸ Include only one message in each e-mail.[46]

(Reprinted with permission from Jane Ranshaw)

The in-house e-mail at **Quaker Oats** is called—what else?—OatMail!

The Idea: Posting Creative Signs

Delightful signs can not only help to create an atmosphere of joy but can also help to celebrate your values. Here are a few examples:

The beatings will continue until morale improves.
—a trucking line

Our company is judged by the people it keeps.
—a bank

Through these doors walk the most skilled and dedicated hospitality professionals in Denver.
—posted above the
employee entrance in a hotel

All children allowed to roam free in this store will be captured and used as slaves.
—Peterson's Ice Cream Store
Oak Park, Illinois

In our work, Stephen Covey and I talk about the concept of an emotional bank account. The idea is that each of us has an emotional bank account. During the day we get deposits and withdrawals in our job. When I ask an audience which they receive the most, without hesitation, all over the world, they unanimously shout, "Withdrawals!"

In a large teleservices center on the East Coast, where there were several hundred employees working in cubicles in one huge room, a group of them got together and made placards on long sticks that read, "I need a deposit!" Whenever they had received a really difficult or insulting phone call, they simply held the sign up high in their cubicle where others on the floor could see it, and those employees who were not on the phone rushed to their aid with a compliment, a treat, or an offer for help! Thus, by asking for a deposit, they received one.

A Caution

Bob Filipczak, in his column "Between the Lines" in *Training* magazine, shares an experience of the lasting impact one's words can have:

> One corporate veteran I interviewed last year told me a story that illustrates how effectively (and effortlessly) a CEO can devastate employee morale. Her team had been working extra hard—long days, weekends, taking work home—to get a project out the door. The day they got it done, the CEO walked through their work area, not to congratulate them, but to complain about how messy their offices were.
>
> Three years later, my source said, the people in her department still remembered the incident clearly. For his part, the CEO in question probably had no idea that anything significant had occurred. Perhaps he didn't even know that these people had just done something extraordinary for his company. Unless he was a sadist, deliberately bent on destroying morale, he was simply oblivious.
>
> The point is, executives' words carry more weight than they realize. How many times have you said or done something that stuck with a group of people for three years?[47]

Think carefully before you speak!

Quick Creative Communication Ideas

▶ Take a team photo to send to employees' families and clients.

▶ Send an important message or good news to all employees in fortune cookies.

▶ Send memos or personal e-mail messages at a time when they don't expect them to let employees know you are thinking about them. Notice what they're doing, their accomplishments, and their difficulties and acknowledge that they are important to your team.

▶ Broadcast an uplifting "Thought for the Day" on voice mail.

▶ Keep a bowl of special candy on your desk. It will contribute greatly to an open door policy!

▶ Kick out the ruts! Go to work a different way. Try a new breakfast cereal. Listen to a different radio station.

▶ Read a new magazine each month, preferably one you've never heard of.

▶ Spend a workday each week at home, in the library, at a customer's, out on the floor—anywhere but in your office.

▶ Schedule breakfast with an employee at least once a week and spend time learning what is important to him or her and finding out how you might be of help to make their job easier. Then ask that employee for honest feedback about your management style.

▶ Give employees a coupon to take their supervisor to breakfast or lunch to discuss: 1. What they really like about their job and 2. What concerns they have and their ideas for solutions. Ask the supervisor to take notes and keep a running list of all employees' answers to look for common themes.

▶ Instead of asking people how they feel about a particular issue, have them draw how they feel about it and create a storyboard. The drawings are usually terrible, but people laugh and important issues come to light.

▶ Arrange seating at meetings based on where you dream of retiring.

▶ Start a "financial billboard" where you post all pertinent financial information to keep employees informed. Once a quarter have a training session where employees can learn what the numbers mean.

▶ Post a brainstorming board. Write out a common sales theme or problem on a colored index card and post it in the center of a bulletin board. Provide white cards on which salespeople or other employees can write their solutions and responses.

▶ When your boss is in a bad mood and you don't want to enter his/her office but you need an answer to a question, fly it in as a paper airplane. That should make him/her smile and the bad mood disappear!

▶ Hold monthly "gripe sessions" where employees can air complaints. It is best to hold these somewhere away from work but on company time. Do not let employees attack individuals.

Notes

1. Gerstner, John. 1994. "Good Communication, Bad Morale." *IABC Communication World*, March, p. 21.

2. Editor. 1995. "Did You Know?" *Meeting and Management Essentials*, Summer, p. 8.

3. Olofson, Cathy. 1999. "Stairway to Information Heaven." *Fast Company*, April, p. 68.

4. Chappell, Tom. 1994. "The Soul of Business." *Executive Female*, January/February. Tom Chappell, 1994, *The Soul of a Business* (New York: Bantam Books).

5. Olofson, Cathy. 1998. "The Ritz Puts on Stand-up Meetings." *Fast Company*, September, p. 62.

6. Editor. *The Motivational Manager,* Sample Issue, p. 14.

7. McGinn, Daniel. 2000. "Mired in Meetings." *Newsweek*, October 16, pp. 52-54.

8. Humphrey, Brad, and Jeff Stokes. 2000. "The 21st Century Supervisor." *HR Magazine*, May, p. 185.

9. Silberman, Mel. 2000. "How to Make Meetings Unusual." *Innovative Leader,* April, p. 8.

10. O'Donnell, Sinara Stull. "Random Acts of Service." *Sam's Club Source,* p. 8.

11. Ho, Rodney. 1998 "Happy <u>Fill in the Blank</u> Day." *The Wall Street Journal,* March 30.

12. Editor. 1999. "Now Hear This." *Entrepreneur,* July 19.

13. Editor. 1996. "Editor's Note." *Training,* July, p. 21.

14. Armstrong, David. 1992. *Managing by Storying Around.* New York, NY: Bantam Doubleday Dell Publishing Group, Inc.

15. McCauley, Lucy. 1999. "Measure What Matters." *Fast Company,* May, p. 102.

16. Price, Bette, and Ritcheske, George. 2001. *True Leaders: How Exceptional CEOs and Presidents Make a Difference by Building People and Profits.* Chicago, IL: Dearborn Trade, p. 145.

17. Ibid., p. 64.

18. Ibid., p. 123.

19. Ibid., p. 47.

20. Hymowitz, Carol. 2000. "Wasted Skills." *Chicago Tribune,* May 28, Section 6, p. 3.

21. Editor. "The Rumor Buster Newsletter." Shaw's Supermarkets of New England.

22. King, Rachel P. 2000. "Nuns Make Action a Habit." *Working Woman,* December/January, p. 20.

23. Herman, Roger. 1998. "Creative Recruiting: Predictions from a Consulting Futurist." *Adult Ed Today,* September-December, p. 12.

24. Ibid.

25. Editor. 2000. "Quick Tip." *Success in Recruiting and Retaining,* December, p. 2.

26. Editor. "How to Find 'Golden Needles' in a Haystack." *Success in Recruiting and Retaining.* Sample Issue, p. 3.

27. Sopensky, Emily. 2000. *The Austin Business Journal,* Dec. 8.

28. Editor. "Drive-by Recruiting Boosts Applications." *Success in Recruiting and Retaining,* Sample Issue, p. 5.

29. Editor. 2000. "Adding Perks Besides Cash Keeps Referrals Coming." *Success in Retaining and Recruiting.* October, p. 5.

30. Ibid.

31. Ibid.

32. Fister, Sarah, et al. 1999. "A Job Hunter's Place Is in the Mall." *Training,* March, pp. 20-21.

33. Ibid.

34. Editor. 2000. "Spice Up Bland Help-Wanted Ads." *Success in Recruiting and Retaining,* August, p. 1.

35. www.thinksource.com.

36. Campbell, Malcolm. 1999. "Meet Your Match: How to Use Meetings to Tap the Creative Force of Your Salespeople." *Selling Power,* March, pp. 80-87.

37. Kaplan, Michael. 1999. "How to Overcome Your Strengths" (sidebar: "Be a Social Worker," *Fast Company,* May, p. 228.

38. Editor. "3 Ways to Trigger Workplace Creativity." *The Lake Report on Positive Employee Practices,* Sample Issue, p. 1.

39. Horowitz, Rick. 1997. "Anniversary Schmaltz."*Chicago Tribune Magazine,* January 5, p. 17.

40. Levinson, Jay Conrad, Smith, Mark S.A., and Wilson, Orvel Ray. 1998. *Guerrilla TeleSelling: New Unconventional Weapons and Tactics to Sell When You Can't Be There in Person.* New York, NY: John Wiley & Sons.

41. Olofson, Cathy. 1999. "To Transform Culture, Tap Emotion." *Fast Company,* April, p. 54.

42. Lublin, Joann S. 1997. "Dear Boss: I'd Rather Not Tell You My Name But...." *The Wall Street Journal,* June 17, p. B1.

43. Editor. 1994. "How to Turn Hints into Hard Facts." *Executive Female,* May/June p. 18.

44. Lublin, Joann S. 1997. Op. cit.

45. Ibid.

46. Ranshaw, Jane. 1999. "Surviving E-Mail—Road Rage on the Information Superhighway." *Training Today,* July/August, pp. 11-12.

47. Filipczak, Bob. 1996. "Between the Lines." *Training,* May, p. 8.

Chapter 9

A = Atmosphere

People may not remember what you say, and they may not remember what you do. But they'll always remember how you made them feel.

—Unknown

While motivating employees directly can be difficult, creating an environment that allows employees to achieve success can make things a lot easier. According to a recent study done by Dr. Gerald Graham, a management professor at Wichita State University, the top five workplace motivators are:

1. Personal thanks from leader
2. Written thanks from leader
3. Promotion for performance
4. Public praise
5. Morale-building meetings[1]

What are you doing as a supervisor or manager in each of these areas to create a motivating atmosphere?

The Idea: Encourage a Creative Environment

The Idea in Action

In an article titled "Creativity in Teams" in *The Inner Edge,* Steven R. Pritzker, Ph.D., writes about being a part of the greatest creative team in television history—the group that produced *The Mary Tyler Moore Show.* It won more Emmys than any other prime-time show. He finds that creative environments, environments where new ideas flourish and people give their very best, share certain features:

▶ Innovative organizations offer a work atmosphere in which everyone can express ideas (**Respect**). The approach of the executive producers created an atmosphere in which the show belonged to everyone, and that resulted in a staff that worked harder and felt prouder (**Reason for Being**).

▶ The leaders in creative organizations are not afraid to let go of the reins (**Atmosphere**). These leaders will seek honest feedback about their behaviors and use it to improve leadership. Creativity will flourish only when ideas are received with as much support as possible; creativity cannot grow in an atmosphere that is controlling, bureaucratic, or inflexible (**Respect**). Leaders are often unconscious of how their controlling behavior causes others to be fearful and "shut down" (**Atmosphere**).

▶ Creative collaboration can grow with differences of opinion (**Empathy**). Fighting is good! But that's not the same as fighting caused by poor communication. Differences of opinion can be beneficial when openly communicated (**Creative Communication**).

▶ Creative organizations make sure to include all members in the process of developing ideas (**Appreciation**)—and use humor to diffuse any tensions (**Enthusiasm**). Thomas Edison started each day with a joke-telling session. A happy, upbeat atmosphere helps foster creativity.[2]

The Idea in Action

What kind of an atmosphere have you created for your team? Here are ideas for a more creative environment:

Create an innovation chamber. Set aside a conference room, cafeteria, hall (anywhere except an office) to use as a space for meeting and exchanging ideas. Set up two or three easels with paper and offer a wide assortment of colored, good-smelling markers and crayons for writing ideas. As people enter the room remind them that "anything goes" and "every idea is a good idea."

Set up a creative corner. Stock the area with books, learning games, creativity videos, and lots of toys. Encourage your employees to spend a little time each week playing in the creative corner to bring out the imaginative child in them. Decorate the room with employees' baby pictures to reinforce that we all need to be more spontaneous.

Post a brainstorming board. Write out a common problem on a colored index card and post it in the center of a bulletin board. Provide white cards on which employees can write and then post their solutions and responses.

The Idea: Encourage Employees' Special Interests

The Idea in Action

Find out people's special interests and encourage employees to get together for a common cause. It may be an interest in cars, home brewing, woodworking, travel, music, or literature. According to an article in *Employee Services Management (ESM) Magazine*, the following activities are wonderful ways to build relationships across the organization and to celebrate people as humans with lives and interests outside of work:

 Gates Rubber Company, Denver, Colorado, encourages art by holding art shows on site, where employees can display and sell their work to fellow employees and the public.
Other companies, like **Jet Propulsion Labs**, encourage art by offering discount tickets to art museums and art galleries.[3]

In recent years, many companies have found it necessary to employ Game Police

Close to Home by John McPherson/Dist. by Universal Press Syndicate

 Jet Propulsion Labs' recreation club, Pasadena, California, formed a music club in which instrument-playing employees hold jam sessions with others interested in similar styles of music. Specialty bands such as jazz and rock are formed within this club, and the members have a wonderful opportunity for extra practice and the sharing of their special talents. Other companies have company choirs and drama teams. They often perform at all-company functions.[4]

 Compaq Computers, Houston, Texas, holds a creative photo contest, with incentives for the winner in several categories. Other organizations encourage starting a photography club.[5]

 Gates Rubber Company, which has sites in many other countries, has founded a Travel Club. One feature of this club is a type of exchange

program in which the employee services department acts as an intermediary for traveling workers. A worker from the U.S. can visit another country and save accommodation dollars as well as getting to meet people from that culture on a more personal basis. Then the favor is returned at a later time by the American worker. What a wonderful way to build global relationships within your organization![6]

Jet Proplusion Labs get groups of employees together for adventure trips—scuba, skiing, river rafting, mountain biking, skydiving, bungee jumping, water skiing. These activities build friendships and help reduce workplace stress.[7]

Citizens Trust encourages many internal employee programs. One example is a monthly reading group to discuss works of fiction. Citizens covers half the cost of the books, buys pizza, and provides a "relaxation room" for the group to meet after work hours. It also sponsors a "Living Well" program, which Adine Mees, director of corporate resonsibility, calls a holistic approach to health that rewards staff for the simple, good things of life—such as reading a book, visiting a parent, hugging, meditating, exercising, learning, teaching, going to the theater, etc."[8]

Schulmerich Bells in Sellersville, Pennsylvania, decided to initiate an activity that would draw together people from various parts of the company. Their answer was clear—a handbell choir. They perform six times a year at senior centers and nursing homes during the noon hours.[9]

The important thing is to listen to your staff, ask them what they want to do and how they want to do it, and then give them support they need in terms of resources, recognition, and responsibility.

The Idea: Hire People Who Are Positive

The Idea in Action

When looking for 500 people to fill positions for a new facility, a **Holiday Inn** interviewed 5,000 candidates. When interviewing, hotel managers excluded all candidates who smiled less than four times during the interview. This criterion applied to people competing for jobs in all categories. Finding the right people at the outset will help create the atmosphere you desire.[10]

Laura Vaughan, New York City's **Tavern on the Green** training director, maintains a strong core of skilled workers in an industry known for high turnover. They average about 425 employees, and about 150 have been there more than 10 years and some more than 20. The priority, Vaughan says, is to find people with *enthusiasm*. "It comes down to the desire to take care of guests," she says. "If we're interviewing waiters, we may ask about dishwashing. The answers tell us if they want to be part of a team or just stay in their box.

"If you want people to give their top performance, to make sure every last spot is cleaned off the crystal, you must treat them with dignity and respect."

Here are some of the ways Vaughan accomplishes this:

▶ The managing director's door is open to every staffer.
▶ They provide free "family meals" for employees three times daily. Workers order from a special menu that includes staff favorites.
▶ She makes the rounds with her smiley-face bucket, depositing candy at server stations or into dishwashers' pockets.[11]

The Idea: Encourage Employees to Create Their Own Atmosphere

The Idea in Action

Dianna Amacker, who works at the **Chicago Mercantile Exchange**, collects international postcards as well as sending herself postcards when she is on vacation. These cards decorate her work area. She says, "When I need a break, I simply take a quick trip to some exotic, faraway place or a favorite vacation spot."

My office is filled with huge collages my daughter made for me of cards, notes, pictures, poems, buttons, and other small items given to me by my audience members. I also have a large, framed photograph of Mother Teresa (one of my personal heroes), framed copies of my book covers, plaques or awards I've won, and—of course—pictures of my husband, children, and grandchildren. I also have a small, framed print from the University of Kansas (where I went to school), a framed print from the Park Royal Hotel in New Zealand (where I spoke), and a poster painted by a dear friend of mine, with the words, "Kindness is Contagious. Catch it!" My bookshelves are filled with books autographed by special writer friends and wonderful small gifts from clients and friends. On the top of my bookshelves, I have dozens of coffee mugs from various clients, some of whom are no longer in business by that name! Finally, on a chair in the room is a darling teddy bear, given to me by a very special friend, who is available whenever I need a hug.

One person has her office decorated with all sorts of Elvis things. She says it's all very gaudy with a good sense of humor! Some people fill their offices with things they collect, while others have objects that remind them of other parts of their lives. Encouraging employees to personalize their own space adds to the human level in your workplace, creating an atmosphere of respect for everyone's individuality.

An article in the August 10, 2001, Sarasota *Herald-Tribune* tells about how **Mercedes Medical**, a medical supply company, improves worker productivity and morale. It lets them bring their pets to work! The company's informal policy has helped reduce absenteeism and turnover by about 25%. They say the pets mostly settle by their owners' desks, creating an atmosphere of "home."[12]

The Idea: Create a Climate of Fun

Women managers who use humor in the workplace are viewed by their

> A fun atmosphere builds a strong sense of community. It also counterbalances the stress of hard work and competition.
> —Libby Sartain, Senior Vice President of HR, Yahoo!

staffs as more effective than those who don't, according to a study, "Humor: A Managerial Tool for Both Genders?" The study was done by Dr. Wayne H. Decker of Salisbury University in Salisbury, Maryland, and also found that male supervisors, in general, got higher ratings than females for sense of humor, enjoying jokes, and telling jokes.[13]

Managers have also discovered that fun in the sales department creates enthusiasm on the street that translates into motivation to get the job done, not because of the money, but simply because it's fun to do.

The Idea in Action

Kris Horner, the CEO of **Auto Glass Plus** in Carrollton, Texas, has created a rollicking sales climate. Often senior management serves lunch to the employees, cutting the pizza, delivering it to their desks, and pouring drinks. Once a quarter, Horner re-creates a relaxing vacation spot on a day projected to be particularly stressful. Employees volunteer weekend hours to decorate the office in the theme, and senior management dresses the part. On "Hawaiian Day" they recorded the highest sales total in the company's history, proving that fun on even a stressful day can produce amazing results. The best news of all is that only five employees have left in the last six years.[14]

Jim O'Connell, senior vice president of sales of **LEGO Systems**, sees having fun as a reinforcement for his salespeople who are mostly on their own. At national meetings he holds beach Olympics and contests for the most creative use of LEGO blocks. Rookie Night, a 15-year tradition at the meetings, is when LEGO newcomers must perform a talent on stage. Although they are shaking in their boots before their performance, the next year they become the most ruthless audience members when the new rookies get on stage! During the fall they have one-week regional contests called Monster Mash (October), Turkey Trot (November), and Festival of Displays (December), when senior management jumps back into the trenches, appointed area spokespersons come up with humorous gibes about the other teams, and shenanigans happen daily. O'Connell believes the underpinning of fun is trust, and as trust is developed, the team becomes stronger.[15]

Matt Weinstein, emperor/founder of **Playfair** in Berkeley, California, encourages sales staffs to pass around a vase of flowers every 30 minutes to recognize individual efforts, learn to play "Happy Birthday" on the telephone key pad, hold a lottery to award the winner a ride to and from work in a limo, switch jobs with management staff, hire a masseuse to perform neck and shoulder massages on demand, and throw a pajama party where business stays open all night.[16] All these activities help to create an atmosphere charged with enthusiasm and delight.

"You can take our standard retirement package, or you can trade for what Carol has behind door No. 2."

Tom Bay, in his former role as senior vice president of **Great American Federal Savings and Loan**, gave each member of his sales team a box of crayons, saying, "Every day is a new color—you choose it." When someone got promoted, they got a bigger box, and sales members strove for the ultimate prize—a huge box of 104 crayons with a pencil sharpener in the side of the box! To reinforce the message, Bay often wrote memos in crayon and staff responded in kind. He reports that his branch became the fastest growing in the organization's history, hitting its six-year goal in less than 16 months. His experience shows that having fun definitely impacts productivity.[17]

In the Orange, California, office of **William M. Mercer, Inc.**, one person gave everybody slippers. Now, everybody wears them to staff meetings and whenever they want to increase creativity. They also post cartoons and let workers fill in their own captions.[18]

A colleague tells this story about fun in the workplace:

> My sister and I worked our way through college at McDonald's. As members of the weekend breakfast crew, we found ourselves scheduled to work on Easter Sunday. No one wanted to work the holiday, and to a man, the crew was grumpy and feeling sorry for ourselves. Our ugly brown uniforms were topped with visors. Someone got the idea of cutting bunny ears out of the white foam breakfast trays and stapling them to the visors. It was a hit! Soon the entire crew had bunny ears. The atmosphere lightened up, and soon we were happy to be working on this special day. But we had one co-worker, Paul, who was still blue. So we made his ears "lop" style (ears pointing down) and put them on his head. It not only cheered Paul up, but we laughed every time we saw him. And the customers loved it!

A women's group once gave a prize for the woman who had the greatest number of shoes under her desk. The winner had over 40 pairs. She hadn't seen how funny it was until she got the prize!

A client writes:

> As a Pilot Debriefer for maintenance at a Tactical Fighter Training Squadron, I debriefed pilots towards mechanical discrepancies. In order to encourage system checks that resulted in zero discrepancies, I began handing out Life Savers lollipops to pilots for "Code I" aircraft. Soon all my "newbies" were looking forward to flying with the Code I Lollipops! Now in retrospect, I see I should have also given lollies to the crew chief and maintenance crew who enabled the plane to fly discrepancy-free.

Violet Lister from **Nationwide Insurance** in Columbus, Ohio, shares her story:

> When I was an employee of Colonial Insurance Company, a subsidiary of Nationwide, the Systems Department had an ugly rubber chicken (with a broken neck, of course) that went to a person who made a "mistake" or "goof." It didn't necessarily have to be work-related. The chicken got passed on to the next recipient fairly quickly! At first when I transferred there and saw the chicken, I thought it was awful to do that, but I soon came to realize how much it lightened up the atmosphere as well as helped solve or fix the problem. Sometimes you'd see the chicken hanging out of someone's backpack (with its head buried) and we all wanted to know, "What did you do now?" I don't know where the chicken is now, but I'm going to try to find out!

Another manager told me that she always keeps Play-Doh on her desk, and she plays with it when talking on the phone. She says it helps her keep her focus.

The Idea: Create an Atmosphere Where Families Are Welcome

The Idea in Action

Freddie Mac, a mortgage company in McLean, Virginia, has begun bringing baby highchairs and booster seats to its employee restaurant. Employees love the highchairs as an effective work and family benefit, and they love bringing their children to have lunch with them. Even the workers without children welcome the young visitors and know many of the employees' children by name![19]

A teleservices company encourages employees to bring their children to work with them to learn what their parents do. They are asked to interview several employees and then write about it. An 11-year-old daughter wrote the following report:

My name is Jennifer and I went to work with my Mom today. I learned what my Mom does at work, and I interviewed four other ladies that work with my Mom. Here is one of the interviews:

This is Rhonda and she is a supervisor. What Rhonda does is reports, payroll, and answering questions from her team members. What Rhonda likes about her job is the people that she works with. What Rhonda doesn't like about her job is no teamwork from upper management and slackers. What Rhonda does besides work is contests, parties, and potlucks. Rhonda works 10 to 12 hours a day. She works 50 to 60 hours a week. She works 5 to 6 days a week. Rhonda would not change her job. The education you need for the job is a high school diploma. Rhonda said yes, she would go back to school to take more computer classes.

When Jennifer finished the report, she said, "I'd really like (the manager's) job when I grow up because all she does is talk on the phone all day!"

What a wonderful way to help children have more understanding of their parents' work and also have a lesson in career planning at the same time. The company feels that the new bond between parents and their children as well as the opportunity to educate the child about their business is well worth the time invested. Perhaps they are even grooming potential new hires!

Employee Services Management (ESM) *Magazine*, a publication of the **Employee Services Management Association**, suggests many ways to involve families:

- ▶ Partner with a local day care center to arrange field trips for school-age children on school holidays. Charge parents enough to cover the cost of the program. Children can bring their own lunch and snack items.
- ▶ Work with a local movie theater to arrange a movie showing on a Saturday morning for employees and their families. Since the theater is not used at that time, they will probably charge little or

nothing for rental. You might even get the movie at the local library to save on expenses.

► Hold a bike rodeo. Use the services of nonprofit agencies like the police department to oversee bike safety.

► Have a "kids clothes closet." Allow employees to use a room and tables and chairs to sell children's clothing, toys, furniture, and books to other employees. Volunteers can be recruited to help set up and price items.

► Hold a used sports equipment sale.

► Offer an Easter egg hunt.

► Hold a Pasta Night for families. Volunteers can cook the meal or work with your food service program. To help defray costs, have a cash bar for drinks. Door prizes make it more fun.

► Organize a bus trip to destination about an hour away—shopping mall, amusement park, ballgame, zoo, etc.[20]

The Idea: Look at Your Physical Work Space

The Idea in Action

Even the design of a workplace can contribute to a positive or a negative work atmosphere, says an article by Julie Wallace in the February 2001 issue of *HR Magazine*. The **American Society of Interior Designers** (www. asid.org) has created FutureWork 2020, a program designed to educate architects and interior designers about the future of the workplace. Its overall message is that environments influence work, and they cite numerous examples of how better design has improved productivity:

► One **Amoco Corp.** facility decreased formal meeting time by 75% and file duplication by 80% after creating an environment to facilitate teamwork.

► At **Monster.com** a life-sized "monster" residing in a purple lobby exemplifies the company's unique work environment. In a company-sponsored study, 90% of employees stated the work environment gave the company a competitive edge, 68% said it affected their decision to join the company, 55% said it influenced their decision to stay, and 62% agreed that it supports creativity.

The article asks, "Does your work environment contradict your corporate goals? If you're trying to promote out-of-the-box thinking within beige, box-like cubicles, it might be time for a strategic redesign."[21]

I often ask my clients what their hallways look like. Most of them are long, gray or beige tunnels of empty, sterile walls. Tom Peters says that if your hallways are boring, chances are that everything you do in your company is boring. I encourage them to be creative with their hallways:

- ▶ Fill hallways with employees' artwork. When you showcase employee talent, you are building self-esteem, encouraging the arts, and creating opportunities for networking. You might even make this into a contest and have employees vote on their favorite work. Encourage artwork of all kinds—painting, sculpture, woodwork, photography, needlework, etc.
- ▶ Use the artwork of employees' children. Have a contest for employees' children, grandchildren, nieces, and nephews to draw a picture of what they think their relative does at work all day. These will be delightful and fun for both employees and customers alike to view as well as family members.
- ▶ Have a "Poster Party" and ask employees to bring their favorite quotation. Then with bright-colored markers and flip chart paper, create inspirational posters to hang in plastic frames throughout the organization. You will find talent that you never knew existed!
- ▶ Rent artwork chosen by an employee committee, changing it every month. You might even choose artwork based on a differ-

ent theme each month and make it an educational experience for employees to enjoy. You could sponsor speakers during lunch to discuss the work or provide fliers about it.

Another example of an innovative atmosphere is documented in the November 1998 issue of *Fast Company* magazine: "The sprawling complex" at the headquarters of **Progressive Casualty Insurance Company** in Mayfield Village, Ohio, "could easily be mistaken for a contemporary art museum. A walkway designed to resemble a stream winds playfully into an underground funnel, thereby creating the illusion of being underwater. Sculptures of Styrofoam clouds, metal origami birds, and cartoonish, floor-to-ceiling evening gowns abound," expressing the distinctive culture at Progessive.

"This is what I get for requesting an office with a window."

Close to Home by John McPherson/Dist by Universal Press Syndicate

Peter Lewis, the CEO, began collecting contemporary art in the early 1970s, finding the works stimulating and innovative—exactly what he wanted Progressive to be. "Plain vanilla walls are uninteresting," he says. "My hope is that nonrepresentational, off-the-wall art sends a message to our people that it's OK to think outside the lines." He even commissions artists to illustrate each year's annual report around a unifying theme. An atmosphere of creativity and openness is carried out everywhere in this "progressive" environment, encouraging employees to be open to new ideas and willing and able to solve difficult customer problems in innovative ways.[22]

What does your physical environment say about your work? Here are some ideas to make your work areas more inviting and fun:

APAC Customer Services, Inc. centers in Iowa have come up with creative ideas to make their workplaces more friendly.

> ▶ The employees of a Cedar Rapids, Iowa, APAC Customer Services facility developed a creative contest to help employees become more familiar with each other. A "Baby Faces" contest was held to give all employees the opportunity to show off how *cute* they were as babies. Employees were asked to bring in a baby picture of themselves. The photographs were then displayed in the center for the contest. Employees were asked to match the correct name to the correct baby picture and vote for the cutest, baldest, funniest, and chubbiest babies.

Quinn & Co., a New York City PR firm, has replaced its conference table with a comfy purple sofa, dubbing it "the dream room."[23]

Rock Island Group, a computer and ISP in Oklahoma City, painted train tracks on its walls. The company, once housed in a historic train station, has a train motif on its logo.

Dr. Gary Kahn, an obstetrician, asked his wife to decorate his waiting room with children's art work. It creates a very special atmosphere.

The president of **Nichol & Co.**, a New York PR firm, gave each employee a camera, film, and two hours off. The result: a 30-piece photo collection for the office called "Manhattan at Work."

At **Federal-Mogul Corporation** in Southfield, Michigan, the walls are decorated with photos of employees at work.[24]

When your employees work in cubicles, it is important to make available some private spaces with telephones. Another option is to make a few cellular phones available for workers to share so they can go elsewhere for privacy. There must always be places of privacy where people can withdraw and ideally where management cannot watch them.

One of my clients whose organizational setup resembled a cube city bought several new Porta-Potties and placed them in out-of-the-way areas near the cubicles. They then encouraged employees who were at the end of their ropes to spend a few moments in their "Time Out" place. Each Porta-Potty had a sign on the front that read "Occupied" on one side and "Vacant" on the other. Employees loved the idea![25]

Whenever employees are moving from an office environment to cubicles, help them adapt to the new surroundings. Alain Hebert, HR director at **InoTech** in Fairfax, Virginia, suggests throwing a grand opening party for the new cube city. Color-code each section with helium balloons, have snacks at each location so people have to visit all of the areas, and ask everyone to bring in a welcome mat and have a contest for the best one.[25]

The Idea: Have Recess

The Idea in Action

The employees of **HLB Communications** in Chicago, Illinois, take an organized play break twice a month. Bimonthly, a different employee organizes a half-hour activity that everybody in the office participates in. Memorable events have included a field trip to the top of the John Hancock building to watch the sunset and a margarita blender party (at the end of the day, of course!). Other times they do things like bowling with plastic pins. The idea came about in a session on how to lower stress levels in the company.

They always begin meetings with five-minute stress-reduction tips. One employee demonstrated stretching exercises that can be done at her desk; another turned down the lights in the conference room, lit a candle, and began a chant. HLB also pays for on-site massages every other week and health club memberships for interested employees. Each year the firm shuts down for a five-day retreat at the American Club in Kohler, Wisconsin, where they have industry seminars one hour and yoga lessons the next. Employees work the hours that best suit their needs, and everyone has a laptop to make such flexibility a real option. Compensation is in the top 10% of communications firms nationwide. The results of all this caring: the company bills far more hours than the industry average.[26]

Every Thursday at 3 p.m., the folks at **Gymboree** in Burlingame, California, ring a bell and declare recess. Some people walk around a lake that's nearby. Others play on the grounds. Foursquare, a school-yard game, is very popular. People from different departments play against each other, so in that way people who might have no interaction come together and have fun.[27]

Workers at **JWGenesis Financial Corporation** in Boca Raton, Florida, can view tapes of classic sitcoms during their lunch hour, courtesy of the vice chairman.[28]

The Idea: Create an Inclusive, Team Environment

In their book *True Leaders*, Bette Price and George Ritcheske share how Lou Smith, President and CEO of the **Ewing Marion Kauffman Foundation**, creates an environment where everyone is valued:

> "I think enduring organizations are inclusive," says Lou Smith. "Not for any reason other than that's how you become a pre-eminent organization. Whey wouldn't I want to capture the input and intelligence and the energy of all of our associates rather than just five people who report directly to me with the privilege of having a senior title? Why wouldn't I want to capture input from the newest associate?"

Smith explains that he has breakfast with all new associates to establish early on that the foundation operates in an environment in which anyone who comes to his office understands that they work within an environment that is not about hierarchy access, but about everyone bringing ideas to the forefront that are important to the organization.

Smith creates an environment that includes three elements that he terms as "the givens" for a successful organization: mutual respect, trust, and integrity. "If you've got those three, you can disagree, but you still respect one another. You know that no matter what the issues are, it's not about personal agendas because our integrity is so high. We are not going to violate any of those. We will make mistakes—we're not perfect—but you can't violate those three."[29]

The Idea in Action

When employees join **DonateTo.com** in Cambridge, Massachusetts, they receive a "toolbox" that the general manager creates. There is Krazy Glue to represent the team sticking together and Tylenol for the inevitable headache. Each week, she stocks the toolbox with something new. The larger symbolism is that the DonateTo.com team is creating a toolbox for people who want to help other people in need—the team's mission![30]

Mark Zagorski of **WorldNow**, a technology company headquartered in New York City, started a monthly "drill." Every month someone is presented with The Team Drill, a clunky old tool that he picked up at a garage sale. The winner must perform a few simple tasks: personalize the drill in some way and devise a new rule for how to care for it. One team member added a Bart Simpson trigger and another made the drill wireless by adding an antenna. At the end of the month the winner passes the drill to the next star. The dented old drill captures their unofficial mantra of "drilling down to solve problems."[31]

The Idea: Create an Atmosphere of Caring

The Idea in Action

APAC Customer Services, Inc. is an organization headquartered in Deerfield, Illinois, that has customer interaction centers all over the nation. For three years I was on retainer with them to help build an atmosphere of service, communication, and caring. This is a story from the APAC newsletter that shows the spirit and caring that is present in their call centers:

> During the winter season, our centers must gear up for inclement weather. However, the record-breaking snows and low temperatures that hit Eastern Iowa January 26th provided an even bigger challenge for APAC employees.
>
> A senior supervisor at one of the Iowa centers was scheduled to be in at 3 p.m. but came in at noon because he felt there would be a "ton of snow" and that people would not be able to get to work, much less get home. What was normally a 20-minute trip for him turned into an hour of battling the blizzard ... but he made it.
>
> The a.m. shift stayed in their seats until after 2 p.m., long after the Iowa Highway Patrol said to "run for cover," and kept servicing our clients. The center manager began giving rides home to the TSRs, some of whom had walked to work that morning, using his four-wheel-drive pickup.
>
> Many of the a.m. Employees had to have their cars physically pushed out of the lot, by hand, so there would be a place for the p.m. shift to park ... if they could get there! The center manager even stayed outside for two to three hours pushing cars out of snowbanks.
>
> The amazing part was that all of the p.m. shift called in, and some actu-

> When you walk into a restaurant you have to feel the energy from the people. You have to feel the spirit of team, you have to know that they are committed to your satisfaction, and we want that to happen in every one of our restaurants.
> —David Novak, Chairman and CEO, Tricon Global Restaurants, Inc.

ally battled their way to their call desks. Many of the APAC employees made major contributions to others in their community who were stuck, providing overnight accommodations, food, etc. The center provided a great example of leadership and spirit, both in the center and in the community. Congratulations on your efforts![32]

Mary Jane Ldreina tells about one of the delightful things they do in their workplace. They have created a "booboo bunny, " a cloth doll made from a washcloth. People in the office pass it around when someone is having a hard time or a bad day. No one says anything. You simply find it on your desk as an encouragement from your co-workers.

The Idea: Help Employees Find Humor in Everyday Life

According to a Hall and Associates survey of personnel executives, 84% said that workers with a sense of humor do a better job. A joyful environment results in fewer sick or mental health days, fewer accidents, lowered stress, better relationships, and higher productivity.

The Idea in Action

In the office:

1. Display a childhood toy or photo of you or your children as a reminder to keep the child in you at work.
2. Keep a stress squeeze ball in your desk. This is especially handy to use when on long phone calls.
3. Have a joy jar on your desk. Fill it with positive, success-oriented sayings, appropriate jokes, and candy.
4. Use a daily joke or positive calendar instead of a plain one and *read it!*
5. Use a Nerf® bat and ball to work out frustrations.

In lounges, copy rooms, or other communal spots:

1. Put up a Humor/Rumor Board. First, make certain everyone knows what appropriate humor is first.
2. Name the office equipment. Talk to it.
3. Keep bubbles, coloring books, and crayons and other childhood toys available for play while copies are being run.
4. Copy someone's hand using the copier. Type on it: "Need a pat on the back? Stand here." Tack the sign on a wall where everyone can lean against it for their "pat on the back."
5. In rest rooms, put up signs that say "Looking good!" Post either on the mirrors or the backs of stall doors.

In meetings:

1. Wear or provide for the group funny hats, deely-boppers, masks, or silly sunglasses.
2. Place tent cards on tables with positive sayings and words of wisdom from famous people.
3. Provide bubble gum, lollipops, ice cream cones, or frozen yogurt. It's hard to be negative when people are enjoying themselves.
4. Place cans of Silly String or water-filled squirt guns in the center of the table—just see what joy erupts!
5. Give each person a small can of Silly Putty to work out their frustrations during the meeting. It's often fun to inquire about the meaning of their artwork at the meeting's conclusion.
6. Make a magic wand that you can use to emphasize how you'd fix things if you could.
7. Play music or funny audio- or videotapes before the meeting starts.
8. Have small jars of bubbles at each place and allow everyone to blow bubbles.

(Reprinted with permission from Sandra Jones Campbell, Ph.D., from "Lighten Up and Light Up the Bottom Line")

Sandy says, "As with communication and leadership styles, each person, each organization has its own humor style. This is a combination of what is funny to the individual and what is appropriate for the setting."[33]

Jeff Ellsworth from the Office of Communications in the **Department of Management and Budget for the State of Michigan** decided to use a little humor to express his frustration after a particularly unsatisfying "moment of truth." He wrote the following lyrics to a song to be sung to the tune of "Santa Claus Is Coming to Town":

Sorry ... Our Computer Is Down

Oh ... you'd better not write
You'd better not call.
You'd better not ask us
We're no help at all.
Sorry ... our computer is down.

We sent you an invoice
You don't understand
And we can't explain it
It's out of our hands.
Sorry ... our computer is down.

You want to do business
You need to know how.
We'd love to assist you
But just not right now.
Sorry ... our computer is down.

We love our computer.
We use it all day
But when we're without it
There's no other way.
Sorry ... our computer is down.

We know what you think.
We're thinking it, too.
The trouble's uptown, though,
So what can we do?
Sorry ... our computer is down.

(chorus)
We hate to make excuses.
But when our server breaks down
It's a devastating blow ... oh ...

Loretta LaRoche of **The Humor Potential** shares the following ideas to bring more humor to your day:

- ▶ **Have a "staff laff."** Gather co-workers once a week and discuss some funny events around your own behavior. Putting other people down is not the purpose. Creating a connection in our common absurdity is.

- ▶ **Create a "Joy List."** Make a list of all your blessings, including people, places, and events. You may want to start with the simple fact that you're breathing. Do this daily, and then read it at the end of each week.

- ▶ **Set up a Humor Corner and Humor Room.** Find a space at home and at work to do this. If a VCR is available, have some funny videos of movies or comedians. Have a basket of silly hats, masks, noses, and wands. Once in a while you may want to put one on while you're having lunch, making dinner, or mowing the lawn.

- ▶ **Do something nice when someone least expects it.** Give the office problem a bouquet of flowers, whether it's a him or a her! Don't put a card in it.

- ▶ **Use a number not a profanity.** Write down all your favorite profanities and then give them a number. If someone is getting on your nerves, just say the number. They'll never know!

(Reprinted with permission from Loretta LaRoche)

She also talks about becoming mindful of the language you use and how it affects your feelings and behavior.[34]

Exercise

The following exercise illustrates how thoughts transform our feelings and behaviors. Take a moment and read the words listed below very slowly to yourself:

Gloom	Torment
Hardship	Rejection
Dread	Darkness
Fear	Sadness
Despair	Pain
Disappointment	Tears
Depression	Anguish
Frustration	Trouble
Melancholy	Misery
Sorrow	

Now please read the list of words below very slowly to yourself:

Joy	Giggles
Silly	Joking
Jolly	Fun
Bright	Exuberant
Cheerful	Gentle
Laughter	Amusement
Hilarious	Gladness
Energized	Pleasure
Merriment	Warmth
Lighthearted	Mirthful
Enthusiastic	

(Reprinted with permission from Loretta LaRoche)

Most of us begin to feel the emotions attached to these words. The first list evokes feelings of loss and sadness. Our body reacts by getting tense. The second list is like taking an antidote. We feel and look better when we have pleasant thoughts.

Quick Ideas for Atmosphere

► Transform someone's cubicle on a special day or occasion—when leaving or returning from vacation (cruise ship), when they receive a promotion (control room) or an award (King or Queen of _____), or the birth of a new baby (nursery).

► Provide coffee, tea, juice, soda, bagels, Danish, as often as your budget allows—every Monday, the last day of the month, or on silly monthly holidays. The book *Celebrate Today* (John Kremer, Open Horizons, 1995) lists all kinds of odd holidays to celebrate.

► Take newcomers around and introduce them to everyone. Have a "welcome aboard" party for all staff on a new employee's first day.

► Post everyone's baby picture and high school yearbook picture along with their current photo in a prominent spot. You might even want to have a guessing contest when you first collect these.

► Play games. Turn hallways into makeshift bowling alleys. Play miniature golf through offices. Distribute toys like Slinkies and Nerf® balls and let creativity flow!

► Provide customizable screen-saver programs for computers to display personal photographs.

► Hold mandatory 15-minute naps.

► Keep a bulletin board to feature one employee's children's art work for a week at a time.

► Create a photo album of all employees. Give one to each new employee.

► Give employees a coupon to purchase something to personalize their workspace. Encourage them to choose something that expresses their passion.

- Have "tea time" every day at 3 p.m. For 10 or 15 minutes, get a cup of tea, coffee, or soda and gather together to share what is going at work, home, or play.
- Take photographs of employees, put them on a bulletin board, and put word bubbles with Post-it® captions on each photo.
- Have a lunch party where everyone who plays an instrument performs. Buy kazoos for those who have no musical talent.
- Send a quick and funny e-mail to a friend before heading to work or catch a morning cartoon with the kids. Enjoying a few minutes of looniness in the morning can change your mood for the rest of the day.
- When a company moved its offices to a new floor, they gave everyone hard hats with a sign, "CLM on the move!"
- Let employees share their talents during lunchtime. This can lighten up the atmosphere and bring new respect to the employees.
- Ask employees to submit several of their favorite recipes along with a favorite funny family story and make a company cookbook.
- Hold an ugly shirt day.

Notes

1. Dr. Gerald Graham, Wichita State University, Wichita, Kansas, as quoted by Bob Nelson, Nelson Motivation, "Motivating Employees in the '90s."
2. Pritzker, Steven R. 1999. "Creativity in Teams." *The Inner Edge*, October/November, p. 12.
3. Cerny, Catrina. 1998. "The Young and the Restless: Serving the New Generation of Employees." *Employee Services Management (ESM) Magazine*, September, p. 14.
4. Ibid.
5. Ibid.
6. Ibid.
7. Ibid.

8. Leigh, Pamela. 1997. "The New Spirit at Work." *Training & Development*, March, p. 31.

9. Editor. 1998. "Employees Make Music Together." *Employee Services Management (ESM) Magazine*, February, p. 5.

10. Editor. "A Smile Will Get the Job." *Communications Briefings*, Vol. XII, No. VI, p. 4.

11. Roberts, Deborah S. "Two Companies Battle High Turnover and Win!" *Employee Recruitment and Retention*, Sample Issue, p. 6.

12. Mille, Margaret. 2001. "Dog Day at the Office—Sarasota Company Lets Workers Bring Their Pets." *Sarasota Herald-Tribune*, August 10, p. 1D.

13. Tyler, Kathryn. 1997. "Humor on the Job—Avoid It to Your Detriment." *Executive Female*, July/August, p. 23.

14. Sturgeon, Julie. 2000. "Fun Sells." *Selling Power*. March.

15. Ibid.

16. Weinstein, Matt. 1999. "Some Fun Ways to Celebrate." *Playfair Newsletter*, April, p. 1.

17. Sturgeon, Op. cit.

18. Lynn, Jacqueline. 2000. "Having Fun Yet?" *Entrepreneur*, May, p. 121.

19. Editor. 1997. "Work Week." *The Wall Street Journal*, December 9, p. 1.

20. Nelson, Cindy. 1996. "No-Cost/Low-Cost Programming Ideas." *Employee Services Management (ESM) Magazine*, January, pp. 6-10.

21. Wallace, Julie. 2001. "Designing the Future Workplace." *HR Magazine*, February, p. 184.

22. Salter, Chuck. 1998. "The Art of Being Progressive." *Fast Company*, November, p. 192.

23. Neal, Victoria, and Torres, Nichole L. 2000. "Trendspotting: Feelin' the Groove with the Latest Trends in 2000." *Entrepreneur*, April, p. 224.

24. Editor. 1997. "A Special News Report About Life on the Job—and Trends Taking Shape There." *The Wall Street Journal*, August 5, p. A1.

25. Poe, Andrea C. 2000. "Attention Undivided." *HR Magazine*, February, p. 64.

26. Dannhauser, Carol Leonetti. 2000. "Attacking Anxiety—When Stress Goes Down, Productivity Goes Up." *Working Woman*, May, p. 40.

27. McCauley, Lucy. 1999. "Measure What Matters." *Fast Company*, May, p. 102.

28. Editor. "Performance Data—News and Numbers." *People Performance*, Sample Issue, p. 14.

29. Price, Bette, and Ritcheske, George. 2001. *True Leaders: How Exceptional CEOs and Presidents Make a Difference by Building People and Profits.* Chicago, IL: Dearborn Trade.

30. Editor. 2001. "Team Rituals." *Extraordinary Team*, Spring, p. 4.

31. Ibid.

32. Editor. 1996. "Blizzard Battlers: Indianola." *APAC Employee Newsletter,* March, p. 2.

33. Campbell, Sandra Jones. 2000. "Seize the Sizzle in Life and Work." *Meeting Update,* December, p. 5.

34. Loretta LaRoche, President, The Human Potential, Inc., 50 Court Street, Plymouth MA 02360, 508-746-3998, fax: 508-746-3398, www.lorettalaroche.com, e-mail: inquiry@lorettalaroche.com.

Chapter 10

A = Appreciation for All

I try to remember that people—good, intelligent, capable people—may actually need day-to-day praise and thanks for the job they do. I try to remember to get up out of my chair, turn off my computer, go sit or stand next to them and see what they're doing, ask about the challenges, find out if they need additional help, offer that help if possible, and most of all, tell them in all honesty that what they are doing is important: to me, to the company, and to our customers.

—John Ball, Service Training Manager,
American Honda Motor Company

Dr. Gerald Graham from Wichita State University, in his study of workplace motivation, found 65 possible incentives. The top motivating techniques reported by employees are:

▶ Personal thanks
▶ Written thanks
▶ Promotion for performance

▶ Public praise
▶ Morale-building meetings

He then reported the frequency of *not* getting these incentives:

> When someone does something well, applaud! You will make two people happy.
> —Samuel Goldwyn

▶ Personal thanks 58%
▶ Written thanks 76%
▶ Promotion for performance 78%
▶ Public praise 81%
▶ Morale-building meetings 92%

His conclusion: "It appears that the techniques that have the greatest motivational impact are practiced the least even though they are easier and less expensive to use."[1]

The Gallup Organization found that 69% of employees say nonmonetary forms of recognition provide the best motivation, according to their 1998 nationwide survey of U.S. workers, commissioned by Carlson Marketing Group. The survey builds on an earlier Gallup research study that confirmed that loyal, engaged employees tend to generate high-performance business outcomes as measured by increased sales, improved productivity, enhanced employee retention, and bottom-line profitability. Their conclusion: give employees the recognition they deserve![2] As many as 25% of good employees who quit, according to a 1998 survey of executives by Robert Half International, Inc., left due to a lack of recognition.[3]

Good managers remember to recognize and praise employees. *Great* managers do it every day. An article in *The Motivational Manager* newsletter shares some proven methods to make sure that appreciating employees becomes a part of your daily routine:

> ▶ **Make employees a part of your weekly "to do" list.** Add the names of the people who report to you to your list of goals to accomplish. Then cross off names as you recognize them.
> ▶ **Use voice mail.** Leave employees voice mail messages praising

them for a job well done. Do it from your cellular phone on the way home.

► **Write notes at the end of the day.** Take a few minutes to write thank-you notes to employees who made a difference that day. (This will also help you to become a more thankful person as you focus on what went right!)

► **At the beginning of the day, put five coins in your pocket.** During the day, transfer a coin to the other pocket each time you praise an employee.[4]

I keep a big letter "A" on my desk as a constant reminder to "Appreciate" others. When I was studying for my master's degree in Adult Continuing Education, one of the interesting things we learned was that adults need to have "anchors," things that help them remember a concept or an idea. Think about what you could use as your "anchor" to remember to appreciate your employees.

The Idea: Call Their Mothers

The Idea in Action

I have recently been sharing a very creative appreciation idea with all of my audiences. Two years ago after I had spoken to a large manufacturing firm, one of the managers stayed to talk with me. He said, "Barbara, I have the lowest-performing team in the whole company. Never once have they ever met their goals. But you got me thinking. I'm going to call and tell you what happens."

Almost nine months later, I received a call from this same man. He was ecstatic! He said, "After you were there, I got the whole team together, and I said to them, 'OK. For any of you who reach your goal this quarter, I'm going to call your mothers!'"

He said for the first time ever, **every single person on his team met their goals!** And he said the calls were one of the nicest things he ever did. Some of the mothers cried, and others were simply delighted. I don't care how old we are, if someone thanks our family for the great job we are doing, it feels wonderful. And all it cost was a few phone calls!

I recently received this e-mail from Jim Gwinn, the Chairperson of the Christian Management Association board:

> I am so thankful for the message you gave at CMA on expressing care and love for others. Have used the "call their Mom or wife to say thanks" idea a few times. It is unbelievable what an impact that has on Moms and then on the person. All whom I have done this for have called me in tears saying, "No one has ever thanked my Mom for my life in that manner." *Thank you* for such an insightful thought. Only wish I had called your husband and told him what a treasure you are and thank him for sharing you with us.

Whose mother, spouse, or significant other might you call today to show your appreciation?

The Idea: Write Letters and Notes

A person who worked in a catering company where hours were long and pay was minimal shared how thrilled all the employees were when the boss posted a letter from a customer who was delighted. He said whenever they felt underpaid and overworked, all they had to do to boost their spirit was to go over to the bulletin board and read that letter. The long-lasting impact: now, whenever he encounters a product or service he enjoys, he writes a letter. His advice to bosses—don't keep letters in a file; place them where everyone can enjoy them. It will work wonders for morale!

The Idea in Action

At **American Italian Pasta Company** they have an accolade system. The CEO, Tim Webster, shares that every week in his staff meeting they handwrite accolades for good deeds, good performance, and exceeding expectations. The person who writes the note signs it and then they all sign it so when someone receives an acknowledgment, it is signed by the whole executive staff.[5]

The sales manager of a large real estate firm in Florida sends letters of appreciation to employees who do something special, and she also encloses a file folder labeled "Success File." She tells them to use it to file any other letters or notes of commendation they receive in their careers, and when they are having a difficult time in their jobs or have goofed up, to reread the letters to prove to themselves that they *are* capable and valuable persons. She says, "You did it before; you can do it again!"[6]

The **Institute of Food Technologists** gives a bookmark to those who have volunteered that reads on one side:

VOLUNTEERS make each day brighter.

On the opposite side it says:

Thank you for being a wonderful VOLUNTEER
Your spirit of community,
Your willingness to share,
Your gifts of time and reliability,
Your comfort and your care,
Your goal of making others' tasks lighter
ADD UP TO A VOLUNTEER WHO MAKES EACH DAY BRIGHTER!

The Idea: Customize Rewards and Recognition

At **Uline**, a shipping company in Waukegan, Illinois, each team leader keeps this sheet for each employee in a special file. Then they use this personal information to customize rewards and recognition.

What Makes You Tick???

We'd like to know what makes you happy! Please fill out this list with your favorites and return it to your team leader. When it comes to a job well done, we aim to please!

Favorite Candy:
Favorite Soda:
Favorite Color:
Favorite Hobby:
Favorite Store:

Favorite Snack Food:
Favorite Sports Team:

Aubrey Daniels, author of *Bringing Out the Best in People,* has each new employee fill out a "Reinforcement Survey," where they list their hobbies and other personal information. Later, when one of his employees does something exceptional, Daniels pulls out the survey and chooses something they will value. Rewards are meaningful only if they are special to that individual. He says, "That's the key to incentives—make them personal." His own passion is collecting golf balls with logos of his clients. His own employees certainly know how to reward him![7]

In the **Waukegan Park District** in Illinois, the custodian was going to have a birthday and planned to come in early that day to do his work. The night before, two employees went through the offices in the building and emptied all the wastebaskets. Then they gave each employee a piece of computer paper and asked them to put a note or birthday greeting in the bottom of their empty wastebaskets. When the custodian came to empty the baskets, he found them completely empty except for a birthday note to him. He was absolutely delighted—and his co-workers found out how very long it takes to empty all those wastebaskets!

At a company in Urbandale, Iowa, the owners displayed appreciation for a long week by attaching personalized notes with a handmade clay pen on each employee's time card. One note read, "You bring smiles to many faces with the caring concern you put into your work. Thanks for a tough week! Pam and Bob." The pen even had artistic smiling faces on it!

BI in Minneapolis, Minnesota, has what they call "Singing Recognition." They have a volunteer choir that can be contacted by any associate to provide a personalized singing recognition. The choir will write a song to a popular tune. The song has specific information included so that the "thank you" is genuine and meaningful. The choir will sing to the associate during a department meeting or whenever the requester would like the recognition to occur. Over 200 BI associates have received singing recognitions from their volunteer choir.

This song was a recognition for Karen Kitchel when she won the Guy Schoenecker Quality Award (named after the founder of the company) to the tune of "Yankee Doodle Dandy":

> You're a Schoenecker Award winner,
> A quality person through and through.
> You worked long and hard on your performance team,
> Now you're receiving your just due.
> Teamwork's what we're all about here,
> Working side by side as one.
> BI is a better place because of all your toil,
> Kudos to you for all you do!

This one was sung to about 90 associates in the Accounting/MIS Division, requested by their vice president and sung to the tune of "The Battle Hymn of the Republic":

> We appreciate the division that delivers what's been sold,
> You'd think that it's not possible, it's magic to behold.
> From turkey, ham or steaks to a little warehouse release,
> We work out little fannies off, for customers we please.
> The system cannot handle this, we cry to deafened ears,
> We go like heck to make it work, without a lot of cheers.
> An IVR for next week's launch, no notice we receive,
> How do we pull it off, you ask, you just would not believe.
> We beckon to your cries for help any hour of the day,
> And answer every question asked in a most professional way.
> Your PC's down, no problem, we can fix it in a jiff,
> It's the coffee that you poured in that that makes
>   your keyboard stiff.

And data, we've got lots of it, all you have to do is ask,
We run this baby 'round the clock, we even multi-task,
And billing, that's no problem, we can invoice on the fly.
We do not have a P.O. yet, we don't ask sales why.
We forecast every sale and more, for optimism reigns,
New systems, that is what we need to play these numbers games,
Reporting to the business units is harder than you think,
They don't understand financials when their performance stinks.
We pay the associates every week, we never miss a beat,
And try to talk to ADP, now that's no easy feat.
We are the best there is, you know, we're really quite a team,
And BI's where it's happening, the best place to be seen!

The Idea: On-the-Spot Rewards

The Idea in Action

At **Busch Gardens** in Tampa, Florida, employees who offer exceptional service to guests receive a "scratch-off" card. These cards are issued on the spot by management and can be redeemed for a variety of rewards, including lunch with the President, leaving 30 minutes early, coming in 30 minutes late, and other things employees say they would like.

SAP, the fourth-largest computer software company in the world, has what it calls "Spot Awards." These can be awarded to any employee by any employee. It is a box of mints with "Thank you for helping us Build the Best" on the top. Each employee receives five boxes each quarter to distribute as they like. They also have Quarterly Recognition, Half-Year Recognition, and End-of-the-Year Awards.

Tavern on the Green in New York City has a program called "Training Bucks." With a budget of $13,500, they printed fake dollars that supervisors could give employees for a job well done. Ten bucks would buy a gift certificate for such vendors as Macy's, The Gap, or Tower Records.[8]

The **Perth Convention Bureau** in Perth, Australia, has "Beyond the Call of Duty" awards. Each staff person is given a certificate that they can award to anyone in the office who has done something extra. The award then gives them a chance to pick a prize from the office treasure chest. They actually borrowed a pirate's treasure chest from a theater company to use for this delightful award.

Family Christian Stores has a card that managers give to employees who have gone the extra mile. It reads "Our frontline is our bottom line."

The Idea: Collect "Wow" Stories

The Idea in Action

In their book *True Leaders*, Bette Price and George Ritcheske write about a delightful recognition process:

> At MascoTech, they created a process for catching people doing something right. "Wow Story is very simple," explains CEO Frank Hennessey. "It's when you see somebody that's doing something that's absolutely incredible and you can't help but say, 'Wow!' We wanted to acknowledge and recognize and reward our people who are living our vision and who are doing those extraordinary things and making a difference. So, we publish stories about them in an internal newsletter." It gives stature to the person that gets coverage, and it also opens up communications as employees call one another to acknowledge what they have read about one another. "People like to be acknowledged for what they do," says Hennessey. "They need to know that you know what they are doing—the contributions that they are making, the sacrifices that they are making, and the successes that they are achieving. People appreciate being recognized."[9]

The **Walt Disney World Dolphin Hotel** in Orlando, Florida, uses *Wow!* Cards—tri-folded, bright-colored wallet cards—for managers to give a quick thank-you note to employees who have *wowed* a customer or co-worker. Occasionally, they also have a visit from *Captain Wow!* who gives them special recognition and encouragement.

The Idea: Personalize Gifts

The Idea in Action

In Vol. 9, No. 1 of *Innovative Leader*, a newsletter published by Winston J. Brill & Associates, an anonymous person writes about appreciation in his organization:

> The vice president of my division has taken it upon himself to give an annual gift to each person in the division. The average cost of the gift is about $50. That, by itself, won't stimulate anyone's innovative abilities. However, what makes this special is that each gift is personalized. The vice president frequently tours the facility and makes sure to chat with each staff member. Somehow, he remembers everyone's name and gets to know something about the person. Either he's got a great memory, or he jots down the information right after a visit. We know he also learns a lot about us through our supervisors.

> Anyway, the gifts arrive at our homes to celebrate our birthdays. Attached to the gift is a personal note signed by the vice president. The note thanks the recipient for a specific contribution, and includes a happy birthday wish. Gifts include a fancy knife (to a gourmet cook), subscriptions to Business Week and Inc. (for a technologist who is becoming interested in the business side of work), and a box of quality jams (after learning that person enjoys big breakfasts; that's why he doesn't eat lunch).

> These presents, more than anything else (including bonuses) in the company, have made this division become extremely dynamic. We would do anything for our vice president, and we will do anything we can to let him achieve his goals, the goals of our division.

> The gifts don't dent the financial columns in any significant manner. The personalization of these gifts, however, does involve a significant time commitment to the vice president. But I'd bet this time commitment is far less than the time that he would have to sacrifice in dealing with unhappy and complaining staff. We achieve beyond our objectives![10]

(Reprinted with permission from Dr. Winston J. Brill)

How are you at giving your employees individualized recognition, attention, and appreciation? Creative and personal rewards mean the most to employees. When you recognize them as individuals, you are giving them the gift they most desire.

A company of 900 employees uses "Thank You" balloons to show appreciation. When someone does excellent work or goes above and beyond his or her job, anyone can fill out a card describing the situation and that card is sent to the human resources department. Once a month, the president of the company reads the card out loud to the whole company and hands out a "Thank You" balloon to the recipient. Each balloon has a ticket inside which the person can take to HR. The ticket qualifies them to draw from the "bingo bin." Depending upon the number on the ticket, the person may receive such things as a coupon for lunch for two or movie tickets for four.

The Idea: Use Post-it® Notes!

The Idea in Action

Donna Cutting, a professional speaker from St. Petersburg, Florida, who focuses on using humor in the workplace, tells about a creative way she and her co-workers were appreciated:

> When I worked as an Activities Director at Park Place Retirement Home in Clearwater, FL, my boss was Dawn Winder. I was one of an incredible team of Department Heads that Dawn brought together with an uncommon sense of caring mixed with high expectations! Dawn had many ways of showing her appreciation to her team, but this is one of my favorites. It's also become one of the most popular ideas that I share with my audiences.
>
> Whenever one of us would come back from a vacation, we would arrive at our desk to find it covered with multi-colored Post-it® Notes! On the notes would be written "We Missed You!" "So Glad You're Back," "It Wasn't the Same Without You," and on and on! No matter how difficult it was to come back to work after a vacation,

Dawn's Post-it® Notes never failed to pump me up and make me feel great about myself, my job, and our team! If one of us had accomplished a goal that we had been working on, the notes would read, "Way to Go!" "Knew You Could Do It!" "Bravo!" "You're Fantastic!" and so on!

Of course, we were not always as nice to Dawn! Whenever she came back from her vacations, our notes to her would read "We left every day at noon," "Donna was really bad," "We closed down for the week," etc. Thankfully, she had a healthy sense of humor!

Dawn recently shared with me how she first used the Post-it® Notes idea. When her children were growing up, she would cover the bathroom mirror with notes on the eve of their birthdays. They would wake up to find messages like "I Love You," "Happy Birthday," "You're a super kid" plastered all over the medicine cabinet, first thing in the morning. Her grown children have told Dawn that they couldn't wait to rush to the bathroom on the morning of their birthday!!!

So inexpensive, so simple, but it's made so many people feel so good!"

The Idea: Give Hershey's Hugs

The Idea in Action

Donna Cutting shares another idea of creative appreciation:

We were always trying to find fun ways to make the entire staff at Park Place feel appreciated. One time, during National Random Acts of Kindness Week in June, we found a way to encourage staff members to recognize each other. We bought packages of Hershey Hugs™ candy and wrapped four or five of them in pretty tissue paper and tied it with a ribbon. Attached were colorful cards that read, "You've been hugged!" Staff members could purchase these cards for a few cents, and fill out the card to be sent to another co-worker. They could be sent anonymously or with the giver's name attached. During the day, Department Heads would deliver the hugs to the recipients.

As you can imagine, all were delighted with their hugs, and employees were tripping over each other to send hugs to their co-workers. This activity was supposed to last one week, but was so well received that it went on for a month. I, personally, spent many an hour putting those "Hug Packages" together, trying to keep up! It was well worth it, to see how excited everyone became over their tokens of appreciation!

The Idea: Write Song Parodies

The Idea in Action

Another idea from Donna:

> One of my personal signatures has always been writing song parodies for special occasions. Whenever any one of my co-workers had a birthday or special event in their life, I would write a song parody that touched on their unique qualities to commemorate the occasion.
>
> One time the parody was for a team member who had just proudly become an American citizen. The parody was written to a medley of Patriotic Songs. Perhaps, more importantly, we also celebrated her accomplishment in this way.
>
> Her entire Department, and all the Department Heads wore Red, White, and Blue for the day. Her office was also decorated to the nines in Patriotic colors.
>
> We held a special lunch in her honor that included hot dogs, potato salad, and of course, apple pie. Her husband was so touched by the celebration that he wrote a lovely letter to all of us thanking us for the love and care we showed to his wife and family!
>
> Personal note: I loved working there! I'm sure you can see why!

The Idea: Have a Gift Closet

The Idea in Action

Kathy Posner of **Comm2**, a public relations advertising firm in Chicago, Illinois, keeps an ongoing "gift closet" to show appreciation to her staff. In the closet, she keeps the following things:

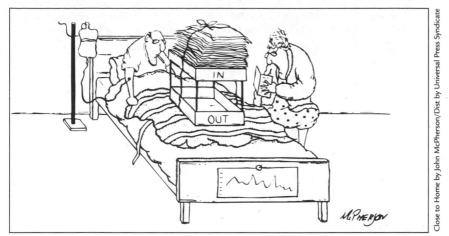

It's from your boss. It says, "Best wishes for a speedy recovery."

- ▶ Umbrellas
- ▶ Leather bookmarks
- ▶ Body shop packages
- ▶ Manicure kits
- ▶ Cigar-related products
- ▶ Silver-plated dresser sets
- ▶ Place card holders that are miniature champagne buckets
- ▶ T-shirts from clients
- ▶ Snapple things
- ▶ Restaurant gift certificates

She says she likes to "give presents constantly. People need the extra incentive and it pumps them up."

She has given such things as limo rides to an area casino for fun and dinner and then a ride back home and toss-away cameras to be used on the weekend so "everyone can share your fun!"

As the holidays approached, she sent the following memo to her staff:

Before we start the hectic Thanksgiving weekend, I wanted to send out the Christmas Wish List and ask everyone to please return it to me with their name on it and the present of their choice circled. If you desire a gift that is not on the list but is within the same range as the gift listed, please feel free to put that gift on the list.

25" color TV
4-head stereo VCR plus
CD stereo system (speakers and cabinet included)
35 mm zoom lens and all that kind of good stuff camera
    (including film and carry bag)
Carpet shampooer and steamer
Man's or woman's business suit
3 extra vacation days
New set of china
Down comforter and duvet cover
Own idea _____

Wouldn't it be fun to work for her?

The Idea: Creative and Unusual Perks and Rewards

The Idea in Action

Fortune **magazine** reported these wonderfully creative rewards:

- ▶ Free rides in the jump seat of company planes (FedEx)
- ▶ Dinner with the president and CEO after 10 years on the job (**Cerner**)
- ▶ Pet insurance (**Timberland**)
- ▶ Three-dollar, on-site haircuts (**Worthington Industries**)
- ▶ Health club reimbursement if you go three times a week (**Synovus Financial**)[11]

Bobcat Construction has some interesting ways to keep employees happy:[12]

- ▶ Employees' children receive a $50 savings bond twice a year when they get all A's on their report cards.

- Employees rotate jobs every Friday for one hour to help combat the we/they syndrome.
- On their work anniversaries employees celebrate with a cake and $100 for each year employed.

Symmetrix, a consulting group in Lexington, Massachusetts, has a point system for rewards and recognition. At the start of every quarter, each Symmetrix team member is given 100 points. Throughout the quarter, team members allocate those points to other team members who they feel have made especially important contributions to their team. At the end of the quarter, employees earn monetary bonuses on how many points they receive. This process teaches team members that everyone brings different skills to a project and all those skills are valuable.[13]

According to *Employee Recruitment & Retention* newsletter, these companies are doing wonderful things to boost employees morale and commitment:

- **AlliedSignal** (now part of Honeywell) offers dry-cleaning services to employees at its headquarters site.
- At **Born Information Services**, employees are treated to a $250 clothing allowance.
- **Whole Foods**, the natural products grocery chain, offers sabbaticals to employees with three years' tenure.
- The investment bank **John Nuveen & Co.** pays most of the college tuition for children of employees who have been with the company for five years or more.[14]

In their book, *The 100 Best Companies to Work for in America,* authors Robert Levering and Milton Moscowitz researched the most unusual benefits that companies offer employees:[15]

1. **Johnson & Johnson** offers newlywed employees an extra week's vacation.
2. At **Leo Burnett** employees receive unlimited sick pay.

3. **H. B. Fuller** gives every employee who graduates college $2000.
4. At **UNUM Corporation** employees receive 30% of their salary in one lump sum at the beginning of each year.

The Idea: Write Poems About Employees

The Idea in Action

Bob Bruce, Human Resource Manager, **Louis Dreyfus Citrus, Inc.** in Mt. Dora, Florida, writes poetry for his employees. Here are a few examples:

Growth

At first there's but a little seed
From which a large tree grows.
Just how much fruit this tree will yield?
At first glance ... no one knows.

But if this tree is fertilized
And given proper care,
It could bring forth a lovely grove
To lead us anywhere.

At Silver Springs, we're like that tree.
We're growing day by day.
We need the help of all of you
To guide us on our way.

We thank you for the work you do
And all the things you give.
Together we'll achieve our goal
And see our future live.

Thanks

Today, the world's so full of fear,
And pain and sorrow, too.
I'd simply like to offer thanks

To you for being you.

It's always such a joy to see
Your very charming smile.
And when a program's set by you,
It's done with class and style.

To know you is an honor, true.
I'm proud to call you friend.
Our friendship is among those things
I pray will never end.

A Note of Thanks

She's just a voice without a face
But pleasant as can be.
So many times she's saved the day
For folks like you and me.

Without her help the calls are hard.
Some numbers we can't find.
At times the load is so intense
You'd think she'd lose her mind.

But many times throughout each day
She shines just like the sun,
When into someone's gloomy life
She brings a little fun.

I "met" her just the other day
And now I'd like to say,
"Thanks, Natalie, for all you do
To brighten someone's day!"

The Idea: Give Silly Awards

In their book *True Leaders,* Bette Price and George Ritcheske interviewed David Novak, the Chairman and CEO of Tricon Global Restau-

rants, who sees his role as a tremendous opportunity to create an environment for happier jobs. He says there are two reasons people leave any company—and it's not because of money. It's because they don't get along with their boss and they don't feel valued. That's why Novak has changed all supervisory titles to "coach" and has made recognition an integral part of leadership development.

The Idea in Action

Tricon Global Restaurants gives out "silly" awards all over the world:

- ▸ At Pizza Hut they give a Big Cheese award.
- ▸ The President of Taco Bell gives the Order of the Pepper award.
- ▸ In Australia they give the Flying Pig award.
- ▸ The CEO for International gives a Golden Glove award.

When Novak was President of Kentucky Fried Chicken, he spontaneously gave away the Rubber Chicken award: "I'd go find a cook in the house who had worked for thirty years and I'd go to my briefcase and get out a floppy chicken. I'd write something on it, like, 'Here's to Bill—Thanks for making great original recipe for 30 years. You're what makes this company really tick! Thank you very much.' I'd bring the whole team together and give him a $100 gift certificate because you couldn't eat the floppy chicken!"

Novak goes on to describe a roundtable discussion in a bottling plant in St. Louis one evening.

> "There were about ten people," Novak recalled, "and I asked these guys to tell me about merchandising. What do we need to do better in merchandising? Who really does it well? And, what do they do?" Everyone started talking about one member of the group named Bob, who was sitting directly across from Novak. "One person said, 'Well, Bob is the best merchandiser in the whole company. In about six hours he showed me more than I learned in six years; he told me how to spin the bottles and how to go and talk to the store manager to get extra display space.'"

Suddenly, everyone in the room was telling Novak why Bob was the best in merchandising. "I looked over at Bob," said Novak, "and Bob is crying—literally crying. I said, 'Bob. Why are you crying?' And what was Bob's response? 'You know, I've been in the company for 43 years—43 years,' he repeated, 'and I didn't know anybody felt like this about me.'" Novak looked around the room and realized there wasn't a dry eye in the place. "I said to myself, 'You know, if I'm ever a president of a company, if I ever have a chance to be a CEO, I'm going to recognize people like you can't believe!'"[16]

The Idea: Make Appreciation a Regular Practice

Go through your weekly planner for the next six months. Write the name of a different employee on each week. During the week that that employee's name comes up, catch him or her doing something right and dish out the praise. You may even decide to do this on a daily basis. Finding ways to remember to thank employees regularly will help create a positive culture.

The Idea in Action

At **Borders Bookstore** in Oak Brook, Illinois, "Secret Shoppers" regularly check out the store. If the store rates in the top 5%, all employees get a $10 gift certificate.

The Director of Human Resources for a large hotel and resort in San Diego, California, describes how they treat their managers:

Each year we plan a fun outing for the mid-managers and managers to promote team spirit. This year they are going to receive an invitation rolled into a scroll, along with a bag of chocolate gold coins:

As a team player, you're worth a bag of gold.
Your value to us cannot be bought or sold.
You deal with issues all day long
And fix whatever is going wrong.

To show we appreciate the hard work you do
We have a fun day planned for you.
So come join your team and watch the ponies race.
There's food and drink to be had and bets to place.
Mark your calendar now for July 28th!
At Noon look for the limo at the hotel front door
And be ready for some fun because there's more in store!
P.S. Dress is casual.

The day of the outing they will be greeted with a glass of champagne as they enter their limo and a gift bag with an "Expect to Win" keychain, engraved business card holder, and a little betting money. They will be chauffered to Del Mar Racetrack to a private table where they can order lunch and drinks as they have fun betting on games. This is one of the ways we try to show our staff how much we appreciate their hard work. It pays off because we have a very low turnover and a high guest satisfaction. We receive many compliments about how friendly our staff is, and the guests keep on returning!

Michelle Berenson from **TCI of Illinois** shares how she recognizes employees: "To let an employee know they did a good job, I give them a package of M&Ms. This stands for doing a job that is Meaningful & Memorable."

Jack Clanton, formerly Vice President and General Manager of the **Farm Bureau Mutual Insurance Company, Inc.**, in Manhattan, Kansas, shares some of the things they do at "Team Mutual" to recognize employees:

▸ **DORPHIE Award.** A small, green thank-you card given to someone who makes you feel good about yourself. "Dorphie" is short for endorphins, which is explained on the back of the card.

▸ **Assorted M&M Thank You's.** Our Mutual Management Team (M&Ms) tries to recognize individuals who have made a significant effort in addressing a business-related or community-related activity (i.e., no overtime on big project, participating in successful charity fund-raiser, or meeting standards for an extended period). The personal note from the manager is given to each individual involved along with a bag of M&Ms candy. We change certificates each year.

▶ **"Thank You" Boards.** These little thank-you cards are used for associates to recognize fellow associates in appreciation for assistance, support, acts of kindness, job well done, etc. "Thank You" posters are located at various areas in the building. Multiple "Thank You" cards are fastened atop the poster and as the cards are removed, the picture and motivational caption emerges from behind. A recipient redeems a "Thank You" from the member of the M&Ms management named on the "Thank You" for small gift items. The transaction makes for fun interaction and good dialogue between the associate and the manager.

▶ **Stair Step.** This award is for educational achievement. When an associate passes a self-improvement course, they receive the small "Stair Step Award" card. The second part of the award is placed in the individual's personnel file for monetary recognition at merit evaluation time. (The "Stair" came from Ralph Stair of Johnsonville Sausage fame.) When an associate makes the effort to learn something new, they increase their value to the company, thus the additional compensation.

The Idea: Form a Foundation

The Idea in Action

At **Lend Lease Corporation**, a global company based in Atlanta, the company set aside $5 million in stock in 1983 to benefit employees. The trust now generates $10 million in annual revenue. As a result, they formed a nonprofit foundation with the sole purpose of supporting the interests of the 10,000 workers at Lend Lease. The vice president of the foundation and three others administer it with the help of

150 employee volunteers, who informally poll their peers on their preferences for menu options.

Employees choose their premiums such as scuba diving, Spanish lessons, home computers, or chair massages, from a menu paid for by the foundation.

They have a "balancing act" program as a part of the menu to help employees better manage their personal lives. They can be reimbursed for movie tickets on certain nights or send flowers at a discount. Under the "community" menu, every employee gets a day off to help a charity of their choice. Most popular is the "personal potential" option, which ranges from emergency elder care, taking family members along on business trips, cooking lessons, and sky diving to setting up a will. One recent survey showed that 95% of employees cite the foundation as a major reason they work for Lend Lease.[17]

The Idea: Involve Everyone

The Idea in Action

Laura Vaughan, the training director at **Tavern on the Green** in New York City, has started a program called "Tavern All Stars," which invites all employees to nominate one manager and six line professionals for recognition each quarter. A secret committee chooses winners who receive a $75 Tavern gift certificate and an engraved brass star. They hold a special celebration at the end of the year.[18]

Success in Recruiting and Retaining newsletter, February 2001, tells about **Viking Freight Inc.**, in San Jose, California, whose rewards and recognition programs all center on the belief that even the simplest reward matters when it's extended to every worker. Here are some of the things they do.[19]

▸ **EZTDBW.** This award is named for the company's slogan, "Easy to Do Business With," and is an employee-nominated award to workers who go out of their way to help co-workers.

▶ **BLTs.** "Breakfast, Lunch, and Talk" involves Viking officers treating groups of five or six new employees to breakfast or lunch and talking with them about work.

▶ **Life Savers.** They are encouraged to give one another a package of Life Savers candy when they get an extra hand from a co-worker to solve a problem.

▶ **Truck Driving Championships.** Company drivers are eligible to participate in driving contests, and then the company sponsors winners and their families with all expenses paid at state and national contests.

Viking reports lower turnover rates then competitors because their employees feel good about their jobs.

In the **City of Valdez, Alaska**, employees are each given a certificate to be used during that year. They are asked to recognize one of their co-workers' efforts for one of two awards:

▶ **"SANTA" Award**—Saved a Needy Teammate's Ass

▶ **"TOP" Award**—Totally Outstanding Performance

They are asked to check the appropriate box, fill out the name on the front, and then provide a brief description of their efforts. These awards are deserving of one "Free Lunch on the Boss," Nancy Peterson, the Assistant City Manager.

Jack Clanton, former Vice President and General Manager of the **Farm Bureau Mutual Insurance Company, Inc.**, in Manhattan, Kansas, shares some of the things they do at "Team Mutual" to include all employees:

I Make a Difference: This certificate was presented to every associate after we reached $1 million saved based on associate suggestions. The purpose was to bring the whole team together to show appreciation for achievement. A company ice cream social was held in connection with the recognition.

Bright Idea. Our answer to the employee suggestion box. Our bright idea box is an opportunity for anyone to offer an improvement idea. Each quarter, we select the best bright idea and make a cash award, engrave the name on a plaque, and put the suggestion in for best Bright Idea of the Year, which qualifies for an additional cash award.

Caught You. A certificate awarded to individuals or a team for some significant accomplishment. This certificate is usually accompanied by theater tickets, football/basketball tickets, a gift certificate to our home town mall, or dinner certificates honored at our finer restaurants. The lower portion is used for accounting purposes while the top becomes bulletin board material.

The **U.S. Department of Energy** had what they call the "Golden Plunger" award. It is given to anyone who "unclogs the system"!

Holiday Inns of Canada has a multi-leveled award system they call the *Apple Program*. Members of the Holiday Inns of Canada team who provide exceptional levels of service deserve special recognition. Now any Holiday Inns of Canada associate, whether employee or guest, can nominate those special people for apple recognition awards. Red, green, silver, and gold apple pins symbolize the program's levels of achievement. Each guest nomination earns the recipient a red apple pin. Each employee nomination earns the recipient a green apple pin. Five red nominations or three green nominations earn a silver apple pin. After receiving five silver apples, the distinguished gold apple award is achieved.

When more than one person deserves recognition, an entire department may be nominated to receive a basket of delicious apples. The Apple Program offers every member of the Holiday Inns of Canada team the opportunity to say "thank you" in a visible, personal way.

BI in Minneapolis, Minnesota, has an *Unsung Heroes Recognition Event*. A company team plans this event to show appreciation for BI associates, who give of their time to help with company-wide volunteering activities. Volunteers are invited to an afternoon of recognition and listen to a special guest speaker. Those attending include volunteers from groups such as Loaves and Fishes (they serve a meal once a month at a center for seniors), Bridging (they help provide quality furniture and household goods for the economically disadvantaged), the BI Choir, BI Tour Guides, the Newsletter Staff, the Corporate Orientation team, and the recycling committee.

BI also has company-wide *Kudos*. For example, following their National Quality meeting, associates return to their desks to find a Kudos "thank you" card signed by the entire business team along with a Kudos candy bar. The purpose is to thank associates for all they do.

A Caution

This letter was written to Dr. Winston J. Brill and was published in his newsletter, *Innovative Leader*, Vol. 9, No. 4, April 2000:

> OK, we're all part of a team. The team wins, we win. The team loses, we lose. Teamwork is what it's all about. That's the corporate "cheer." Most of our bonuses and salary raises are directed to teams rather than individuals. Thus, each team member is treated as the "average" of the team.

> This new pressure to be a great team player seems, in many cases, to work against the company's objective—to be a winner in a very competitive market. I'll give you a personal example. All by myself, I thought of a new process through which the cost of production of our main product would be decreased by 15%, a major contribution. That was the idea part.

> Next, we had to test the idea (it worked!) and reduce it to practice. Of course, many people and many talents were involved in those steps. With other people's ideas, we finally brought the new process on-line and the company is reaping the benefits.

> My supervisor, a "team player," acknowledges the great team effort by "everyone." We even had a catered fancy lunch attended by the CEO and other big shots who congratulated "the team." My name wasn't mentioned once. It was always "the team." The only single

person that could be associated with this process was, by default, the team supervisor. He, by the way, initially didn't believe the process would work and tried to talk me out of getting the other team members involved.

Now, I'm happy for the company and happy for my team. But I'm miserable about me. This was the most important contribution I've ever made at work. I'm bitter that I haven't received appropriate recognition. Am I just a selfish person, more interested in myself than the team's success? Yes, I am! And I think anyone else would be just as selfish. Isn't it human nature to want to be openly acknowledged for a very important idea?

I'll tell you one thing. I'm not as effective as I had been. My bitterness clouds my current work. I certainly am not looking forward to contributing the next great idea. Why put up with the usual negativity that comes with it? Let's all be average; that's the way we're treated.

Do you over-emphasize team playing? Be careful.

—Anonymous[20]

(Reprinted with permission from Dr. Winston J. Brill)

> Our employees very clearly articulated that—assuming that the basics were in order, that they were paid fairly and that their workplace was a good place to work—what really drove them to do their best was performing meaningful work and feeling valued for doing it.
> —Helen Drinan, former President and CEO, Society for Human Resource Management

An article by Laura Lawson in *HR News*, August 2000, titled "Team Rewards Start with Business Objectives," shares some of the lessons learned by Jerry L. McAdams of **Watson Wyatt Worldwide** in studying 79 team incentive plans:

▶ Everything starts with business objectives.
▶ Customize a plan to your company.
▶ What you reward people for tells them what your company values.
▶ Have lots of winners and few losers.

- ► Involve employees in selecting award winners.
- ► Anticipate how the program will "play out" in countries other than the U.S.
- ► Administration is everything.
- ► Payoffs are in the eye of the beholder.
- ► The introduction, operation, and management ownership of the plan are critical.

He shares one critical aspect of a reward program **Great Plains Software** has for its project management teams, a "Friends List." Weekly, team members create a list of colleagues who aren't on the team but who helped with the project. These "friends" are thanked and also can share in the monetary rewards.[21]

If you have team reward plans, evaluate them with these criteria in mind to avoid de-motivating your employees like the one above.

Kim Smithson, president of the **National Association for Employee Recognition**, says, "Companies need to have an atmosphere where employees are being recognized and a system of recognition that is consistent and fair."

This is a letter I received from an audience member that shows how little things can make a difference:

Dear Barbara,

I so enjoyed your talk this week at the SHRM conference. The opening speaker on Monday gave each of us a challenge to either write or call an individual who had made a difference in our lives. However, I would not have taken the time to write or call my special person without hearing your presentation. I wrote a letter to an uncle who had made a difference in my life after his brother, my Dad, had been killed in a Kansas tornado. I was 13 at the time. I had always treated him with respect but had never spoken or written the words to let him know of my appreciation.

It costs so little to show just the smallest amount of appreciation to others we work with. My department consists of five employees. We have a short meeting each Monday just to start the week right. At this meeting each one is asked to share how they were able to go beyond the expected to help another employee. The best situations are those that completely change the attitude of the employee and not just solve their problem. We also have Post-it® notes with "Thanks" or "I noticed" preprinted at the top which anyone may use to place on employees' desks or hand out to employees. My last company gave out carnations to recognize birthdays. The manager would present it, and everyone that person came in contact with would ask, "Why the flower?"

Enclosed is one of the products we manufacture. Because you are on your feet a lot, I thought you might appreciate these stockings. Let me know if they help those tired legs!

Sincerely,

Joe Hoffman

Quick Appreciation Ideas

▶ Give an employee a surprise day off.

▶ Write and perform a song about your employees.

▶ Have a surprise "Queen/King for the Day" celebration for someone who is always there to support others.

▶ Send flowers to an employee's spouse, parents, or significant other, thanking them for the great work that employee is doing.

▶ Use candy names as ways to appreciate employees. When they have met a sales or other goal, give them a Skor bar. If they have gone the extra mile, how about a package of Extra gum? If they have done something really valuable for the team, choose a $100 Grand candy bar. If they always make everyone laugh or keep their spirits high, give them a Snickers. If you go to a good candy store, you can personalize something for each person on your team.

▶ Find a key employee on your staff who enjoys and is good at making employees feel good and make employee recognition a formal part of his or her job description.

▶ Ask each employee to write down at least eight things they would like for rewards or recognition—at least two that cost no money, two that cost from $5 to $50, two that cost from $50 to $200, and two dream things.

▶ Have a senior manager wash an employee's car.

▶ Take out an ad in the local paper celebrating an employee.

▶ Give an employee a pair of painter's gloves with the fingers dipped in red paint as the "I work my fingers to the bone award."

▶ Send each employee a glass container. Then give them a different kind of candy to fill it every month.

▶ On the employee's birthday let them choose from five different envelopes, each with something they have suggested they would like for a reward.

▶ Keep an "Appreciation Box" on your desk so employees can let you know what others have done for them.

▶ Help one of your star employees run for an office in a trade association. If they win, take away some of their responsibilities so they can handle the extra work they've taken on.

▶ Have an "Achievements Box" in your work area where employees can write down whenever something positive happens. At the end of the week, read each entry to employees.

▶ The CEO of a very large company decided to shake hands with every single employee during Christmas week to thank them for their hard work that year.

Notes

1. Dr. Gerald Graham, Wichita State University, Wichita, KS.

2. Jasniowski, Ron. 2000. "Bring Out the Best in People—and Keep Them!" *Innovative Leader*, February, pp. 8-9.

3. Ibid.

4. Editor. "Make Recognizing Employees Part of Your Daily Routine." *The*

Motivational Manager, Sample Issue, p. 1.

5. Price, Bette, and Ritcheske, George. 2001. *True Leaders: How Exceptional CEOs and Presidents Make a Difference by Building People and Profits.* Chicago, IL: Dearborn Trade, pp. 146-147.

6. Editor. "Give Employees 'Success Files.'" *The Motivational Manager,* Sample Issue, p. 2.

7. Daniels, Aubrey. 1994. *Bringing Out the Best in People.* New York, NY: McGraw-Hill.

8. Roberts, Deborah S. "Two Companies Battle High Turnover—and Win!" *Employee Recruitment & Retention,* Sample Issue, p. 6.

9. *True Leaders,* p. 146.

10. Anonymous. 2000. "Knives and Rewards." *Innovative Leader,* January, p. 11.

11. Editor. 1999. "News You Can Use." *Training & Development,* April, p. 12.

12. Smith, Greg. 1999. "News You Can Use—Good Place to Work." *Training & Development,* April, p. 12.

13. Editor. "3 Ways to Trigger Workplace Creativity." *Positive Employee Practices,* Sample Issue, pp. 1-2.

14. Editor. "Best Practices." *Employee Recruitment & Retention,* Sample Issue, p. 5.

15. Levering, Robert, and Moskowitz, Milton. 1994. *The 100 Best Companies to Work for in America.* New York, NY: Doubleday.

16. *True Leaders,* pp. 37, 135-136.

17. Dannhauser, Carol Leonetti. 2000. "The Right Rewards." *Working Woman,* July/August, p. 41.

18. Roberts, Deborah S. "Two Companies Battle High Turnover—and Win!" *Employee Recruitment and Retention,* Sample Issue, p. 6.

19. Editor. 2001. "Widen Recognition to Reward Everyone." *Success in Recruiting and Retaining,* February, p. 5.

20. Anonymous. 2000. "It Was My Idea, Not His!" *Innovative Leader,* April, p. 11.

21. Lawson, Laura. 2000. "Team Rewards Start with Business Objectives." *HR News,* August.

Chapter 11

R = Respect

If you lead through fear, you will have little to respect; but if you lead through respect, you will have little to fear.
                              —Anonymous

If you take a couple of drops of human dignity and respect—just a couple of drops—and put them on an employee, and *if* they believe you, they'll swell up just like a sponge.
                              —Tom Melohn, former CEO,
                              North American Tool & Die Co.

According to a recent survey by MasteryWorks, a consulting group in Annandale, Virginia, employees do not ultimately base their decision to change jobs on financial factors. Instead, trust plays a key role in the decision. If employees feel that they haven't built a trusting relationship with their employers, then they most likely will move on quickly to another job, the survey found.[1]

Surveys have found that most employees leave an organization because of ineffective relationships with their immediate supervisors. In other words, employees stay with organizations where they feel respected and valued, where they are recognized for their contributions, and where they are encouraged to develop their skills and talents.

> Too many leaders today don't develop their people. They've stopped investing in them. They've focused on technical core competencies only. I think one of these days we're going to pay the price for it.
> —Tom Melohn, former CEO, North American Tool & Die Co.

Alignment Strategies, Inc., interviewed 500 successful managers from a cross section of industries who were identified as having quality relationships with their employees to find what they did that made a difference in employee retention.

These supervisors were found to engage in similar practices, all of which show deep respect for the individual. Some things they did were:

- ▸ Set mutual expectations.
- ▸ Provided frequent feedback.
- ▸ Avoided generalities or stereotypes in communicating.
- ▸ Shared personal experiences and cultural knowledge of the organization.
- ▸ Acted as advocates and provided visibility and exposure for employees.
- ▸ Were accessible and encouraged "straight talk about the bad news as well as the good news."
- ▸ Knew and appreciated the employee's work.
- ▸ Coached and developed knowledge and skills.
- ▸ Recognized and rewarded superior performance.[2]

Most of the supervisors focused the relationship on job performance but emphasized that they spent time getting to know the values and personal interests of their workers. They reported that trust was higher when they connected with their subordinates personally as well as professionally. All of these practices show deep respect for the individual. Are these practices you use with your employees?

The Idea: Listen to Employees

The Idea in Action

Learning to listen to employees is one of the most powerful ways of showing your respect as a supervisor or manager. Just letting employees talk is not the same thing as really listening. Ann Hambly, the Managing Director of **Prudential Asset Resources**, says in *True Leaders*:

> Listening, to me, makes me feel there is an openness that I can go back and tell people things that maybe a boss who didn't listen would not. I give every single person equal access to me if they want to come in and meet with me. I give them the same respect I would my boss. My motto has been to treat everyone—every single person— with the same level of respect you would expect. There should be no distinction if they are the receptionist, the secretary, or the file clerk. They are still people doing a job that is important to your success, and if you think they're not, try moving them out for a week.[3]

Listening is an active skill and you must work at it. Here are five things to improve your listening skills:

- **Put your work away.** If you remove temptation, it will be easier to focus on the employee.
- **Bite your tongue.** Never ever interrupt an employee when he/she is talking to you.
- **Smile and lean forward.** If the employee is standing, ask them to sit if possible. If not, stand up yourself so that you are on the same eye level. A smile invites the employee to share and sends a message that they are important to you. Also use direct eye contact to create rapport.

> ▶ **Always ask questions, even if you don't have any.** This tells employees that you have been listening.
> ▶ **Start your own comments by paraphrasing the employee.**[4]

At **Borders Bookstore** in Oak Brook, Illinois, managers really listen to employees. After hearing employees' concerns, a decision was made that no one ever works at one station for more than two hours. They rotate around. That way no one gets bored, and they learn all the jobs in all areas.

During the holiday season, their busiest time of the year, one day the manager put a form in everyone's mailbox. It was a small "fill in the blanks" questionnaire that read:

Today I was really frustrated because _____.
Today would have been much better if _____.

Then everyone's answers were discussed in a staff meeting.

Rich Flanagan, retired President of Borders, had what is called a "Flanagan Form." On it any employee can turn in any comment or question and the answer is published in the next employee newsletter.

The Idea: Provide Enriching and Ongoing Training

Providing enriching and ongoing training is one of the ways organizations can show respect for their employees. Because employees value training, they'll be more loyal to a company that provides it, which certainly impacts budget-minded senior managers. One employee said, "I was going to invest possibly years of my life at a company, so I wanted it to show that it was willing to invest in me." Jack Lowe, the CEO of **TD Industries**, "I think if you pull somebody out of their workday and put them in a pretty good training program, you have said something to them about how valuable they are."

This kind of thinking is what builds loyalty.

Thomas Mahan, vice president and senior consultant with **Saratoga Institute** in Santa Clara, CA, says, "We read a lot in the press that employees aren't loyal today. We found [in interviewing 60,000 employees who had quit their jobs in 1998] that there is an emergent population that defines loyalty differently. They tell us that their loyalty is tied to their confidence in their ability to do the work required in the company in the future. They're saying, 'Teach me the things that will keep me employed here.' As a result, their motivation is tied to education, mentoring, and growth opportunities. This is probably the first time since World War II that training and human capital competence are the leverage."

Mahan goes on to say, "We found that if the American workforce has the training it wants, 12% will leave their current company anyway. However, if they don't get the training, 41% will leave. It you have a company of 1,000 employees, that means employee turnover will cost you $14.5 million a year."[5]

The Idea in Action

At **SAS Institute**'s boot camp, employees of the software developer in Carey, North Carolina, get technical training, but they also work on business ethics, time management, and leadership skills. Annette Holesh, personnel director, says that when they decided to revamp their boot camp program a few years ago, they looked at numbers. "The industry average turnover is 22%. Our turnover (now) is just 4%. We figure that saves us $50 to 60 million a year." An interface analyst with SAS agrees: "Just that the company is willing to invest in me motivates me to give back. I feel that a lot of people want a company to really value them. Training and development are one way a company shows that."[6]

The Horn Group, a San Franciso-based public relations firm, has created a "personal development fund." They offer employees cash that they can spend on any type of training they feel would help them do their jobs better.[7]

The Container Store offers 240 hours of formal training to an employee during their first year in an industry that averages eight. Kip Tindell, one of the co-founders of the company, notes that most retailers do not spend a lot of time training new employees because the turnover rate in the industry is so high. Their dedication to training, however, has actually lowered their turnover rate by building the people and giving them the tools they need to truly take care of customers.[8]

 Lucent Technologies in Naperville, Illinois, has a goal of offering its employees 50 hours of training each year. Each employee designs his or her own "personal development plan" with the assistance of a coach from Human Resources.

They offer some wonderfully interesting training programs to their employees:

- ► "Wholeness in the Workplace: Connecting Mind, Body, and Spirit"
- ► "What Are You Rushing To? Creating a Life on Your Own Terms Right Where You Are"
- ► "How to Increase Your Creativity in the Midst of Chaos"
- ► "Dialogue: Skills for Learning Conversations"

These classes are offered through "IdeaVerse," a virtual organization within Lucent whose mission is "to help Lucent Technologies create and sustain a climate that supports creativity, innovation, and team effectiveness."[9]

Think about what kind of training you are providing for your employees. The vice president of product management for a New York City-based outplacement and human resources consulting firm says, "In most cases, career derailment is not because of technical skills but interpersonal skills. People are looking to fill that gap." As you offer your employees excellent training on both the business and the human levels, you are not only creating the kind of employees you want in your workplace, but you are also showing that you value them as whole persons.[10]

Company chairman Lloyd Fegman didn't have much patience for
what he considered to be dumb questions.

One of the most creative kinds of training being used by organizations to attract new hires is "reality-based" training.

At **Whirlpool Corporation** newly hired salespeople in groups of seven are actually sent to live in a house near corporate headquarters in Benton Harbor, Michigan, for two months, with two weekend breaks to return home. The idea is to become intimately familiar with Whirlpool brands, washing dozens of loads of clothes, cooking meals, and washing dishes, all with company-made appliances. They also compare Whirlpool products with those of competitors and shop for appliances at local stores. Many recruits say they chose Whirlpool over other job opportunities because of this creative training, and all but one of the first group of "Real Whirled" trainees are still with the company and several have been promoted.[11]

BI in Minneapolis, Minnesota, sponsors a Learning Fair for all associates. They are able to spend an afternoon visiting booths around BI to learn about training that is available and other new initiatives. The invitation to the Learning Fair had a drawing of a frozen brain on the cover and the following explanation:

> It's the middle of another Minnesota winter, and, as we all know, wind chills of –25 tend to slow things down a bit ... including BI brain power. But just because it's cold outside, doesn't mean we can't *heat things up!* As part of BI's continuing commitment to quality, the learning team wants to fire up associates with a CAMPUS-WIDE LEARNING FAIR.

> BI keeps growing, and that makes it difficult for associates to keep abreast of all the terrific training opportunities and capabilities. A diverse selection of groups within BI will conduct informational sessions throughout the afternoon. As you visit these groups, you will receive a stamp for each group you visit. (Look in your mail one week prior to the event for a Learning Fair Passport in which you'll collect your stamps.) Acquire 10 stamps, and you'll quality for a $400 SWEEPSTAKES AWARD to be applied toward an outside training class of your choice!

> As you dart from one building to the next in the cold of February, you'll discover a heated discussion of BI training in each conference room. Jump start your brain, and attend the BI Learning Fair!

The Idea: Find Out What Makes Your Employees Feel Respected

The Idea in Action

In his article, "Roll Out the Red Carpet of Retention," professional speaker and author John Blumberg suggests the following exercise:

> Regardless of the level or background of one's job, does your work environment promote employees truly demonstrating respect for one another? Probably the easiest way to compile action ideas for this category is to look in the mirror. What are specific actions that help *you* feel respected?

> Ask employees to look in the mirror, asking them to convert the word "respect" into specific action ideas, ideally ones that are measurable. You will then have an excellent foundation of actions to build upon.[12]

Try to generate ideas that are very basic and quantifiable such as "being on time," "keeping promises," "giving everyone a chance to contribute." Then use this list as a guideline for the way you will treat one another on your team.

The Idea: Build Camaraderie and Respect

The Idea in Action

Joe Hill shares two interesting ideas to build camaraderie and respect within your team in his article, "7 Ways to Motivate Your Staff."

- ▶ Let someone else be the boss and rotate. Employees can have a tremendous amount of fun and will benefit through a learning experience with this technique. This may be the only chance for some employees to experience a leadership role in the workplace. Not only does this technique allow for role changing, it also allows employees to become more of a team with you! (You may get to see what they really think of you when they assume your role.)
- ▶ Create an "assistant" assistant manager and rotate the job. They could help you train new employees or other managerial duties, freeing up your time. This technique will create a team atmosphere, and lower stress levels as everyone has an opportunity to participate. It is also a great learning experience.[13]

Alice Errett, the owner of a cleaning franchise called **The Maids** in Kansas City, Kansas, demonstrates an exemplary model of respect in the way she treats employees. In a tough labor market in an even tougher business (very few people these days are willing to work that hard, in an unglamorous job for very little money), Errett has discovered the key to finding and keeping good employees.

An article in the *Johnson County Business Times* describes Errett:

She stumped for employees at job centers, on street corners, in grocery stores, in churches, and just about anywhere else she could find willing workers in Kansas City, Kansas. She went to pick them up if she had to. She showed them respect.

Mrs. Errett's ability to attract and retain workers all comes back to the underlying respect she has for her employees, who have been beaten down so much that they're slow to trust anyone, let alone a white business owner in suburbia. "I believe that no matter who you are, if you're white, black, Hispanic, Asian, or whatever, you should be treated fairly," she says. "It doesn't matter where you're from."

She decided at the beginning that she couldn't be bound by traditional ways of doing things if she were going to survive in labor-starved Johnson County. Errett's revelation

> Treat employees like partners, and they act like partners.
>
> —Fred Allen

was this: treat workers with respect and do what you can to take care of them, in and out of the office. Treating workers with respect is the easy part, but taking that extra step to extend a helping hand is something most business owners are afraid to do.

Most of her employees live in the toughest areas of Wyandotte County. Many are Hispanic and don't speak English. Some are African American and don't speak Spanish. Quite a few have difficult home lives. Almost all are financially strapped.

She's not running a charity, however. She grossed just under $1 million in 1999. Here are some of the things she's done for her employees:

- ▶ Forged a public-private partnership with transit officials to subsidize a bus that picks up her workers in Kansas City, Kansas, and deposits them at her office front door.
- ▶ Furnished a living room in the office complete with sofas, a television, a VCR, and a few photo albums lying around to make it feel like "a home away from home."
- ▶ Put a full-service kitchen in the office so workers can fix breakfast or dinner for themselves or their families. The company provides a simple breakfast such as bagels and cream cheese for all employees.

- Set up a bilingual library of periodicals and books for her employees to read. All workplace materials are in both Spanish and English. She also encourages her employees to read to their children!
- Became an expert in day care and sick-child referrals, in car loans, and even bail bond resources.
- Trained employees in household budget management.
- Provided teambuilding and interpersonal skills training classes to help workers get along with each other.
- Paid for her employees' flu shots and vitamins.
- Rotated employees as the "greeter" at the door. Their job is to get a smile out of every worker who arrives. For this "extra" job, the person gets $20.
- Included diapers and formula as employee benefits.
- Held English as a Second Language classes on site.
- Transported workers to GED and college classes so they could earn degrees.

To sum up her respect for her workers, Alice Errett says, "I will do everything in my power to make it possible for the people who work for me to be healthy and be here." In addition to lending a hand, she also is giving unskilled workers much needed job training. And as a result, she has earned many loyal employees!

Jane Conley, president of the Merriam Chamber of Commerce in Johnson County says, "I assure you that Alice is giving a lot better service to her clients because of what she does for her employees. Her employees are reliable, trustworthy, and just as interested in keeping her in business as she is."[14]

The Chicago Bakery supervisors at the **Nabisco, Inc.** bakery in Chicago authored a booklet titled "125 Ways to Empower People." Here is the introduction:

As a part of the continuous improvement process, *empowerment* is a critical step in employee ownership. We must use the *empowerment* process to give all Chicago Bakery employees the knowledge, authority, skills, and incentive to achieve our business goals and job satisfaction.

Most organizations "talk" about *empowerment*, while here at the Chicago Bakery, we're "doing" something about it! At a recent supervisors' off-site meeting, all of the bakery supervisors did a short "brainstorming" session to come up with ideas that they could do now as steps on the empowerment road.

The ideas in this book are a collection of their practical suggestions that can be done immediately. It also leaves space to add 25 more ideas that are specific to each supervisor's area.

Empowerment is a process that takes time, patience, education, and understanding. Each supervisor will find and use their own ideas as well as build on others to keep us moving in the right direction.

Here are a few of their ideas:

▸ Ask a department, other than your own, for ideas on how you can better support them.

▸ Invite an employee to one of your management meetings.

▸ Invite a different department manager to meet your employees and update them on "what's new" and Q & A.

▸ Educate employees about the business (cost of cans, packaging, and raw materials, for example), tell them a little every week, and post it too.

▸ Talk about mistakes and what can be learned—remove the fear.

▸ Let go! Don't jump in right away. Let employees try to solve the problem first.

▸ Write up someone for doing something *good*.

▸ Get line employees involved in end-of-shift meetings to review problems from previous shifts.

▸ Ask for help!

▸ Ask an employee, "If you had to make a recommendation for _____, what would it be?" and then listen.

- Take a hike. Walk around to relieve stress. Make sure you're a healthy person—it makes for better relations and clearer thinking.
- Pay attention to the "middle" people, too, not just the stars and troublemakers.
- Create a fun department award like the "golden broom" for good housekeeping, the "golden safety kit" for safety, etc. Make it a traveling award.
- Give positive feedback daily. Pick someone different every day.
- Put up an "idea board" in your area that anyone can write suggestions on at any time.
- Let hourly employees conduct safety meetings. Do it gradually with your coaching.
- Ask, "How can I support you?"
- Ask employees what task they'd like to learn to help them do their job better. Then jointly find a way to make that happen.
- Buy an employee a cup of coffee to say "thank you." Sit down and just talk to get to know him/her better.
- Foster an environment that encourages questions and follow through by asking for employees' input as *partners*.
- Share business information. Perhaps post the e-mail newsletter on a bulletin board weekly.
- Have a positive attitude about this new concept and new ideas—and show it.

(Reprinted with permission from Nancy Cobb, HRD Manager, Nabisco Corporation)

The Idea: Educate Employees on the Company's Business

The Idea in Action

An article in *The Motivational Manager* tells how one company taught its employees where company dollars go:

At Artists' Frame Service in Chicago, Illinois, employees knew what the company charged customers and that their pay was only a fraction of that. The CEO wanted them to understand that the difference between invoice prices and their salaries wasn't all profit. So the employees were treated to a demonstration of the company's expenses, illustrated as portions of a hypothetical $100 order.

As the presenter explained where the money was going, different departments came forward to claim the proceeds of the sale. An oversized $5 bill, for example, was disbursed to cover the cost of the company's Yellow Pages listing, which costs roughly 5% of its receipts. The pile of cash was whittled down as claims were made by rent, health insurance, and other fixed and operating expenses which many employees don't think about. When all the bills were paid, $5 remained.

The demonstration improved morale by giving workers an understanding of the company's expenses and challenged them to look for ways to save the company money. Now that they understand how lean a company has to run to stay competitive, buyers are ordering in bulk and watching inventory carefully, and clerks are finding ways to handle orders more efficiently.[15]

How might you use this idea to teach your employees where the dollars go?

59% of employees in an Ernst & Young LLP survey said the best way to motivate employees is for managers to show them how their jobs help the company make money. And 77% of the managers in the same survey agreed.[16]

The Idea: Create a Code of Conduct in Your Work Team

The Wall Street Journal reports a study at the University of Delaware and Penn State University that most companies claim to have ethics codes but only 50% of these firms require workers to acknowledge these codes or sign off on them.[17]

One way to increase respect in your work team is to create a work-group code of conduct. Whenever you are a part of an ongoing team, committee, or other group that will be working together for a prolonged length of time, it is crucial to the effectiveness of the team to establish a code of conduct, listing the specific behaviors you will use in interacting with one another. It is also critical that each member of the team participate and agree on the final version. I even suggest having each member sign the code and posting it in their regular meeting room or central work area as a reminder of their commitment.

The Idea in Action

I spent two days working with the training team of the Electronic Commerce Division of **Rockwell International**. As a part of this work, they created their team Code of Conduct.

Code of Conduct

Be on time for all meetings.
- ✔ Have an agenda with time limitations
- ✔ Stick to agenda/time frames
- ✔ Assign meeting roles

Communication process
- ✔ State problems (feelings/facts)

Possible solutions
- ✔ Your recommendations

Time limit for floor
- ✔ OK to shelve topic
- ✔ Everyone speaks
- ✔ Individual responsibility
- ✔ Try time limit up front

Leave personal disagreements aside.
Listen when others talk.

> **Be open with concerns.**
> **Treat everyone with professional respect.**
> **Keep the slate clean.**
> **Do not say anything negative or unkind about the training delivery team.**
> **Share what has been done well (2-5 times more).**
> **Demonstrate loyalty.**
> **Share information with all team members—FYI.**
> **Evaluate ideas, not people.**
> **Practice positive intent.**
> **Focus on the situation, not the individual.**

Their manager shared with me that the morale of the team has been much higher, that meetings have become much more pleasant and efficient, that there is a new spirit of creativity and fun in the workplace, and that they are truly beginning to function as a team. They have decided to begin each meeting with "Hurrah" time and have even come up with a reminder to keep them on track with the behaviors in the code—when someone is not following the behaviors, they use the phrase *"Check your code!"* They are even thinking about having buttons made with this slogan.

The customer service team at **Viscosity Oil** in Willowbrook, Illinois, established this code of conduct, each individual signed it and posted it in their common workspace:

- ▶ If someone has a problem with another person, come directly to that person.
- ▶ Don't put your finger in someone else's face.
- ▶ No back stabbing—don't say negative things about anyone.
- ▶ If someone comes to you with a problem, don't share it with others.
- ▶ Everyone come to work with a smile and *keep it!*

The employees of the **Waukegan Park District** in Waukegan, Illinois, created an Employee Code of Values to reflect how people should be treated in their workplace to create effective personal and professional relationships. This is their Employee Code of Values:

- I will offer assistance when a co-worker is obviously in need of help. I will be proactive and will not wait to be asked to lend a helping hand.
- I will listen and communicate effectively with co-workers.
- I will go directly to the source of concern or of miscommunication.
- I will recognize and accept compliments!
- I will be positive—maintain a positive mental attitude, a "yes we can" attitude.
- I will treat co-workers with respect and be courteous.
- I will have a sense of humor.
- I will be part of the solution—not part of the problem.
- I will treat everyone fairly and equally. I will recognize that people of diverse backgrounds have differences.
- I will be honest and trustworthy.
- I will respect others' time, workload, priorities, and deadlines.
- I will be realistic in my expectations.

The U.S. Department of Energy Environmental Programs Group, Argonne National Laboratory in Argonne, Illinois, created the following Code of Conduct:

- Listen while others are speaking. Listen to suggestions.
- Follow the Golden Rule.
- Provide constructive feedback.
- Be responsive to customers' needs.
- Presume good intentions.
- Assume the best of co-workers.
- Share information with affected partners.

- Be on time for all meetings. End on time.
- Acknowledge contributions.
- Show courtesy to all individuals.
- Honor commitments.
- Avoid memo and e-mail wars.
- Confirm understanding of messages.
- Respect personal time.

They also created a "Human Level" Code of Conduct:

- Bring a treat on your own birthday.
- Friday is dress-down day.
- Show and Tell hobbies once a month.
- Have a "Fax of the Month" cover sheet.
- Buy someone lunch when they do you a favor.
- Smile frequently.
- Have more informal gatherings.
- Create a Humor Board.

The **Council of Logistics Management** in Oak Brook, Illinois, created their Code of Conduct:

- Take responsibility for your actions and be more accepting of others' mistakes.
- Don't initiate gossip or repeat gossip.
- It's more important to find a solution to a problem than to lay blame.
- Do unto others as you would have them do unto you.
- Respect one another.
- Look at the big picture.
- Clarify communications.
- Worry about what you're doing and not what everyone else is doing.

It is best to have an outside facilitator lead the process of developing a code of conduct because it can be an emotional one, and a strong trust level must be developed to allow people to express deep feelings and concerns and to be honest in expressing the behaviors they desire in a working relationship. This often involves leaving "old baggage" behind and starting anew in these relationships, so it is crucial that *every member of the team* commits fully to these behaviors as the guide for how they will work together in the future.

The Idea: Give All Employees Business Cards

In today's society a business card indicates that you are successful, and having a card of their own gives employees a sense of pride and value, no matter what their position is. Also, with excellent computer printers, the cost of creating business cards is negligible.

One of my clients, a manufacturing company with a strong commitment to customer service, gave each of their employees business cards, including office staff, telephone reps, custodial people, stock persons, truck drivers, and workers on the line. On each person's card was the customer service term "Manager of Moments of Truth" below their name. This small gesture raised morale and impacted productivity almost immediately. As the president of the company said, "I don't care if they only give the cards to their mothers. We value them, and we want them to know that!"

The Idea in Action

Lois Ketay, CMM, office manager of **Cardiothoracic-Vascular Surgeons** of Cincinnati, Ohio, promotes professionalism and pride in her ofice by providing business cards for all the staff members, according to *Briefings on Practice Management* newsletter. "Our receptionist is more than just a receptionist—she's an appointment secretary. That title goes on her card, and she sends her card along with a letter and a map to new patients so they know who they've been communicating with," says Ketay. Everyone in the office has a title and that goes on their cards. "A job title makes the employee realize that his or her position is important to the practice, rather then simply another staff job that anyone could easily fill."[18]

Titles can also be motivating. A front desk supervisor in one office has her title on her business card— "Director of First Impressions."

> The way to attract and retain good people is to give them interesting work to do, interesting people to do it with, and treat them like the responsible adults they are.
> —Charles A. O'Reilly III and Jeffrey Pfeffer
> *Hidden Value: How Great Companies Achieve Extraordinary Results with Ordinary People*

Another person's title is "Problem-solver." Margo O'Malley at **Honeywell, Inc.**, has the intriguing title of "Positive Environment Specialist." One of my favorites is a young man in the restaurant at the **Red Lion Hotel** in Denver, Colorado, whose title is "Sandwich Mason." Some managers have even changed the title of supervisors to "Coach" to suggest the importance of developing their people.

The Idea: Encourage Individual Employee Career Development

"The company is responsible for providing the environment in which people can achieve their full potential, and employees are responsible for developing their skills," says Raymond V. Gilmartin, CEO of **Merck & Co.**, in an article titled "We Want You to Stay. Really" in *Business Week* magazine June 22, 1998. "That's the key to our ability to attract and retain new talent, and it defines the new employment relationship as I see it today."[19]

The Idea in Action

International Paper Company wants to let employees know that IP cares about their long-term future, so they rolled out a new program for their 13,000 white-collar workers. Managers must sit down with employees every year, according to Carol Roberts, vice president for people development, and discuss their career desires, separate from the annual performance review. This special attention helps employees feel they are valued and important to the company as well as helping them plan their own personal career path.[20]

An article in *Harvard Business Review*, January-February 2000, shares a way companies can collaborate to help employees in their career development:

> Cascade Engineering, a plastic parts manufacturer in Grand Rapids, Michigan, has teamed up with a local Burger King to coordinate recruiting. Applicants who do not have the skills necessary for Cascade's production positions but who otherwise seem like good workers are offered jobs at Burger King. Successful Burger King employees who begin looking for more skilled positions are offered vocational counseling at Cascade. The prospect of moving to Cascade provides an incentive for people to join and stick with Burger King, and the Burger King employees become a dependable labor pool for Cascade. The career development that individuals would have experienced within a single company now takes place across two companies.[21]

The Money Store recently hired on-site career counselors. The vice president of recruiting says that the program is meant to give people a sounding board infused with advice. The sessions are all confidential.

Dow Corning has designed a "career fitness" program to help employees see opportunities in-house to grow their careers. This program can teach even the newest recruits how to navigate different job functions so they won't have to leave the company to find something better.[22]

In a newsletter called *Positive Leadership*, **Lawrence Ragan Communications, Inc.** suggests several creative ideas to help employees manage their careers:

> ▶ Host monthly "Career Development Days" with employees. Set

aside one day a month to sit down one-to-one and discuss where they are in their careers, what they want to do, what skills they'll need to get there, and what opportunities are available.

▶ Start a "Professional Development Club." Assign each of your employees a different industry-related trade publication. Once a week, have a "Reading Meeting" in which you ask employees to share any interesting stories, trends, or products they've read about.

▶ When you attend a conference, take detailed notes, and turn them into a presentation for employees.

▶ Ask managers who are experts from areas such as accounting, finance, budget, etc., to conduct in-house seminars on different topics for your employees and offer to do the same for theirs.

▶ Be a "mentor headhunter" and help your employees find mentors within the company.[23]

The Idea: Consider Younger Workers

The Idea in Action

It is important to respect differences in our workforces. Lawrence J. Bradford and Claire Raines, authors of *Twenty-Something: Managing & Motivating Today's New Work Force,* have prepared a list of what turns younger workers off and on:

Turn-ons

▶ Recognition and praise

▶ Time spent with managers

▶ Learning how what they're doing now is making them more marketable

▶ Opportunities to learn new things

▶ Fun at work—structured play, harmless practical jokes, cartoons, light competition, and surprises

▶ Small, unexpected rewards for jobs well done

Turn-offs
▶ Hearing about the past—especially yours
▶ Inflexibility about time
▶ Workaholism
▶ Being watched and scrutinized
▶ Feeling pressure to convert to traditionalist behavior
▶ Disparaging comments about their generation's tastes and styles
▶ Feeling disrespected[24]

Generation Y college students, those born after 1977, in a survey reported on the **WomenConnect** Web site, said the top two things they wanted in their first jobs were "A fun work environment" and "Growth opportunities."[25]

The Idea: Use "After the Fact" Exit Interviews to Get Employees Back

Don't necessarily end retention efforts when key employees leave. Sometimes when you call them back and tell them you miss them, you may be able to retrieve a good employee who got away!

The Idea in Action

Sprint and **Anheuser-Busch** call those who have left the company to ask them to participate in interviews six months after they have left. They ask, "What really made you leave?" setting the stage to ask them if they might like to return.[26]

The Idea: Everyone Is Important

The Idea in Action

A client writes:

> During my second month of nursing school, our professor gave us a

pop quiz. I was a conscientious student and had breezed through the questions, until I read the last one: "What is the first name of the woman who cleans the school?" Surely this was some kind of joke! I had seen the cleaning woman several times. She was tall, dark-haired and in her 50s, but how would I know her name? I handed in my paper, leaving the last question blank. Before class ended, one student asked if the last question would count toward our quiz grade. "Absolutely," said the professor. "In your careers you will meet many people. All are significant. They deserve your attention and care, even if all you do is smile and say 'hello.'" I've never forgotten that lesson. I also learned her name was "Dorothy."

This is an important message for managers and supervisors to remember!

Roger D'Aprix, a noted authority on corporate communications, has developed a model to help managers lead employees from the very important "me" level to the "we" level. The first three questions are "me-based" and ones everyone must be able to answer before moving to higher levels:

▶ What's my job?
▶ How am I doing?
▶ Does anybody care?

Then the questions become "we-focused":

▶ How are we doing?
▶ Where do we (our team) fit in?
▶ How can I help?[27]

Using this model with your employees will help you communicate to them that each of them is important and valuable, and they are also an essential part of a larger team.

The Idea: Real Life Lessons

This was part of a real life memo sent to all support staff. See how it would make you feel if you worked for this organization:

Items of Concern

▶ All filing is to be done on a daily basis by each member of the support staff. No exceptions.

▶ Everyday check every item in your *in box*. They are not dumping grounds.

▶ All desks are to be cleaned and left neat every day. This will avoid clutter and force you to comply with #2.

▶ Files are to be kept in the file cabinet. Only those files you are currently working on should be on your desk.

▶ We are not machines. Please read all documents before you take them to personnel for review. We waste far too much time re-reviewing.

▶ Everyone should be aware of the phones. Answer them.

▶ I don't want to have to have you all turn in a daily productivity sheet, but I will if I feel it is warranted.

▶ Postage is for firm use only. Log in personal use and reimburse the firm.

▶ No job is below anyone. Do what it takes to get the job done. If you won't, I know I can find people out there who will.

▶ All personal calls and errands are to be done on your own time.

▶ We will have a meeting when I get back to go over all of this.

Look at every memo you send or email you write and ask if it is respectful of your employees.

The Idea in Action

In a June 2001 article in *Fast Company* magazine on the **U. S. Military Academy**, which was recognized for Grass Roots Leadership, Christina "CJ" Juhasz, '90, director in online ventures, Merrill Lynch, shares a critical leadership lesson:

> I led a team of incoming plebes during basic training. I thought I had

to lead the way that I saw others doing it—with stress and shouting, like a traditional drill sergeant. Well, my unit performed very badly. And they hated me. That experience shook me up. I realized that leadership isn't rule-based. It isn't about stress. It's about inspiration, about setting and communicating a vision. It's about gaining trust. Once you have someone's trust, once you get them on the same sheet of music, they don't want to disappoint you. The leading becomes very easy.[28]

Christina learned to understand the value of respect!

Quick Ideas to Show Respect

▶ Recommend or share books, videos, movies, music that you like with employees. Ask for suggestions from them as well. Have a personal "lending library."

▶ Never, under any circumstances, belittle an employee or gossip about them.

▶ Always say "Good morning" to all employees. In our research we found that 7% of the frontline and professional staff we interviewed had left a job because their supervisor or manager did not greet them in the morning.

▶ Periodically stand at the door at closing time and thank each employee for being there that day.

▶ Be a colleague rather than a boss. Refer to your employees as "associates."

▶ Have a one-on-one career counseling session with each of your employees once a year. Find out what they enjoy doing most and what they would like to be doing one year from now, five years from now, and 10 years from now. Keep notes and find ways to help them meet these goals.

▶ Celebrate learning! Keep a monthly log of what you learn each day and encourage employees to do the same.

▶ Ask for more feedback on what you're doing.

▶ Say "Go for it!" more and "What if it doesn't work?" less—to yourself and to those around you.

▸ Listen to *everyone*. Ideas can come from anywhere.

▸ Start a reading club. Once a week or month have a "reading meeting." Have each employee to bring an article that they think could have an impact on how the organization does business. Then have them summarize and discuss it with the rest of the group.

▸ Give employees a book or subscription to a magazine on something that interests or intrigues them.

▸ Allow them to attend a class or conference that excites them.

▸ Every Friday afternoon, write down three things that you learned from your employees that week.

▸ Schedule regular career and/or personal development discussions to get in touch with employees' needs, motivations, and aspirations.

Notes

1. Leonard, Bill. 2001. "Building Trust Is Key to Retention Factor." *HR Magazine*, May, p. 29.
2. Dixon-Kheir, Catherine. 2001. "Supervisors Are Key to Keeping Young Talent." *HR Magazine*, 46:1, January, p. 139.
3. Price, Bette, and Ritcheske, George. 2001. *True Leaders: How Exceptional CEOs and Presidents Make a Difference by Building People and Profits.* Chicago, IL: Dearborn Trade, p. 68.
4. Editor. "Keep Employees on Board with Training." *Employee Recruitment & Retention*, Sample Issue, p. 8.
5. Olesen, Margaret. 1999. "What Makes Employees Stay." *Training & Development*, October, pp. 48-52.
6. Ibid.
7. Editor. "Create a Personal Development Fund." *Employee Recruitment & Retention*, Sample Issue, p. 5.
8. *True Leaders*, p. 132.
9. Editor. "Keep Employees on Board with Training." *Employee Recruitment & Retention*, Sample Issue, p. 5.

10. Olesen, Op. cit.

11. Editor. "Reality-Based Training Attracts New Hires, Leads to Promotions." *Success in Recruiting & Retaining*, Sample Issue, p. 5.

12. Blumberg, John. 2000. "Roll Out the Red Carpet of Retention." *The Resume,* February.

13. Hill, Joe. 1998. "7 Ways to Motivate Your Staff." *Adult Ed Today,* September/December, p. 37.

14. Editor. 1997. "Maid to Order Solutions." *Johnson County Business Times,* September 29/October 12.

15. Editor. 2000. "Employees Need to Understand Where Company Dollars Go ... So Show Them." *The Motivational Manager,* Sample Issue, p. 1.

16. Editor. 2000. "Money Motivates Learning—How the Company Makes It, That Is." *The Motivational Manager,* Sample Issue, p. 9.

17. Editor. 2000. "Ignoring the Code of Ethics." *The Motivational Manager,* Sample Issue, p. 9.

18. Editor. 1995. "Employee Business Cards Boost Professionalism." *Briefings on Practice Management,* September, p. 2.

19. Bernstein, Aaron. 1998. "We Want You to Stay. Really." *Business Week,* June 22, pp. 67-72.

20. Ibid.

21. Cappelli, Peter. 2000. "A Market-Driven Approach to Retaining Talent." *Harvard Business Review,* January-February, pp. 103-111.

22. Branch, Shelly. 1998. "You Hired 'Em. But Can You Keep 'Em?" *Fortune,* November 9, p. 250.

23. Editor. *Positive Leadership*, Bonus Issue.

24. Bradford, Lawrence J., and Claire Raines. "Understanding Young Workers." *Communication Briefings,* Vol. XII, No. VI, p. 2.

25. www.womenconnect.com.

26. Branch, Shelly. 1998. "You Hired 'Em. But Can You Keep 'Em?" *Fortune,* November 9, p. 250.

27. Grensing-Pophal, Lin. 2000. "Follow Me." *HR Magazine,* February, p. 39.

28. Hammonds, Keith H. 2001. "Grassroots Leadership: U.S. Military Academy." *Fast Company*, June, p. 114.

Chapter

R = Reason for Being

I long to accomplish a great and noble task, but it is my chief duty to accomplish humble tasks as though they were great and noble. The world is moved along, not only by the mighty shoves of its heroes, but also by the aggregate of the tiny pushes of each honest worker.
　　　　　　　　　　　　—Helen Keller

Workers want more than a paycheck for the large part of their lives that they spend on the job; they want their lives to be a source of satisfaction, creativity, and development. They will respond with extraordinary dedication to work they see as their own.
　　　　　　　　　　　—Lawrence Perlman,
　　　　　　　　　　　Chairperson and CEO, Ceridian

A challenge for all organizations is to discover how to engender the emotional energy of their frontline workers. These workers are often unskilled and paid little, and their work can be unexciting, repetitive, and boring. Because their work is unchallenging and they often see little chance of advancement, many of them work at a "job," for a paycheck, and are not engaged or emotionally connected with the organization and its long-term goals. Finally we're realizing that their impact on customers and profits is enormous, and we must find ways to give them a sense of purpose, meaning, and value in their work. Only then will they become committed to the organization and feel good about themselves and the important work they are doing.

> (Values are becoming important) because people are no longer willing to have a church and state mindset about work and personal life. Today, people look at the whole picture: Who am I as a person, who am I as a dad, and who am I as an employee?
> —Thomas D. Kuczmarski, author, *Values-Based Leadership*

When *Fortune* magazine placed Southwest Airlines in the top five of its 100 best places to work in the U.S. in 1998, 1999, and 2000, one of the major reasons was because of responses from employee interviews, according to Libby Sartain, then Vice President of People: "The employees said things like: 'I believe I can make a difference as an individual here,' 'My supervisor notices when I do a good job,' and 'I am valued as an individual and for my work.'" When employees were asked if they planned to be working at Southwest in five years, nearly 100% said "yes," a response which was off the charts compared with other organizations interviewed.[1] Because it has given its employees a deep sense of purpose and "Reason for Being," Southwest Airlines has dedicated, committed employees who are giving their very best to their jobs and who are passionately loyal to the organization. This sense of purpose and value is a gift supervisors and managers can give to their staff every day.

Value Others

Whenever we can let another person know how valuable they are, we are giving them a very special gift. Several months ago I walked into the women's rest room at O'Hare Airport en route to one of my speaking engagements. There was a lady there who was cleaning. She was all hunched over with a grim, downhearted expression on her face, ever so slowly going through the motions of cleaning the sinks and mirrors

I walked up to her, touched her on the arm, and said, "Thank you so much for keeping this washroom clean. You're really making a difference for all of us who travel." She immediately perked up, smiled a huge smile, and began cleaning with zest! By the time I left, she was handing out towels to all the women who were washing their hands. It brought tears to my eyes. What was the little thing I did? In that one statement I told her she was of value and her work was important, the gift we all desperately need in our world today.

As supervisors and managers, you have the opportunity to make this difference in an employee's life every single day!

The Idea: Create a Sense of Pride and Purpose

The Idea in Action

Fortune magazine recently surveyed organizations that have done a good job of keeping their star performers, according to an article in *Workplace Visions* newsletter. They learned some valuable lessons that relate to an employee's sense of purpose and value:

- ▶ Foster a sense of family and community so people feel they are working for a cause as well as a company (**Valero Energy**, San Antonio, Texas, 2,993 employees).

- ▶ Allow all employees, no matter how junior, decision-making authority. In a service industry, that gives you an edge over the competition (**Home Depot**, Atlanta, Georgia, 216,000 employees).

- ▶ Trust your employees to balance the demands of work and life, and give them the opportunity to do so (**SAS Institute**, Cary, North Carolina, 4,135 employees).[2]

At a seminar in Boston, Debbi Fields, the founder of **Mrs. Fields**

Cookies, shared some of her "beyond the normal bounds of business" practices that have given her the winning edge:

- ▶ If her cookies are not sold within two hours, they're donated to charity.
- ▶ Her guarantee is written on every bag.
- ▶ She only hires people who love cookies.
- ▶ She makes people sing "Happy Birthday" during their job interview.
- ▶ She hires attitude over ability.
- ▶ She gives employees all the cookies they want to take home.
- ▶ She often gives out samples in the streets.[3]

All of these things create goodwill, loyal employees, great relationships, and new customers. Today there are more than 600 Mrs. Fields Cookies stores in seven countries—and the number is growing.

Bob Nelson, author of *1001 Ways to Reward Employees,* in his newsletter, *Rewarding Employees*, tells of ways that companies can give their employees a sense of purpose and pride:

- ▶ All employees at **Apple Computer** in Cupertino, California, who worked on the first Macintosh computer placed their signatures on the inside of the product.
- ▶ Employees at **Cooper Tires** of Findlay, Ohio, are allowed to stamp their names on the inside of the tires they produce to recognize them for their contributions.
- ▶ **Federal Express** in Memphis, Tennessee, inscribes the name of an employee's child in large letters on the nose of each airplane it purchases. The company holds a lottery to select the name and flies the child's family to the manufacturing plant for the christening.[4]

PeopleSoft, a California software firm, created a series of ads featuring its employees. These "people profiles" were designed to attract passive job seekers as well as to honor employees. They contained full-page spreads on employees' unusual accomplishments and interests.

The Idea: Share Your Values

The Idea in Action

Federal Express values time so much that they lock the doors at the starting time of a meeting. This demonstrates in a very concrete way to employees how important time is to their business.

The mission statement of **Keller Williams Realty** in Naperville, Illinois, says: "Keller Williams is founded on the principle that people make a difference. What makes Keller Williams so unique is our focus on who is our partner—our associate. We have built our culture around what our associates believe is best for their careers." What a wonderful commitment they have made to their staff!

Much has been written about **Southwest Airlines** and rightly so. They have created a culture that is based on a sense of belonging and purpose. This is their mission statement:

The Mission of Southwest Airlines

The mission of Southwest Airlines is dedication to the highest quality of Customer Service delivered with a sense of warmth, friendliness, individual pride, and Company Spirit.

To Our Employees

We are committed to provide our Employees a stable work environment with equal opportunity for learning and personal growth. Creativity and innovation are encouraged for improving the effectiveness of Southwest Airlines. Above all, Employees will be provided the same concern, respect, and caring attitude within the organization that they are expected to share externally with every Southwest Customer.[5]

Service Master in Downers Grove, Illinois, has four objectives in their mission statement:

- To honor God in all we do.
- To help people develop.
- To pursue excellence.
- To grow profitably.

These four statements tell employees clearly what the values of the company are. Think about what a sense of purpose and belonging it would give your employees to create a mission statement for your work team or department.

The Noel Group, a privately owned travel company based in Stevens Point, Wisconsin, wanted to find a way to both celebrate internally the basic good values each of their employees brings to their organization and also tell their customers, vendors, friends, and relatives what a unique company they are. As a result, they asked their employees to share their own personal values, and they collected these pieces of personal wisdom into a small book of quotes and photographs entitled "Foundations." The company then distributed the book to employees, customers, vendors, and business colleagues.

"The response has been extremely positive," says John Noel, president of the 160-employee company. "Employees appreciate the recognition 'Foundations' offers, which says to them, 'We're proud of our employees.' The book has also helped further trust and deepen relationships with customers and vendors by showing them what type of company we are. Many have even ordered additional copies of the book."

23 employees contributed, and some of the examples include:

- Fear is the reverse gear of faith.
- Go look out a different window.
- Magnificent opportunities are sometimes disguised in impossible situations.

The small profit on each book is donated to the company's "Make a Mark" humanitarian program, which builds orphanages, schools, and clinics worldwide. People give the books to job candidates, potential customers, waitresses, and even taxi drivers, and with each copy they celebrate the company's real "foundation"!6

An article in the *Positive Leadership* newsletter suggests that you find an executive in your company whose values and principles you admire and who lives these principles every day. Then ask that person to speak to your employees and to cover such topics as the importance of ethics in business, how to make principled decisions, some of the ethical situations facing the company, and some real-life examples of how principles have helped the executive's career. Then hold a discussion afterwards, asking employees how these ideas apply to their daily work.

The Idea: Tell Your Company's Story

The Idea in Action

Tomaso's Pizza in a small town in Iowa has an insert in each of its pizzas that tells the customer "The Tomaso Story":

> Dear Friend:
>
> My story begins with the first pizza I ate in 1965. I remember eating at Naso's in the 1500 block of 1st Avenue NE. My drum teacher, R.L. Smith (yes, that Smitty), took a few of us from the small band at St. Matthew's School. I ate a plain cheese pizza and was not impressed.
>
> In high school my family ordered many pizzas, mostly from Naso's and Tony's. By the time senior year (1969) came around, I was a weekend fixture at Tony's. Life was good. Tony's was action central and that was there I wanted to be.
>
> For college I went to Mankato State in Mankato, Minnesota. I wanted to get away from home and 250 miles seemed like a good distance. My favorite pizza in college was Pagliai's. Since I discovered Pagliai's in Minnesota, I often ate at the home base Pagliai's in Iowa City.
>
> What happened?
>
> The world became "modern." Chain pizza stores were located in each quadrant. Now we could all drive a short way and get the same pizza. Dough was shipped in frozen and thawed at the store. Precooked

sausage (little uniform pellets) showed up on uniform circles of dough. Vegetables were minced in a meat grinder. Consistency was in, but something terrible had happened!

We Forgot About Quality.

I say "we" because my family and I ate a lot of those pizzas. As I perceived the quality slipping, I said, "That's it. I can't take this any more. I want a real pizza." (I can be irrational at times!) Real pizza is hard to find, so I decided to ...

Make My Own at Home.

My first efforts were a bit of a trial. My kids, Nick and Abbey, would not eat them, my wife Kathy ate some but offered a lot of suggestions, and our dog Amy loved every bite! I had to refrigerate the leftovers for Amy since my production outpaced her consumption!

When Nick and Abbey started eating my pizzas, I knew I was improving. When they asked me to make them for their friends, I really knew I was on the right track! Six years of trying different recipes gave me an understanding of Tony Naso's words to me at age 88, 23 years after he retired. Tony said, "This is a complex thing. The combination of the right dough, the importance of a good sauce, and high quality toppings give you a lot of variables to get screwed up."

This is the reason average pizza is easy to find and real pizza is an adventure to seek out. I didn't start flour flying six years ago so I could go public and serve you today. It just happened.

If Tomaso's has a place in the pizza world, it is because God has put enough good thoughts in my heart and enough good people in my life to help me.

Tomaso

P.S. Please come back and visit. (Go to the kitchen door on the right side of the bar.)

Note: Handwritten on the inside top of the pizza box is a note from Tomaso:

Marshalls,

Thanks for ordering this pizza. If you have any comments, please call my home phone and tell my tape (phone number).

Grazie,

Tomaso

Have you ever written your organization's story? Do you use this to motivate both customers and employees?

The Louisiana/Southern Mississippi Chapter of the **Special Libraries Association** found a wonderful way to share their stories. Chapter members were invited to submit "stories" of experiences from their library careers. Later the Chapter met with the SLA Student Chapter and other students and faculty of the University of Southern Mississippi Department of Library Science.

Everyone who attended was given the booklet containing the stories written by the Chapter members, titled "What Do You Remember Most?" Some of the members told their stories to the group at the meeting. The Chapter felt it was an opportunity for the students to gain some insight into the "real world" and for all "veteran" librarians to learn from and share with each other.

Here are two examples:

I'll never forget one night when this young man walked up to the reference desk. He came to my side, huddled with me, opened his book and pointed down to a long list of references. Quietly, but emphatically, he queried, "Who is this guy named Ibid? ... He sure has written a lot of stuff!"

Exhilarating times ...

* * *

Perhaps the most satisfying part of being a librarian comes when a patron praises you for finding "the treasure" that no one else was able to locate. Sometimes it's serendipity; sometimes it's skill; and sometimes it's a combination of the two. Most every librarian has experienced the wonderful high which comes from stretching one's abilities and locating that special piece. I remember the feeling and generalities of a number of such conquests but time has blurred most of the details.

Bobbie Scull

Has your organization ever collected your workers' stories?

A well-known drug company has created videos of people who have used their drugs, called "Stories from the Heart." Showing these videos to all employees helps create a sense of purpose and mission in the important work they are doing as they see in a powerful and poignant way how the drugs they manufacture directly impact the lives of real people.

Is there a way for you to tell your organization's story through video?

The Idea: Find the Path That Fits the Culture of Your Organization

The Idea in Action

In an article in *Harvard Business Review,* Jon R. Katzenbach and Jason A. Santamaria share the results discovered by researchers at McKinsey & Company and the Conference Board who for three years studied companies known to engage the emotional energy of frontline workers. Their research found that there are five distinct managerial paths that result in committed, high-performance frontline workers:

- ▸ **The Mission, Values, and Pride Path.** Emotional energy is generated by mutual trust, collective pride, and self-discipline. Frontline employees commit themselves to the organization because they are proud of its aspirations, accomplishments, and legacy; they share its values. Organizations that follow this path are the U.S. Marine Corps, 3M, and the New York City Ballet.
- ▸ **The Process and Metrics Path.** Emotional energy is generated by transparent performance measures and standards and clear tracking of results. Frontline employees commit themselves to

the organization because they know what each person is expected to do, how performance is measured, and why it matters. Organizations that follow this path are Johnson Controls, Hill's Pet Nutrition, and Toyota.

▶ **The Entrepreneurial Spirit Path.** Emotional energy is generated by personal freedom, the opportunity for high earnings, and few rules about behavior; people choose their work activities and take significant personal risks. Frontline employees commit themselves to the organizations because they are in control of their own destinies and they savor the high-risk, high-reward work environment. Organizations that follow this path are Hambrecht & Quist, BMC Software, and Vail Ski and Snowboard School.

▶ **The Individual Achievement Path.** Emotional energy is generated by intense respect for individual achievement in an environment with limited emphasis on personal risk and reward. Frontline employees commit themselves to the organization because they are recognized mostly for the quality of their individual performance. Organizations that follow this path are FirstUSA, McKinsey & Company, Perot Systems.

▶ **The Reward and Celebration Path.** Emotional energy is generated by recognition and celebration of organizational accomplishments. Frontline employees commit themselves to the organizations because they have fun and enjoy the supportive and highly interactive environment. Organizations that follow this path are Mary Kay and Tupperware.

The authors of the article looked in detail at the Mission, Values, and Pride Path as it is implemented by the **U.S. Marine Corps** and discovered five practices that other organizations might adopt in order to fire up their employees:

Practice One: Overinvest at the outset in inculcating core values. Most new hires get a very brief introduction to their company's values before they are asked to demonstrate them on the job. By contrast, the Marines' 12-week training is focused entirely on inculcating the values of honor, courage, and commitment, and it is delivered by the organization's most experienced and talented people who see the job as an honor. Because of the intense focus on values, the Marines build a sense of belonging to a noble cause.

Business application of this principle:

- ▶ Spend quality time on the organization's values at the beginning of orientation.
- ▶ Assign orientation training to your most talented and experienced managers and increase the training time enough for new hires to absorb and buy into the values. In some organizations, the CEO or President conducts the orientation training to show his/her commitment to those new employees and to the importance of values to the organization.
- ▶ Continue to focus on the values after the training ends.

Practice Two: Prepare every person to lead, including frontline supervisors. According to the authors, "The policy of training every frontline person to lead has a powerful impact on morale. The organization's belief that everyone can and must be a leader creates enormous collective pride and builds mutual trust."

Business application of this principle:

- ▶ Embrace the notion that a great many frontline workers can lead and thus should be trained to do so.
- ▶ Support the idea that every frontline supervisor deserves extensive leadership training.
- ▶ Create informal leadership partnerships by assigning newly appointed managers, ad hoc, to work with more experienced veterans in the running of a division or a department.

Practice Three: Distinguish between teams and single-leader work groups. Too many executives put together single-leader work groups and call them "teams," which confuses and de-motivates people and undermines the performance of small groups. In business real teams are rare; rather, most work is done by single-leader work groups, which rely entirely on their leaders for purpose, goals, motivation, and assignments, and each member is accountable solely to the leader.

The authors define a real team as "drawing its motivation more from its mission and goals than from its leader. Members work together as peers and hold one another accountable for the group's performance and results. In a real team, no individual member can win or lose; only the group can succeed or fail."

Business application of this principle:

▶ Understand the differences between the two.

▶ Apply this knowledge to managing the front line and be clear in your assignments of each.

Practice Four: Attend to the bottom half. In most businesses attention is focused almost exclusively on the people who have the greatest potential. By contrast, the authors cite a colonel who made it a point to get to know every member of each class of

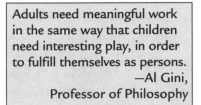

Adults need meaningful work in the same way that children need interesting play, in order to fulfill themselves as persons.
—Al Gini,
Professor of Philosophy

300 officer candidates while serving as commanding officer. They say, "The impact of this principle is powerful. Personal attention means that floundering Marines are caught before they hit bottom." Salvaging underperformers makes good business sense, both because of the shortage of frontline workers and the cost of replacement and also because of the positive energy it engenders in the workplace as a whole.

Business application of this principle:

▶ Hire frontline supervisors with experience in counseling or teaching or train supervisors to work with the bottom half.

▶ Invest in training and development programs focused on employees who are at risk.

▶ Evaluate supervisors on that dimension of their jobs.

Practice Five: Use discipline to build pride. An organization can use discipline as control and punishment or as an opportunity to build pride. For example, the Marines use discipline to mold a positive self-image by helping them discover what they are capable of when they apply themselves and then discovering that they can accomplish more than they ever thought possible. Every "mission, values, and pride" company studied encourages self-discipline in order to build pride. Both Marriott and Southwest Airlines employees are "driven by self-discipline and group-discipline—an ardent desire to follow the rules in order to make themselves and the organization proud."

> Commitment comes about only when people determine that you are asking them to do something that they really care about.
> —Peter Senge,
> author of *The Fifth Discipline*

Business application of this principle:

▶ Make an executive decision never to be content with enterprise-imposed, top-down discipline.

▶ Encourage self-discipline by calling attention to workers who demonstrate this quality.

▶ Display shortfalls, especially those that are apparent to customers.[7]

Here are some ideas of things various organizations are doing to apply these principles:

▶ At **KFC** headquarters in St. Louis, Missouri, a frequently traveled hallway called the Walk of Leaders is home to mounds of memorabilia commemorating great moments in the company's history, such as the opening of the company's first store and the introduction of new menu items.

▶ The authors tell a legendary **Home Depot** story illustrating the organization's commitment to honesty between executives and the front line:

Several years ago, the Home Depot hired a former homemaker to work in an outlet's millwork department—a job that required expertise and technical knowledge. Her managers promised that she would receive all the training required to make her a success if she promised to commit to meeting the needs of the department's customers— demanding contractors who were prone to frequent and unpleasant displays of impatience. Both the management and the employee kept their ends of the bargain.[8]

- At **Marriott** a week-long examination of company values culminates in new employees role playing in realistic scenarios that require them to apply the company's values when making tough decisions.
- **Southwest Airlines** posts hundreds of documents and photos highlighting the company's accomplishments in the lobby of its headquarters building.
- **Marriott** prominently displays letters from customers praising superior service as well as posting all guest complaints for every employee to see.
- **State Farm Insurance Company** hires former high school teachers as supervising agents.
- **Primerica Financial Services** has hired former high school football coaches as agents because they have skills in teaching and knowledge of how to keep talented but undisciplined young people on track.
- **GE** routinely surveys frontline employees on job satisfaction and hold supervisors accountable for the results.
- **Southwest Airlines** turns its plane around in less than half the time of many of its competitors as a result of employee self-discipline and the group-discipline practiced by its work groups. The authors say,

Employees undertake their tasks with fervor, not out of fear of punishment, but out of a desire to make their airline the best. It is common to see baggage handlers, flight attendants, and pilots scrambling to beat the clock and encouraging others to do the same. Sometimes crew members actually help bagage handlers, and vice versa—something unheard of at other airlines.

▸ **Marriott** housekeepers drive themselves—and one another—to get rooms clean in less than 24 minutes, and bellmen hustle to get guests checked in and to their rooms with no delays or complaints, another outstanding example of the power of self-discipline and group-discipline and the pride these frontline workers feel.[9]

The Idea: Learn What Your Employees Love

One of the ways we find a sense of purpose in our lives is by discovering what it is that "turns us on," what we have a passion for, what we love. As you begin to find out the passions of those people with whom you work, you will find a new kind of bonding occurring. You are connecting with what is most important in another person's life.

Here are some questions to ask your employees:

1. What do you love to do during idle time?
2. When you're in a bookstore or library, which sections draw your attention?
3. In school, what were some of the topics you chose to write papers on?
4. What do you think about when your mind is wandering?
5. Do you have a hobby or a collection?

See if you can find any patterns in the answers employees give to the following questions. Just caution them to be sure that these are things they really love, not things they "should" love!

▸ Three of my favorite books:
▸ Favorite magazines:

▶ Favorite TV shows:

▶ Favorite movies:

> People can smell emotional commitment ... from a mile away.
>
> —Tom Peters, *The Pursuit of WOW!*

As you learn more about each employee's preferences and passions, you will be more creative at helping them find ways to transfer that passion to the workplace, perhaps through special projects, new job assignments, small group sharing, or even setting up a weekly display of employees' talents to celebrate each person's unique contributions.

The Idea: Practice Job Sculpting

The Idea in Action

Really great employees can do well in almost any job, so the only reason they will stay, according to Timothy Butler and James Waldroop, authors of an article titled "Job Sculpting: The Art of Retaining Your Best People," is if their jobs fit their *deeply embedded life interests*—that is, their long-held, emotionally driven passions. They have identified eight different life interests of people drawn to business careers:

▶ **Application of Technology.** These people are intrigued by the inner workings of things and are curious about finding better ways to use technology.

▶ **Quantitative Analysis.** These people see running the numbers as the best, and sometimes the only, way to figure out business solutions, and they see mathematical work as fun.

▶ **Theory Development and Conceptual Thinking.** Nothing brings more enjoyment to this group than thinking and talking about abstract ideas.

▶ **Creative Production.** These people are seen as imaginative, out-of-the-box thinkers, and they seem most engaged when they are brainstorming or inventing unconventional solutions in new situations.

Close to Home by John McPherson/Dist by Universal Press Syndicate

The Transit Authority makes a desperate attempt to promote a friendlier atmosphere by hiring hospitality hostesses.

▶ **Counseling and Mentoring.** These folks love to teach, which translates in business into counseling or mentoring, allowing them to guide employees, peers, and even clients to better performance.

▶ **Managing People and Relationships.** These people enjoy dealing with people on a day-to-day basis and derive a lot of satisfaction from workplace relationships. However, they focus much more on outcomes than the counseling and mentoring category. They are less interested in seeing people grow than in working with and through them to achieve the goals of the business.

▶ **Enterprise Control.** They are happiest when they have the ulti-mate decision-making authority. They find satisfaction in making the decisions that determine the direction taken by a work team, a business unit, a company division, or an entire organization.

▶ **Influence Through Language and Ideas.** Some people love ideas for their own sake, but others love expressing them for the sheer enjoyment that comes from storytelling, negotiating, or per-suading. They feel most fulfilled when they are writing or speak-ing or both!

It is not uncommon for managers to sense that an employee has more than one deeply embedded life interest. Most people in business have between one and three. "Job sculpting" is the art of matching peo-ple to jobs that resonate with the activities that make them truly happy. To do this, managers need to listen more carefully when employees describe what they like and dislike about their jobs.

The authors say,[10]

> Once managers and employees have discussed deeply embedded life interests—ideally during employee performance reviews—they can work together to customize future work assignments. In some cases, that may mean simply adding another assignment to existing respon-sibilities. In other cases, it may mean moving that employee to a new position altogether. ... Skills can be stretched in many directions, but if they are not going in the right direction—one that is congruent with deeply embedded life interests—employees are at risk of becoming dis-satisfied and uncommitted. ... In fact, one manager went through three companies before realizing it wasn't the company he needed to change but his work. ... To turbocharge retention, you must first know the hearts and minds of your employees and then undertake the tough and rewarding task of sculpting careers that bring joy to both.

Quick Ideas to Promote a Reason for Being

▶ Ask employees to list all the things they really like about work-ing on your team. Then post them in a common area.

- Help employees move their careers forward. Post job openings and promote from within as often as possible.
- Include support staff as part of the team.
- Encourage employees to trade jobs with someone else in the organization at least once a quarter.
- Celebrate each employee's anniversary with the company in a personalized way. Find out something that is important to them (their family, a hobby, a favorite food or place, a hero or heroine, a collection, a dream) and tie that in in some way.
- Ask each employee who was his mentor or the person who most influenced his life or who was his favorite teacher. When that employee excels, write a thank-you note to the person who helped him/her.
- Ask each member of your staff to write a personal mission statement. Answer the questions: "Who am I?" and "What am I here for?" Then have them write a paragraph describing their professional ambitions and goals. Ask them if they are in alignment with their mission statement.
- Develop a mission statement for your own work team.
- Ask employees to write up their personal views of career satisfaction. Have them prepare a few paragraphs on what kind of work they love and then have them describe their favorite activities on the job. Afterwards discuss what they have shared.
- Reward the families of hard-working employees. Send their spouses a card or a dinner or movie voucher to let them know that you don't take the extra time their family member is putting in for granted.
- Give support staff a small budget of perhaps $100 a month. They may use it for anything to benefit the department—special supplies, treats for the department, or fun decorations.
- Put a shoe box on the end of your desk and ask employees to

submit ideas, either signed or unsigned. Then hold a monthly "Idea Meeting" and go through the ideas to determine which ones will work and which ones won't.

Notes

1. Leonard, Bill. 2001. "Ready to Soar." *HR Magazine*, January.
2. Society for Human Resource Management. "Advice for Keeping Your Top Talent." *Workplace Visions*, p. 7.
3. Editor. "From the Top: Debbi Fields' Recipe for Management Success." *Women as Managers,* Vol. 98, No. 1, p. 3.
4. Nelson, Bob. "No-Cost Recognition." *Rewarding Employees*, Vol. 3, No. 6, p. 3. www.nelson-motivation.com.
5. Freiberg, Kevin, Freiberg, Jackie, and Peters, Tom. 1998. *Nuts!: Southwest Airlines' Crazy Recipe for Business and Personal Success.* New York: Bantam Doubleday.
6. Lukara, Alissa, 248 Meadow Drive, Ashland OR 97520, 541-488-3120, e-mail: alukara@mind.net.
7. Katzenbach, Jon R., and Santamaria, Jason A. 1999. "Firing Up the Front Line." *Harvard Business Review*, May/June, pp. 107-117.
8. Ibid.
9. Ibid.
10. Butler, Timothy and Waldroop, James. 1999. "Job Sculpting: The Art of Retaining Your Best People." *Harvard Business Review,* September/October, pp. 151, 148, and 152 and www.hbsp.harvard.edu/products/hbr/sepoct99/99502.htm.

Chapter 13

E = Empathy

Each of us really understands in others only those feelings he is capable of producing in himself.
—André Gide

Juliet Schor, the author of *The Overworked American*, says that everyone is working harder and longer today, in fact, an extra month per year, to be exact. 58.5 million workers are traveling more than 45 minutes just to get to their jobs![1] Families and Work Institute (FWI) found that 88% of us say we work very hard, and that hard work causes negative spillover into the rest of our lives. For example, 26% of American workers feel emotionally drained by their jobs, 28% don't have the energy to do things with family or others, and 36% just feel used up at the end of the day.[2] Thus, anything organizations can do to relieve some of this stress is desperately welcomed by employees.

When employees are struggling to balance the demands of their jobs with their personal responsibilities, the results are often lost productivity, absenteeism, and turnover. Wayne Page, benefits practice leader for the Southeast with The Hay Group, a management consulting firm in Atlanta, says in an article in *Entrepreneur* magazine, "Anything you can do to reduce stress will help employees focus on the task at hand." He suggests creating a survey or series of focus groups to find out where your workers need help, and then develop a program to provide the specific assistance people want. Some organizations you will read about even contract with an outside concierge service to help employees.[3] As a supervisor or manager, it is important to begin to understand what specific needs your employees have and then think about creative ways you might help them relieve some of the stress in their lives. When you develop this kind of empathy, everyone will win!

Another way to promote empathy in your organization is to create opportunities for employees to do something for others in the community. According to a survey done last year by the Points of Light Foundation, a community service group, 81% of companies include volunteering in their overall business strategies, compared with only 31% in 1992.[4] National Volunteers Week is usually scheduled during the seond or third week of April. Does your organization encourage volunteering and support community service projects? If not, this is the time to begin!

The Idea: Encourage Service to Others

The Idea in Action

Nancy Bruner-Koontz, events manager at **Janus Funds**, Denver, Colorado, oganizes volunteer groups for youth-at-risk organizations such as the Boys & Girls Clubs of America and Big Brothers/Big Sisters of America. Other organizations do community service projects with groups like Adopt-A-Highway and Habitat for Humanity. The University of California at San Francisco (UCSF)-Empact! helps raise money in the AIDS Walk by getting a group together through their newsletter.[5]

 At **Tom's of Maine** the policy is that employees should try to give 5 % of their work time to some kind of community service or volunteer project. This encourages employees to explore their gifts as they help others.[6]

 Ashland Chemical in Dublin, Ohio, gives scientists company time to make presentations to science classes and also dedicates space for a group of students to meet to do science research. They also donate used fitness equipment from their fitness centers to a United Way agency that sponsors fitness centers for inner-city families.[7]

 Digital Semiconductor employees donate hundreds of backpacks full of notebooks, pens, socks, and other school supplies to needy children.[8]

 The Rockport Company organized a group of employees to paint the storage facility for a local food pantry.[9]

 BI in Minneapolis, Minnesota, has many volunteer groups. Some of these groups help those in the community and others are internal volunteers. Here are a few of them:

- ▶ **Bridging Team.** The team raises money as well as communicating, coordinating, and staffing monthly household goods collections of items donated by BI associates. Their goal is to provide quality furniture and household goods for the economically disadvantaged.
- ▶ **Corporate Orientation Team.** This team has been volunteering for a number of years to help new associates learn about what's important at BI. They cover benefits, telephones, our history and culture, and quality and customer satisfaction.
- ▶ **Loaves and Fishes Team.** Since 1992, the Loaves and Fishes team has served a meal once a month to anyone that wishes to

join them at Creekside in Bloomington. On an average night they serve 75 meals. They also collect donations from BI associates.

▸ **Recycling Committee.** Their mission is to reduce waste at BI through recycling and use reduction, education, and reward as their main tools. Through the year they reward associates with goodies such as caramel apples, cookies, state fair coupon booklets, calendars, etc., and they visit individual departments, as needed, and do educational stints in addition to their cardboard crunching, can crushing, and dumpster diving all around BI!

▸ **Tour Guides.** They take time from their regular work schedule to act as hosts to their clients to showcase their BI campus and explain how BI's departments work together. They know the ins and outs about everything from accounting to the warehouse!

▸ **Singing Recognition Team.** This group sings throughout BI. You give them the words to use and they'll match them to a tune. They have sung to over 150 associates in team meetings or at their desks.

The Idea: Help Your Community

The Idea in Action

The **University of Utah Hospitals and Clinics** in Salt Lake City, Utah, have a community outreach project called "Project Dehydration":

> Summer heat and rising temperatures have had an adverse effect on our community. The Crossroads Urban Center has informed us that people living on our streets, in tents, cars, and motel rooms have been found to be suffering from severe dehydration. Are you in a position to help?

> A single contribution from the following list of suggested items could make a tremendous difference for those less fortunate: we need healthy beverages that are non-carbonated so they don't require refrigeration, and that are prepared in single-pack and non-breakable containers.

Here are some suggestions: bottled water, fruit or vegetable juice, sports drinks, such as Gatorade.

In addition, the Center also recommended donations of new or gently used plastic sports bottles and baby bottles.

Please bring your donations to the drop boxes located in the Front Lobby or Cafeteria from July 17-August 31.

 Another project sponsored by the **University of Utah Hospitals and Clinics** was called "Blue Jeans for Babies—Saving Babies Together" to collect money for the March of Dimes:

Stickers are $5.00 (good for wearing jeans on a single day)
You can show your support by purchasing sweat, golf, or T-shirts and stickers March 28–April 27.
Long sleeve T-shirts $15.00
Sweatshirts $20.00
Golf shirts $20.00
(Purchase of a sweat, golf, or T-shirt is your ticket to wearing jeans on Wednesdays and Fridays throughout the campaign.)

They also sponsored a March of Dimes "Walk America" on April 28, 2001.

 Deluxe Data Systems in Milwaukee discovered a way to help the community while cleaning out their files. They call it the "Pound for Pound Campaign." For every pound of old files one of their employees discarded, the company agreed to donate one pound of food to charity. Bins were set up around the company and more than 26,000 pounds of old papers were thrown away and, consequently, $6000 of food was donated to the needy.[10]

BI in Minneapolis, Minnesota, has a monthly feature in their company newsletter which highlights how associates reach out to the community.

The Idea: Provide Benefits That Impact Employees' Personal Lives

When you provide ways to help employees in their personal lives, you are creating not only loyal employees but loyal families. Young male workers, especially, highly value work/life benefits. A new Harris Poll shows that seven in 10 would trade money for family time. This was true of 70% of 1008 men in their 20s and 71% in their 30s but only 26% of men over 65 agreed. Four-fifths of the men ages 20 to 39 said that having a work schedule that allows them to spend more time with family is more important than challenging work or a high salary. 63% of young women rate family time as more important than any other career factor.[11]

A new survey by Hewitt Associates presents some key findings for benchmarking your organization:

- ▶ 57% of employers surveyed offer flextime and 47% offer part-time employment.
- ▶ 90% of employers offer some type of child care benefits to employees.
- ▶ 47% of employers offer elder care assistance.
- ▶ 52% offer some type of on-site personal service to employees.
- ▶ 37% of employers provide financial security programs to help employees make decisions about their retirement and investments.
- ▶ 75% of employers provide employees with education opportunities.[12]

The Idea in Action

Genentech, a San Francisco-based biotech firm, has a subsidized day care center that stays open until 10 p.m. once every three months for what it calls "Date Night." The program is so popular that it *takes less* *than three minutes* to fill all the spaces after the date is announced. Parents pay $20 for one child and $16 for each sibling, and about 50 children in their pajamas show up for each Date Night.[13]

A small, Illinois-based company called **Fel-Pro, Inc.**, provides an interest-free cash advance of up to $2250 for full-time employees to "finance" a home computer. The staffer must pay the cash advance within a two-year period through payroll deductions. To date, Fel-Pro has financed computers for 367 employees. Employees are very appreciative of this program because the perk benefits their families as

> I believe that man will not merely endure: he will prevail. He is immortal, not because he alone among creatures has an inexhaustible voice, but because he has a soul, a spirit capable of compassion and sacrifice and endurance.
> —William Faulkner

well. And Fel-Pro managers say it's a definite convenience for staffers to have access to up-to-date technology at home. Not only does this perk help improve employee computer skills, but it also makes it easier for employees to work at home when a child is ill or they have a tight deadline.[14]

Fel-Pro, listed many times as "one of the best places to work," also offers an in-house, free career-counseling program for the purpose of *keeping* employees, not just for helping them cope when downsizing hits. Their goal is to forge a partnership with employees so that if they decide to build their career elsewhere, they can have help. Most of the staff, however, use the center to learn the mechanisms to move ahead in Fel-Pro. The company also provides a year-round daycare center for preschool- and kindergarten-aged children (started in the early '80s), after-school care, tutoring and summer camp for staff members' children, and tuition reimbursement for outside education. In addition, it awards a $1000 bonus to any Fel-Pro employee upon completion of an advanced degree. The company also provides extensive internal training and improvement programs and offer scholarships of up to $3,300 per year for four years to any employee's child accepted at an accredited college or trade school.[15]

Nucor Corporation, a Charlotte, NC, steel manufacturer, has offered $2200 a year toward college tuition for all children of full-time workers for up to four years. It recently expanded the benefit to reach all workers and even decided to include the spouses of employees, who can receive $1100 a year for up to two years. Nucor president, John Correnti, said in a recent article in *Investor's Business Daily* that the benefit keeps employee turnover "practically at zero."[16]

(Your company can offer a smaller dollar amount and still get similar results. Showing that tuition and employee-development benefits are important to a firm goes a long way in attracting and retaining qualified workers.)

Here are some examples of conveniences you may choose to offer to your employees to give them more time with their families:

- Bill payment center
- Video drop box
- On-site photofinishing
- Prescription service
- Sell stamps
- Sell bus tokens

Other ideas to help employees are:

- Aerobics classes
- Nutrition seminars
- On-site flu shots
- Self defense classes
- Smoking cessation programs
- Weight Watchers classes
- Toastmasters classes

- ► Walking program
- ► On-site chair massages
- ► Cancer prevention programs

The Idea: Show Understanding of Personal Issues

The Idea in Action

Another way to boost morale and retention is to be understanding of personal situations.

- ► When my son, Garrett Glanz, and his wife Ashley recently had a new little daughter, **Microsoft** in Redmond, Washington, gave him four weeks' paid paternity leave. A very special feature of this family perk is that it does not all have to be taken at one time.
- ► **Country Companies**, an insurance company in Minneapolis, offers its employees an option they call "Choice Time." Workers who need occasional extra hours off can take them without spending sick or vacation leave, as long as they make up the time before the weekends and avoid overtime. This perk has helped retain several of the firm's working moms, who also take advantage of flextime so they can be home from work by the time their kids leave school.[17]
- ► **Accenture** has a "7 to 7" travel policy. No one is required to leave home before 7 a.m. Monday, and all employees are encouraged to fly back home by 7 p.m. Friday. This shows workers that they care about their personal lives and families.[18]
- ► According to an **AMA/Ernst & Young** survey of senior human resources executives, companies are finding that investing in employees and "giving them a life" via flextime and sabbaticals are more effective retention tools than cash payoffs. "Our database shows that companies with flexible work arrangements

which reflect employee needs and concerns have a real advantage," added Deborah Holmes, Director of the Office of Retention at Ernst & Young, which sponsored the AMA study. "They know that it takes more than money to keep employees. If companies help employees balance their lives between job and family without penalizing their career development, people are less likely to leave for a few more dollars."[19]

Flavor Dynamics, Inc., a Somerset, New Jersey maker of flavorings for coffee beans, recognized that some workers struggle with the cash-flow problem of needing to pay a large amount of money twice a year for auto-insurance bills. They have decided to offer employees a chance to buy auto insurance through a payroll-deduction program every two weeks so they don't have the shock of owing big money twice a year.[20]

The Idea: Help with Employees' Everyday Needs

The Idea in Action

Making life easier can be more valuable to people than extra cash. Employee assistance programs now exist that offer concierge services such as grocery shopping, dry cleaning, laundry, "meals to go," and household repairs and maintenance. By helping employees accomplish mundane "household" chores at work, time away from the office can be spent in a more relaxing, enjoyable manner—which translates into a happier, more loyal workforce.

Campbell Soup Company offers its employees a variety of life assistance services: childcare, elder care, education/hobby classes, and on-site medical care.

A story in the *Success in Recruiting and Retaining* newsletter tells about **Wilton Connor Packaging** of Charlotte, North Carolina. They found that most of the employees did not own washers and dryers and had to take public transportation to laundromats, so this is what they did:

> The company started a full-service laundry benefit for its 500 workers which lets them drop off their wash in the morning and pick it up at the end of the work day. The cost to the company and its workers is paltry: Workers pay $1 a basket and a quarter for each pressed item of clothing, and the company chips in an equal amount. Costs are kept low by guaranteeing the laundry service regular business.
>
> Wendy Walker, the firm's HR manager, says the perk is "the most popular thing among our employees." Along with two other creative perks tied to its specific work force—a staff handyman to help employees with minor home repairs and tutors for employees with school-age children—the laundry perk has helped to keep the firm's turnover at next to nothing—1% a year.
>
> Walker told *Human Resource Executive*, "People know that this is a fair company and a good company to work for because we have sensitivity to our employees' everyday needs."[21]

At **Continental Airlines** the CEO recognizes that in order to be successful they must make their employees happy. That is why they have done such things as modernizing breakrooms and cafeterias and give them an extra floating holiday and an expanded 401(k) program, and awards of Eddie Bauer Edition Ford Explorers for perfect attendance. He says in their airline magazine, "These things don't come

> The valuable contributions that casual friends make in the workplace include aiding productivity, fostering a greater sense of teamwork, providing a sounding board, and helping workers feel they are part of a corporate "family."
> —Jan Yager, Ph.D., *Friendshifts*™

cheap, but they are well worth our investment. ... What really counts, of course, is the end result of all these efforts, and that's the award-winning service you receive because our employees are happy."[22]

Datex-Ohmeda, a Tewsbury, Massachusetts-based anesthesia and critical care company, realized that the incentive their employees appreciated most was the gift of time. As a result they signed up with Boston-based corporate concierge Circles. Now all 1700 North American workers and their spouses can call or send an e-mail request for help. Employees can make unlimited requests for such things as dental appointments, household help, hard-to-get tickets, or planning weekend getaways, and these requests are filled in a couple of days. The company personalizes its rewards while keeping its cash outlay manageable. The benefits manager estimates that because employees' nagging concerns are soothed, the firm saved 280 work hours in the first quarter alone. They also provide a dry cleaner and a mobile on-site car wash and detailing operation.[23]

CIGNA, a health care, insurance, and financial services corporation, has a Working Well Moms program that provides comfortable, discreet places for nursing employees to pump milk. They also include at no charge: advice from a lactation consultant, access to a hospital-grade electric breast pump, a carrying case with milk storage system, bottles, breast shields, and hygienic tubing, and literature on nursing topics. A spokesperson says that the program has reduced infants' illnesses and, thereby, mother's absenteeism by an estimated 27%.[24]

The Rockport Company in Marlborough, Massachusetts, keeps a fleet of mountain bikes for employees to burn off steam and calories during lunchtime. Exercising during lunch re-energizes employees for a productive afternoon. They are also planning to have a reflexologist onsite during specific times to administer foot massages to employees.[25]

According to a story in *The Wall Street Journal*, **Cape Cod Potato Chip Company** in Hyannis, Massachusetts, even offers a "day care" service to provide temporary shelter for Tamagotchis, Nano Babies, Giga Pets, and other varieties. The popular toys, which beep when they need food, water, or exercise, have been banned from many schools, so many young owners risked leaving them to "die" for lack of care. The marketing director said, "We make potato chips so kids are important to us. This is a great way we could do something for them."[26]

According to an article in *Success in Recruiting and Retaining* newsletter, December 2000, Julie Ferrier at **OneSoft** in McLean, Virginia, acts as the company "mom" to help make employees' lives better. She arranges for dry-cleaning pickup, has an iron and ironing board and sewing kits, sells stamps, and even addresses wedding invitations. She says, "Employees can go anywhere and get any amount of money, but I think it's the little perks that keep people."[27]

> Today's leaders are reinventing everything but themselves. Yet, this is why so many attempts to revolutionize business fail. Unless executives realize that they must change not just what they do, but who they are, not just their sense of task, but their sense of themselves, they will fail.
> —Tracy Gross,
> *The Last Word on Power*

A number of large companies have hired a full-time concierge or corporate errand runner to help busy employees with personal business. They do such things as making restaurant reservations, puchasing tickets, tracking down gifts for special occasions, hiring baby sitters, tracking down recipes, and planning anniversary getaways. Lack of time for personal business has become a major gripe in many companies today, and many organizations feel that having a concierge available has improved morale and lowered stress in significant ways.

Quad/Graphics, Inc., in Pewaukee, Wisconsin, offers many forms of "hidden paychecks." An on-site medical facility offers no-cost care for employees and their families. They also offer interest-free loans to purchase or repair a car, discounted bus service to company plants, 24-hour on-site daycare, a fitness center, free legal advice, and on-site EAP and tuition for education.[28]

Wilton Connor Packaging in Charlotte, NC, has provided its employees with a full-time handyman who does home repairs when Wilton's workers don't have time. The company pays the handyman's salary while the employees pay for all parts and materials. The original idea was to help the company's lowest-paid workers manage high labor bills for home repairs, but middle-level workers who are strapped for time also appreciate the service. However, it is off-limits to top managers who can afford to pay market rates for household repairs.

Some other things that other organizations do for their employees:

- Pack gourmet meals to take home.
- Provide an on-site car mechanic.
- Employ a psychologist who makes desk calls.
- Provide help with adoptions.
- Have a miniature golf course and a basketball hoop.
- Provide workout equipment.[29]

The Idea: Encourage Flexible Hours

According to an article in *Success in Recruiting and Retaining* newsletter in July 2000, Randstad consultants found in a study of more than 6000 North American employees that 51% of employees would stay in their current jobs rather than switch if their employer offered flexible working hours. 62% prefer a boss who understands when they need to leave work for personal reasons over one who could help them grow professionally. Most surprisingly, 51% of employees surveyed prefer a job that offers flexible hours to one that offers an opportunity for advancement. The bottom line: "Employers can gain a critical advantage in recruiting and retaining employees by examining ways to integrate flexibility into all corners of the organization." Two of the simplest:

- Allow for a portable office with Internet and wireless technology.
- Offer nontraditional schedules beyond the 9-to-5 workday.[30]

The Idea in Action

 Forsyth Medical Center in Winston-Salem, North Carolina, decided to try a new way to retain nurses and recruit new ones: give them the same schedule as their school-age children. They now have the option of working for either 12 months a year or just nine. They keep their benefits but do not earn pay during the summer.[31]

At **Columbia Bank** in Columbia, Maryland, bank tellers can now choose to take off the summer while keeping their jobs, vacation time, and benefits. Such leaves are approved as long as a replacement teller is available. Employees report higher job satisfaction and the bank boasts high retention rates as a result.[32]

Ernst & Young is so zealous about keeping employees that it has created an *Office for Retention*. A poll of all employees on flexible schedules found that 65% would have left the firm without them.[33]

 BI in Minneapolis, Minnesota, gives associates the opportunity to work summer hours. In Minnesota, the winter is long and cold. Summer hours allows the associate to work one hour longer Monday through Thursday and then have Friday afternoon off to enjoy!

A fun, flexible workforce with lots of lifestyle perks is a strong pull, especially for many young recruits. **Northrop Grumman Corporation's** generous vacation package, flexible work schedule, and company sports leagues have enticed many college students who sacrifice big money in favor of lifestyle perks. One college graduate who went to work for Northrop Grumman says that another employer could double his salary, but he'd probably decline if it meant giving up the perks![34]

The Idea: Encourage Employees' Spiritual Growth

The cover story of the July 9, 2001, issue of *Fortune* magazine is titled "God and Business—The Surprising Quest for Spiritual Renewal in the American Workplace," by Marc Gunther in which he states:

> Depending on how the question is asked, 95% of Americans say they believe in God. When the Gallup Poll asked Americans in 1999 if they felt a need to experience spiritual growth, 78% said yes, up from 20% in 1994; nearly half said they'd had an occasion to talk about their faith in the workplace in the last 24 hours.[35]

Faith-based companies employ the whole person, not just workers for eight hours. They promote respect, learning, and listening throughout the company, and their mission transcends the bottom line.

According to the Fellowship for Companies for Christ, there are 10,000 Bible and prayer groups across America that meet regularly, and Buddhist reading groups are also growing in population.

Companies such as Taco Bell, Pizza Hut, and Wal-Mart are now hiring Army-style chaplains who minister to any employee's religious needs, no matter what the faith basis. Members of these 24-hour "God squads" visit the sick, deal with nervous breakdowns, respond to suicide attempts, and officiate at weddings and funeral services for their companies.[36]

According to Mark Dress, founder and president of Inner Active Ministries, a nonprofit organization in Wake Forest, North Carolina, that provides chaplains to businesses, there are at least 4000 workplace chaplains, also called corporate or business chaplains, in the U.S. today. These chaplains work interculturally and across faith groups and can do things that no one else in the organization has time to do, such as go to traffic court with an employee, encourage an employee who's having a bad day, attend funerals of associates and their children and help with funeral arrangements, counsel employees during a crisis, or even help with a major conflict between two departments or between two individuals within a department. They are available to meet with employees at work, off-site, or even in jail. They also often direct employees to other forms of help. For many employees who don't know where to turn, the chaplain is the first go-to person whom they can trust.

David Koonce, the director of HR and civil service for the City of Lufkin, Texas, says about having a workplace chaplain, "If we can reach the employee from a mental health perspective and use the chaplaincy program to do that, then we believe that will have a positive impact on lost time issues, sick time, personal days off, absenteeism of any sort, and health insurance cost reduction." Most organizations that have chaplains feel that not only does having corporate chaplains affect mental health but it also boosts productivity, morale, and retention because it shows that the organization cares.[37]

The Idea in Action

Xerox Corporation sponsors "vision quests" and "spiritual seminars" for its employees at all levels, from senior managers to clerks.

Deloitte & Touche offers prayer groups at its many locations.

A number of New York law firms conduct Hebrew classes and Talmud studies at lunchtime.

Aetna International encourages the virtues of meditation classes.

BI in Minneapolis, Minnesota, sponsors a Support/Prayer group. Each Monday morning there is an opportunity for associates to gather together for support and prayer for themselves and other BI associates or family. This group provides BI with a sense of community. About 25 associates attend these gatherings.

The Idea: Invest in Employees Who Are at Risk

The Idea in Action

Marriott has a six-week program called Pathways to Independence that is specifically designed for frontline workers who are former welfare recipients or who were hired from the ranks of the homeless. This program offers instruction in life skills such as opening a bank account and using public transportation, work skills such as cleaning a hotel room efficiently, and even etiquette such as grooming and time management. This training pays off in retention rates, according to an article in the May-June 1999 *Harvard Business Review* titled "Firing up the Front Line":

> In the Washington, D.C. area, the percentage of new employees remaining on the job longer than one year was higher among Pathways graduates than among comparable workers who hadn't had training—75% versus less than 65%.[38]

The Idea: Put Employees First

The Idea in Action

Scott Kerslake, CEO of **Athleta Corporation**, a women's sports apparel company in Petaluma, California, urges his employees to put themselves and their personal needs before their jobs. He has 60 employees and sales are $18 million for the current fiscal year. Instead of treating employees as objects, he has created a culture that allows them to be honest.

The CEO shows his staff respect by allowing them to tell the truth about what is important in their lives. His sensitivity comes from his experience as a trader on Wall Street in New York, where he had to slip away to take a short run, even though he worked till late at night.

Because of this philosophy, Kerslake believes, his company has grown 500% over last year and turnover is less than 1% in an industry where the average is 38%. Employees are loyal because he treats them as responsible adults. The staff is cross-trained and fills in for each other when personal needs arise. Those who need time off work willingly in the evenings or weekends as necessary.

Employees tell how they are able to take time from work for such needs as infertility procedures, taking the dog to the vet, and rearranging work schedules so that marriage partners can have one day a month off together. Being able to take the time you need for things in your personal life builds honesty, respect, gratitude, and loyalty.[39]

Charles Garfield, in his book *Second to None: How Our Smartest Companies Put People First,* writes about what Mike Conway, the president of America West, says about helping employees:

> It is not unusual for somebody to be in my office, for example, with a shoebox full of bills. We will just pay off all the bills. We put the employee on a program that they can handle, paying the company back over an extended period of time at a very nominal interest rate, far better than they could get at a bank.

They are really putting their money where their mouth is when they say they care about employees![40]

> When company executives get involved in charity work, it send the message that the leaders are invested in their community, that there's more to life than making a profit and that they care about their employees having balanced lives.
> —Dr. Ann McGee-Cooper, author and business consultant

In a story written by Michael Ryan for *Parade Magazine* about a catastrophic fire that nearly destroyed all of **Malden Mills** manufacturing plant in Lawrence, Massachusetts, on December 11, 1995, it seemed certain to put its 3000 employees out of work. Then, the owner, Aaron Feuerstein, did something that astonished his workers. He announced that he would keep all of his 3,000 employees on the payroll for a month while he started rebuilding the

90-year-old family business. In January, he announced he would pay them for a second month, and in February he said he would pay them for a third. By March, most of the employees had returned to full-time work. The first time was a surprise, the second time was a shock, and the third time he did it brought tears to everyone's eyes. It cost Feuerstein several million dollars.

When asked how he was different from other CEOs, Feuerstein said, "The fundamental difference is that I consider our workers an asset, not an expense. I have a responsibility to the worker, both blue-collar and white-collar. I have an equal responsibility to the community. It would have been unconscionable to put 3000 people on the streets and deliver a death blow to the cities of Lawrence and Methuen. Maybe on paper our company is worth less to Wall Street, but I can tell you it's worth more. We're doing fine."

In talking to people in the plant, it was discovered that Feuerstein had arranged for heart bypass operations for several workers, and he offers free soft drinks and breaks when the summer heat drives up temperatures to over 90 degrees on the manufacturing lines. He said, "I could get rid of all the workers who earn $15 an hour and bring in a contract house that will pay their laborers $7. But that breaks the spirit and trust of the employees. If you close a factory because you can get work done for $2 an hour elsewhere, you break the American Dream."

The devotion with which his employees do their work is a testimonial to the respect Feuerstein has for them. Before the fire, the plant produced 130,000 yards of fabric a week. A few weeks after the fire, it was up to 230,000 yards. People became very creative and were willing to work 23 hours a day. It is these workers, said Feuerstein, who are responsible for his company's recovery.[41]

The Idea: The Graduation Pledge Alliance

Research indicates that workers of the future will strive to find meaning in their lives by evaluating the quality of their jobs, what their organization stands for, and how it lives out its corporate values. Does a particular job reflect the employee's personal goals, values, and beliefs, and is the organization honest, socially aware, and environmentally responsible?

The Idea in Action

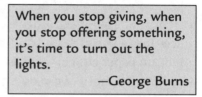

In an article in the December 2000 issue of *HR Magazine* titled "The Graduation Pledge Alliance," Sharon Leonard writes about a movement that started in 1987 at **Humboldt State University** in Arcata, California, and is now housed at Manchester College in North Manchester, Indiana. The Graduation Pledge encourages new graduates to put their ideals first by carefully deciding where they will work.

> When you stop giving, when you stop offering something, it's time to turn out the lights.
> —George Burns

The alliance's voluntary pledge is simple and straightforward: "I pledge to explore and take into account the social and environmental consequences of any job I consider and will try to improve those aspects of any organization for which I work."

Leonard says, " Students who take the pledge must determine what social responsibility means to them as they consider whether a company believes in such things as workplace accessibility, contributes to local charities and social change efforts, values diversity, engages in environmental responsibility, and respects workers' privacy." Sample questions they can ask during a job interview are:

- ▶ Is there an employee assistance program or other source of support?
- ▶ Is there support for child care and other kinds of dependent care?
- ▶ Are there opportunities for community service with co-workers?

- ▶ What is the organization's record on occupational health and safety? Waste handling?
- ▶ How are products packaged? What efforts have been made to minimize solid waste?
- ▶ What programs does the organization have to contribute to the surrounding community?

Students are urged to be change agents within their organizations and throughout their careers. The Graduation Pledge Alliance Web site (**www.manchester.edu/academic/programs/departments/Peace_Studies/files/gpa.htm**) reminds students that "job satisfaction is more than just a paycheck. Some ideas for workplace improvements include: recycling programs, mentoring programs, workplace flexibility, wellness programs, diversity programs ... and promoting joy and celebration. If your workplace doesn't have these things, create them!"

Leonard reports that Manchester College estimates that more than 30 colleges have formed Graduation Pledge Alliances on campus recently. What a marvellous movement to foster social responsibility and empathy for others while one is true to one's own beliefs and ideals in selecting one's work! While each person who takes the pledge has a choice in the job he or she decides to take, it also emphasizes that one can create change wherever he or she may be.[42]

The Idea: Involve Families in Your Work

The Idea in Action

The **Society for Human Resource Management** in Alexandria, Virginia, holds an annual Take Our Children to Work Day. Besides learning what employees of the world's largest HR management did for a living, on April 27, 2000, the participants got a chance to hear and see what life might be life if they were to become a judge, police officer, veterinarian, or dentist.

The **Ms. Foundation for Women** started this day of career inspiration and aspiration for girls in 1993 with "Take Our Daughters to Work Day" to give girls a sense of their own potential. Their official theme for 2000, for example, was "Free to Be You and Me." At Ernst & Young the girls created a "Me" Map about themselves to learn the importance of diversity and accepting each other's differences. They also participated in a spoof of the TV show "Jeopardy" in which they guessed about famous women in various fields.[43]

This kind of activity does a great deal to foster empathy and understanding of various careers, whether it is called "Take Our Daughters or Kids or Children to Work Day." It is especially meaningful for the children of the employees who work in that organization to learn more about what they do and to experience their parents' workplace in person. The more a child feels a part of a parent's or relative's whole life, the more understanding they will be when they may have to share that loved one's time with the organization.

Nursing Spectrum, a professional magazine reaching one million nurses, sponsored a contest for children and grandchildren of their subscribers. This was the ad they placed in their magazine:

Calling All Kids—Grandkids, Too!

What so you see when you think of a nurse? Nursing Spectrum is looking for children, ages 4 to 11, to draw a picture illustrating what a nurse is to them. Winners will be awarded a $50 gift certificate from Toys "R" Us—just in time for the holiday season! We'll select four budding artists, one in each of the following age ranges: 4 to 5, 6 to 7, 8 to 9, 10 to 11. The winners will also be featured in the December issue of *Nursing Spectrum*.

What a delightful way to include their readers' families!

Inland Steel of Chicago invites employees to bring their spouses when they hold regular meetings where employees can ask questions of top management. This sends a special message: "We realize how important your family is to you, and they are important to the company as well."[44]

The Idea: Provide Financial Help for Employees

The Idea in Action

An article in the March 2001 issue of *Success in Recruiting and Retaining* newsletter states that 74% of employees at growing businesses say they are "very" concerned about the financial future for themselves and their families. And only 21% of these employees believe that their employers are concerned about that, according to a study by the **Principal Financial Group**.

The article suggests some low-cost tips:

▶ Don't make new hires wait to join the company 401 (k) plan. According to the Profit Sharing/401(k) Council of America, 37% of plans now let employees begin contributing during their first month on the job; 52% let them sign up after three months.

▶ Offer financial perks for free.

▶ The "Get the Facts on Saving and Investing Campaign" has a spea-kers bureau that will make work site presentations on financial topics at no cost—**www.americanpayroll.org/new56.html**.

The **American Savings Educational Council** offers free resources on financial planning to employers and individuals—**www.asec.org/tool-shm.htm**.

Make sure people know how good they've got it. Tell them how valuable your 401 (k) match is and explain your tuition reimbursement program using what one company calls the "drip irrigation" approach: a daily e-mail newsletter, messages on paychecks, and prescheduled mailings of premiums and benefits reminders. The idea is to maintain a constant trickle of communication to improve retention.[45]

The Idea: Consider Elder Care Provisions

According to the Families and Work Institute, by 2002, 42% of all workers will be elder care givers. In the U.S., about 22.4 million households include caregivers of people over age 50. 72% are women, and most of them also work outside the home. When Genesis Health Ventures and the National Association for Female Executives polled more than 800 NAFE members who perform elder care, 89% of respondents reported increased stress. One fourth said the strain had adversely affected their career. Only 19% believed their employers supported them "a great deal." In order to boost morale, retention, and productivity, organizations need to seriously consider helping these employees. Some of the benefits suggested are meal

Knowing that her manager would never allow her to leave early to watch her son's soccer game, Wendy hires a body double.

delivery, legal help, research on nursing homes, transportation, and adult day care.

SAS Institute in Cary, North Carolina, has an elder care coordinator.

American Express, **PricewaterhouseCoopers**, and **Texas Instruments** have invested more than $100 million toward employees' child or elder care needs through the American Business Collaboration for Quality Dependent Care. Participants can sign up their parents for transportation or back-up care.

At **Eli Lilly**, an Indianapolis-based pharmaceutical firm, employees can take a leave of absence for up to three years to care for an elderly parent. It is not all paid, but a job is guaranteed upon return. Other options they provide are flextime, part-time work, and job sharing. They also offer an on-site support group for caregivers.[46]

Novartis Pharmaceuticals helps staff with research on social care options and also contributes to certain types of care, such as an attendant in the home or senior day-care centers.

Organizations that support elder caregivers will reap the rewards. Lost productivity from higher turnover, increased absenteeism, and reduced workload requests yield an estimated annual loss to U.S. employers of $11.4 billion to $29 billion, according to a 1997 survey by MetLife.[47]

Resources: Family Caregiver Alliance (caregiver.org) and Elder Care Locator (**www.eldercare.gov**) 800-677-1116.

The Idea: Consider Employee Assisted Housing

The Idea in Action

Employer-assisted housing programs can attract new employees, keep current ones on board, and bolster morale. EAH, according to the *2000 Benefits Survey* by the Society for Human Resource Management, is a relatively rare benefit with only 6% of employers offering mortgage assistance and 3% providing down payment assistance. However, since the strong economy has driven housing prices higher (from 1997 to 1999 prices jumped 16%), this benefit is one that can greatly improve recruitment and retention as well as helping local communities, and at the same time it shows that employers care about their workers' lives outside of work.[48]

G1440 Baltimore, a Web applications firm, provides its employees with $1,000 grants and lends them "whatever else they need for the down payment and closing costs," says Matt Goddard, president.

Bank of America in Charlotte, N.C., set up a home ownership counseling center, which is especially valuable for first-time buyers. Counselors examine employees' credit reports and financial situations and provide guidelines on housing the employee can afford.[49]

Other options are forgivable loans, repayable loans, and interest rate buy downs.

The Idea: Tailor Recruiting and Retention to Life Stages

According to an article titled "The 'Family Guy' Lives: Young Men Will Trade Money for Time" in the *Success in Recruiting and Retaining* newsletter, researchers at the Radcliffe Public Policy Center in Cambridge, Massachusetts, found the following:

- ▶ 80% of men between the ages of 21 and 39 rank family time at the top of the list of employee benefits they desire, compared with 85% of women in the same age group. (Total: 84% of men and women in their 20s and 30s favor a family-friendly workplace above all.)
- ▶ 71% of the men polled said they would gladly trade pay for more time with their families. Researchers said that men in their 20s are 7% more likely than women of similar age to give up pay for more family time.
- ▶ 79% of men and women in their 40s most value work that is challenging and rewarding.
- ▶ 86% of men and women in their 50s and older focus on enjoyable work relationships.

Keeping these values in mind, an organization can offer different benefits for different age groups as well as a combination of programs and enhancements that will appeal to each of these desires.

The most interesting and unexpected result of this study is that men just entering the workforce are much more likely to put family ahead of pay.

Three companies that particularly appreciate family men:

- ▸ **Deloitte & Touche** encourages fathers to take paternity leave and use flexible hours.
- ▸ **Merrill Lynch** held a seminar on fathers and adolescents, broadcast to field offices.
- ▸ **Charles Schwab & Company** held a session on balancing work and family that attracted more men than women.[50]

Another interesting finding from a study on relocation is that the major barrier to relocating today is family ties. 87% of those polled cited this reason as the major obstacle to their leaving their present jobs. 65% cited the spouse's employment as a barrier. In 1993 the cost of living was the number-one barrier to relocating, while today it ranks as number three, so we can see younger worker's values have changed to a much more intense focus on the family.[51]

At the June 27, 2000, annual conference of the Society for Human Resource Management in Las Vegas, Richard Pimentel, senior partner of Milt Wright & Associates, Inc., shared ways to retain Baby Boomers:

- ▸ Cross-train them for lateral job moves so they feel more secure.
- ▸ Ask them to mentor younger employees to help create meaning in their work.
- ▸ Have an EAP that will help with family problems.
- ▸ Develop a return-to-work plan for non-occupational diseases and injuries.
- ▸ Help them stay productive despite medical problems.
- ▸ Give them benefit options so they can choose what they need.[52]

Quick Ideas for Empathy

▶ Make every effort to attend visitations when employees have lost a loved one. If you can't attend, send someone else from management.

▶ Send flowers to employees' homes for births, deaths, marriages, and long illnesses.

▶ Remember their birthdays and celebrate with an invitation to lunch, part of the day off, a card from you, or a personalized gift.

▶ Give a get-well call to an employee who has an extended illness. Let them know they are missed and cared about.

▶ Be aware of what is going on with employees' families and ask about them periodically. Give them a pre-paid phone card to call family members.

▶ Take the most difficult co-worker you know out to lunch. Try to see the world from their perspective.

▶ Some organizations provide such things as on-site haircuts, shoe repair, free breakfasts, dry cleaning pickup, and dinner to go to save employees time so they can be with their families.

▶ Have an annual "Take Your Parents to Work Day."

▶ Invite your employee's whole family to dinner to thank them for a job well done, especially if the employee has worked overtime on a special project.

▶ Have a 15-minute "listening time" with each employee once a month. Keep notes on what they share, but your job is simply to listen.

▶ Give pagers to women who are in the late stages of pregnancy and to their spouses so they can be in constant contact with each other.

▶ Provide English as a Second Language classes during work hours.

▶ Have someone design a Web site for an employee's family.

▶ Give employees one "leptosis" day a year. This is a day they can take off to do anything they would like. The only stipulation is that they must tell you they have "leptosis" when they call in so that if there is an emergency or a huge time crunch, you can ask them to please have leptosis another day.

▶ Give employees "stress buster" coupons, good for a few hours off to do something fun.

▶ Give employees one paid day off to do volunteer work of their choice. Then have a "volunteer fair" where everyone can display what they chose to do.

▶ Consider such benefits as pet care for employees who are going on vacation and offering an oil and lube change in the company parking lot.

Notes

1. Editor. 1999. "Time-Stressed Consumers?" *Entrepreneur,* December, p. 98.

2. Ibid.

3. Editor. 1997. "Getting Personal." *Entrepreneur,* December, p. 120.

4. Magistro, Nicole. 2000. "225,000,000,000." *Working Woman,* April, p. 88.

5. Cerny, Catrina. 1998. "The Young and the Restless: Serving the New Generation of Employees." *Employee Services Management (ESM) Magazine,* September, p.13.

6. Chappell, Tom. 1994. "The Soul of Business." *Executive Female,* January/February, p. 75.

7. Helson, Cynthia M. 1997. "Warming Your Employer's Image." *Employee Services Management (ESM) Magazine,* October, p. 10.

8. Ibid.

9. Ibid.

10. Editor. "Cleaning Files for Charity." *Communications Briefing,* Vol. XII, No. VI, p. 8.

11. Editor. 2000. "Don't Neglect to Market Work/Life to All." *Success in Recruiting and Retaining,* July, p. 4.

12. Editor. 2000. "Flexible Benefits Lead Companies' Competitive Arsenal." *Success in Recruiting and Retaining,* July, p. 7.

13. Editor. 2001. "Babysitting of Company's Dime Gives Parents a Break." *Success in Recruiting and Retaining,* January, p. 5.

14. Editor. "Low-Cost Perk Employees Love: Financing Home Computers." *Success in Recruiting and Retaining,* Sample Issue, p. 5.

15. Leigh, Pamela. 1997. "The New Spirit at Work." *Training & Development,* March, p. 29-30.

16. Editor. "Helping Pay Tuition Keeps Turnover to Zero." *Success in Recruiting and Retaining.* Sample Issue, p. 5.

17. Editor. "'Choice Time' Is Top Choice for Working Parents." *Success in Recruiting and Retaining,* Sample Issue, p. 5.

18. Editor. *Employee Recruitment & Retention.* Sample Issue, p. 5.

19. AMA Research Report. "Retaining Employees a Top Concern." Source: www.amanet.org/research/specials.

20. Editor. 1999. "Small Companies Find New Way to Retain Employees." *The Wall Street Journal.*

21. Calandra, Bob. 2000. "Finders Keepers." *Human Resource Executive,* June 2.

22. Bethune, Gordon. 2000. "Recipe for Success." *Continental,* February, p. 8.

23. Dannhauser, Carol Leonetti. 2000. "The Right Rewards." *Working Woman,* July/August, pp. 40-41.

24. Editor. 1997. "Coffee—Uh, Milk—Break." *Training & Development,* November, p. 10.

25. Helson, Cynthia M. 1997. "Warming Your Employer's Image." *Employee Services Management (ESM) Magazine,* October, p. 10.

26. Sessa, Danielle. 1997. "These Lucky Electronic Pets Can Sing I'll Be Home for Christmas." *The Wall Street Journal,* January 11.

27. Editor. 2000. "Quick Tip." *Success in Recruiting and Retaining,* December.

28. Editor. 1998. "Offer Your Employees Hidden Paychecks." *Smart Workplace Practices,* February, p. 1.

29. Editor. 2000. "Everyday Perks Aid Retention of Low-Wage Work Force." *Success in Recruiting and Retaining*, August, p. 5.

30. Editor. 2000. "Flexible Workplace Ranks Tops; 'Soft' Benefits Win Out." *Success in Recruiting and Retaining,* August, p. 2.

31. Editor. 2001. "'Anything-Goes' Flexibility Keeps the Hard-to-Recruit on

Board." *Success in Recruiting and Retaining*, February, p 5.

32. Editor. 2000. "'Summers Off' Program Retains Valuable Workers." *Success in Recruiting and Retaining*, November, p. 5.

33. Branch, Shelly. 1998. "You Hired 'Em. But Can You Keep 'Em?" *Fortune*, November 9, p. 250.

34. Poe, Andrea. 2000. "What's on the Table?" *HR Magazine*, May, p. 54.

35. Gunther, Marc. 2001. "God and Business." *Fortune*, July 9, pp. 59-80.

36. Gini, Al. 2000. "Religion in the Workplace." *The Works*, Summer, p. 21.

37. Grensing-Pophal, Lin. 2000. "Workplace Chaplains." *HR Magazine*, August, pp. 54-60.

38. Katzenbach, Jon R., and Santamaria, Jason A. 1999. "Firing up the Front Line." *Harvard Business Review*, May/June.

39. Kleiman, Carol. 2001. "Flexible Workplace Makes Honesty the Best Policy." *Chicago Tribune*, January 9.

40. Garfield, Charles. 1992. *Second to None: How Our Smartest Companies Put People First*. New York, NY: McGraw-Hill.

41. Ryan, Michael. 1996. "They Call Their Boss a Hero." *Parade Magazine*, September 8.

42. Leonard, Sharon. 2000. "The Graduation Pledge of Alliance." *HR Magazine*, December, p. 214.

43. Blackburn, Kimberly. 2000. "Daughters' Day Is Going Co-ed at Many Organizations." *HR News*, June, p. 5.

44. Editor. "Invite Spouses to Meetings." *Positive Leadership*, Sample Issue, p. 1.

45. Editor. 2001. *Success in Recruiting and Retaining*, March.

46. Doheny, Kathleen. 2000. "Elder Care, Younger Care." *Working Woman*, April.

47. Wells, Susan. 2000. "The Elder Care Gap." *HR Magazine*, May.

48. Editor. 2001. "Home Is Where the Kitchen Is." *HR Magazine*, February, p. 16.

49. Tyler, Katherine. 2001. "A Roof over Their Heads." *Hr Magazine*, February, p. 42.

50. Editor. 2000. "The 'Family Guy' Lives: Young Men Will Trade Money for Time." *Success in Recruiting and Retaining*, August, p. 3.

51. Editor. 2000. "Family Ties Sink Transfers." *Success in Recruiting and Retaining*. August, p. 6.

52. Editor. 2000. "Baby Boomers—Handle with Care." *HR News*.

Chapter 14

E = Enthusiasm

The tragedy of life is what dies inside a man while he lives.
—Albert Schweitzer

It may be obvious, but what we've observed again and again is that
personal enthusiasm is the initial energizer of any change process.
And that enthusiasm feeds on itself. People don't necessarily want
to "have a vision" at work or to "conduct dialogue." They want to
be part of a team that's fun to work with and that produces results
they are proud of.

—Peter Senge

In their book, *Finding & Keeping Great Employees*, Jim Harris and
Joan Brannick believe that it is the organization's culture that will
determine the success of any program designated to enhance the selec-
tion and retention of excellent employees. The authors present four
categories into which most organizations can be placed in terms of
their core concept:

- **Customer Service**—the underlying purpose is to create a customer solution.
- **Innovation**—the underlying purpose is to create the future.
- **Operational Excellence**—the underlying purpose is to create a process that minimizes costs while maximizing productivity and efficiency.
- **Spirit**—the underlying purpose is to create an environment that inspires employee excellence.

> Enthusiasm is that kindling spark that marks the difference between the leaders in every activity and the laggards who put in just enough to get by.
> —Johann Friedrich Schiller

Harris and Brannick suggest that finding and keeping great employees requires a match between the employee, the job, and the organization's culture. Interestingly, the fastest-growing core culture is spirit. In this organizational culture, competitive advantage is gained through unleashing people's limitless energy, creativity, and enthusiasm. However, each of these culture categories must be driven by enthusiasm for the organization to be successful. When employees are enthusiastic about their organization and the job that they do, no matter what the core culture, they give their very best, and they are committed to staying.[1]

The Idea: Encourage Social Interaction

We need to find more reasons in our organizations to celebrate and to enjoy one another. Programs encouraging social interaction can boost morale and foster cohesiveness, benefiting both employees and company.

The Idea in Action

Chambers & Chambers Wine Merchants in San Francisco get the entire staff together every Friday afternoon for bread, cheese, and wine. The 4:45 Club, as they call it, gives them a chance to taste new wines or specials the company is offering. Even better than the social interaction and learning about the new products is the perk that the employees then can purchase the wine at a discount.[2]

> I always come to work full of enthusiasm, smiling, and generally pleasant. It drives the others crazy trying to figure out what it is they're missing!
>   —a reader in Missouri

Compaq Computers has a club strictly for social events so that employees can find new friends. Through the program, new employees, especially, may have an easier time adjusting. The club watches Monday Night Football, attends concerts, goes tubing, participates in wine-tasting and murder mystery dinners, enjoys comedy clubs, art museums, and much more.[3]

Nancy Bruner-Koontz at **Janus Funds**, Denver, Colorado, holds holiday parties and celebrations that are fun and different. One time she hired a '70s retro band to play for their Christmas party. She also held Latin dance lessons during a picnic, themed "Fiesta Latina." Trying something new keeps employees delighted.[4]

Rebecca Preston of the **Perth, Australia, Convention Bureau** shares that every Friday they have what they call "Four Thirsties." It is a time when their leader, Anne-Maree, feels they deserve to come together as a team for drinks, to relax and share the week's activities. Rebecca says this time is very special for the team to connect and feel good about what they have accomplished.

During vacation season, a Dallas unit of **Sprint** holds "Fun Fridays" with such events as "exchange-a-plant-with-a-co-worker" day and a social where managers in aprons serve sundaes.

Employees at **Nike Corporation** in Beaverton, Oregon, stop work at 4:30 on Thursdays, drink beer and soda, and then kayak across a lake, race bikes, and compete in a 600-yard run.[5]

> A mediocre idea that generates enthusiasm will go farther than a great idea that inspires none.
>   —Mary Kay Ash

BI in Minneapolis, Minnesota, has a Fun QIT (Quality Improvement Team) that plans company-wide events to bring fun and joy to the workplace. In addition, any proceeds from these events benefit a local organization. Here are some of the events they have sponsored:

▸ January—Chili cook-off. This was an opportunity for associates to get to know each other during lunch time while sampling a variety of chili made by associates. BI provided beverages, crackers, and prizes for the hottest, most unusual, and best overall chili.

▸ February—Valentine's Day. Over 3000 candy hearts with personalized messages were distributed among peers. The Fun team sold the hearts for 50 cents and delivered them to desks on Valentine's Day. $1200 was donated to the Minneapolis Crisis Nursery as a result.

▸ March—Potluck Lunches and Daffodil Day. This was a time to get together and support the American Cancer Society. The start of spring was celebrated with an indoor picnic where associates could treat themselves to a bunch of daffodils. Over $1000 was contributed.

▸ April—Book Sale. Associates donated used books, videos, and music which were sold for $1 or less to other associates. All proceeds went to Bridging, an organization that provides household goods to the needy.

▸ May—Surprise. A surprise bag of fun toys and treats was placed on the desks of all associates early one morning in May.

▸ June—Dunk the Director. Directors and vice presidents volunteered to be in the dunk tank where associates have a chance to dunk them.

Here are some other ideas of things the group has sponsored:

▸ Shamrock Search Contest. Four-leaf clovers were hidden all around the BI buildings.

- Green Jeans Day (can wear jeans with something green).
- Nerf® basketball contest with food shelf collections.
- March Madness. Flower seed on every desk the first day of spring with a contest for the best flower by 4th of July.
- "Thank You" Month. "Thanks" Post-it® notes were distributed to all associates with a memo from the president.
- Holiday celebration and cube-decorating contest.
- Mid-Winter Blues. Weekly Blues Busters (stress tips). Blues Brothers video brown bag lunch. Blues costume contest with blues music by the BI band. Blue jeans every Friday in January.
- Ice Cream Break. Surprise ice cream bars on front lawn with "We treat you right!" theme.
- Dog Days of Summer 1. Hot dogs and chips picnic lunch on lawn with "Dunk the Director."
- Dog Days of Summer 2. Employees bring in their dogs for a dog wash.
- Olympic event. Associates participate in an all-building scavenger hunt with Olympic challenges in each building.

One other suggestion:

- Elvis Appreciation Day.

The Idea: Create a "Hoopla!" Culture

The Idea in Action

John Pearson, the CEO of the **Christian Management Association**, tells of how he began to create a "Hoopla!" culture in his organization:

> As a CEO, "Hoopla!" never came naturally to me. I always felt we had too much to do and too little time. But one year I attended a workshop on "How to Put Fun into the Workplace" and got a $10,000 idea.
>
> One day I announced that we'd provide lunch for our team of 11 in the conference room the following Wednesday. Everyone eagerly arrived on time, but instead of sandwiches in their brown bags, they

found them bulging with candy.

"Oops," I bluffed, "the deli made an error. Well ... we'll have to go out for lunch." I took them to a great restaurant where I had already made reservations. We ordered from the menu and had a relaxing meal. But it was just the start!

After dessert, I gave everyone a sealed envelope with these instructions: "In your envelope is cash that you MUST spend in the next 60 minutes at the mall next door. You must spend the money ONLY on yourself. Buy whatever you'd like. Cash that you don't spend, you must return to me. We'll meet at the fountain for 'Show and Tell.' If you're late, you owe me 50 bucks. Ready. Set. GO!"

Staff members leaped out of their chairs and ran through the mall. Each envelope contained $50, and not one person returned any money an hour later! (And before I left the mall, several shoppers asked if we had any openings at our organization!)

That day is still a vivid memory for team members—and the goodwill it created lasted a long time. It was the right time and the right event for the right team. They felt appreciated.

If you're the leader or manager, and you're not the spontaneous, creative type—then bestow on someone the bonus title of "International Vice President of Hoopla!" Give this party person a team and a budget and let them loose.

The amount of time and resources your spend on "Hoopla!" is directly proportional to the morale and spirit of your staff.

In Appendix C, you will find a "Hoopla!" rating test that you can do monthly to see how your organization is measuring up.

The Idea: Give Personalized Awards

The Idea in Action

Linclay Corporation, a St. Louis-based real estate management firm, rewards employees on their 10th anniversary with a tribute created especially for them, says Bob Nelson in his book, *1001 Ways to Reward Employees*. Committees made up of employees who know the recipient well are formed two to three months in advance to plan the gifts.

The committee interviews the spouses, parents, children, and friends of the recipient to get an idea of what the employee would appreciate. Members take it very seriously. A racing enthusiast at the company, for example, was given a share in a limited partnership in a racehorse for his 10-year recognition.

The company sets a $2000 budget on the gift and the employee committee arranges it. "Traditional recognition programs motivate the recipients," said Mike Lee, the director of human resources. "But this program, because other employees are involved, motivates everyone."[6]

Do you know what the passion of each of your employees is?

The Idea: Hold Team-Building Meetings

The Idea in Action

Employease, a young, Atlanta-based firm that helps companies like MindSpring and Ocean Spray automate their HR, benefits, and payroll operations, has a monthly all-hands meeting called "First Friday." The meeting, which includes financial results and sales updates as well as anything-goes presentations and lots of fun, is described as a "raucous, creative embodiment of its mission."

The meeting is designed to make their strategic mission tangible and real in a fun, creative atmosphere. Mike Seckler, co-founder and VP of strategic marketing, says in an article in *Fast Company* magazine:

> First Friday is a mix of straight talk, town-hall discussion, and vaude-ville. After we welcome new employees, members of the management team discuss financial results and operational news. If the topic is our next big release, then we'll talk about how critical it is that we make our deadlines. Next, teams give presentations on our new strategic partnerships, our recent successes, and our benchmarks. Because we don't want the meeting to be predictable, we let the teams decide the format of each presentation. Thus, the business-development team is known for its clever yet on-target skits.

One of the best practices of these meetings is new-employee stand-up. New employees stand up in front of the whole group and share their background and why they decided to join Employease. They always get a standing ovation, which reminds everyone of just how special this company is. Everything they do in these meetings embodies the enthusiasm they have for their mission and vision. Mike says, "We're not a great company if we're not having fun!"[7]

The Idea: Add Fun to the Workplace

William Fry, a psychiatrist at Stanford who is a leading humor researcher, claims laughing 100 times a day is equivalent to 10 minutes of strenuous rowing. Wouldn't you rather laugh? Physiologically, when you belly laugh, your throat goes into uncoordinated spasms, sending blasts of air out the mouth at 110km/hour. The body starts pumping adrenalin, the heart rate increases, and the brain releases endorphins and enkephalins—natural pain killers. The lungs pump out carbon dioxide, tears cleanse the eyes, and your muscles relax and release tension. You may be a mess, but you feel terrific! Humor boosts the immune system and reduces hormones that cause stress. We all need to have more fun at work to be at our best.[8]

The Idea in Action

April Fool's Day (April 1) is now officially International Fun at Work Day. Organizations such as **Sprint**, **EDS**, and the **California Polytechnic Institute** have gotten into the spirit by staging ice cream socials and parking lot beach parties. Others come to work barefoot, have a costume contest, or bring their pets in for a playdate. This day of fun promotes team building, creativity, and productivity. Does your workgroup celebrate a Fun at Work day?[9]

On National Fun at Work Day, **Grafton Public Library** in Grafton, Ohio, partied for 12 hours straight, honoring a different employee every hour.

A Business Conference Call, Inc. in Chaska, Minnesota, had "Backwards Day" on which the employees dressed, walked, and even talked backward.[10]

Jim Warda, author of *Where Are We Going So Fast?*, writes a weekly column called "Where Are We Going So Fast?™—Online." One day, he announced to his readers that he was declaring "Take Your Inner Child to Work Day." This is what he found on that day:

> Walked into the department to find Tom and Susan running through the cubes, playing tag. Joe, my usually conservative and careful colleague, was drawing out hopscotch lines in the hall. Hank and Bill were making paper airplanes, trying to see whose could fly farther. And everywhere, productivity soared. Why?
>
> Because, like children, people were all saying what they felt. In meetings, if an idea was presented that didn't yet make sense, someone would say, "Hey, Rick, that idea doesn't yet make sense." However, if the idea was a good one, high fives were exchanged all around and then a cake and balloons were brought in to celebrate.

He goes on to say:

> For me, I learned something important on "Take your Inner Child to Work Day." I learned that we're all still seven-year-olds inside. And that seven-year-old can be demanding, pounding on your brain and your chest, wanting to be let out every once in awhile. So, I try to let him out a little every day. The hard part is getting him back in!

Katherine Lyons, the founder of **The Society for Ladies Who Laugh Out Loud**, tells about a CEO with a flair for theater who arrives at work once a month as a different personality. She says it raises morale.

She once arrived as the Wizard of Oz. No costume. Just subtle hints throughout the day that a wizard was in their midst. She had researched this ahead of time: the idea was to help others see that they already possessed what they wished for.

Throughout the day messages and gifts appeared on people's desks. Someone who was timid deceived a framed Certificate of Courage. A gruff and grumpy fellow found a heart-shaped box hidden on his cluttered desk. In it were scrolled messages, each speaking of kindnesses he had shown others. Another person received a framed diploma certifying the recipient had earned a Doctorate of Diligence and Dedication.

Everyone quietly received something from the great wizard, including one women who, after a terrible upheaval, had been struggling to find "home." She received small red-sequined shoes and a plane ticket. According to Katherine, she DID click her heels!

(Reprinted from Katherine Q. Lyons, The Society for Ladies Who Laugh Out Loud, www.ladieslaugh.com)

In their book, *True Leaders,* Bette Price and George Ritcheske write about what is done for fun at **The Container Store**:

> The Container Store borrowed the idea of a Fun Committee from Southwest Airlines. The committee gets together and decides to do things that are just for fun. Among the past year's events were a chili cook-off and a Wizard of Oz costume party where even the co-founders dressed in costume. On the day we arrived at the corporate office for our interviews, a team of employees in coordinated t-shirts had just finished forming a human arch to send off a group of visiting school kids. They cheered and re-established the arch for us and greeted us with the same enthusiasm![11]

Ameriking, one of the franchisees in the Burger King system, encourages fun sales-building tools in their stores. Every other Saturday, one of the managers and his team have a

> Success is going from failure to failure without a loss of enthusiasm.
> —Winston Churchill

magician who performs during the day. They have increased their Saturday sales by 50%, and everyone has been having a lot of fun! The manager has also added a bike raffle to this event. Customers put their names in for the raffle during the week, and the lucky ticket is pulled on Saturday, creating a lot of repeat business and an air of excitement.

Scott Gengler, the President of **Energy to Change** in Milwaukee, Wisconsin, shares "10 Ways to Have Fun at Work" in his newsletter, *LaughLines*:

1. At lunchtime, sit in your parked car and point your hair dryer at passing cars to see if they slow down.
2. Page yourself over the intercom. Don't disguise your voice.
3. Insist that your email address be zena-goddess-of-fire@companyname.com.
4. Encourage your colleagues to join you in a little synchronized chair-dancing.
5. Develop an unnatural fear of staplers.
6. Put decaf in the coffee maker for three weeks. Once everyone has gotten over their caffeine addictions, switch to espresso.
7. Finish all your sentences with "… in accordance with the prophecy."
8. dontuseanypunctuationorspaces
9. Put mosquito netting around your cubicle.
10. Hum when you ride in an elevator.[12]

(Reprinted with permission from Scott Gengler)

The Idea: Create a Culture of Joy

The Idea in Action

Doug Merritt, the co-founder of Icarian, Inc., an online company in Sunnyvale, California, that provides software for businesses to manage their workforce, wants to create a company that balances extremely hard work with a lot of fun. He has implemented many fun programs and perks for employees, but his most creative program is "Icarian dollars."

Each month the company allows each employee to spend $50 to improve the workplace. Employees pool their money to fund a project or a charity by charging $50 to their expense accounts. Icarian dollars have paid for foosball and pool tables, wind chimes for the lobby, company ski and rafting trips, soccer and roller hockey leagues, and charity events. Both Merritt and his employees feel that these dollars help promote teamwork and fun.[13]

The Idea: Have Theme Meetings and Celebrations

The Idea in Action

Beverly Schnepel, the former Chairman of the **State Women's Committee of the Iowa Farm Bureau Federation**, tells about some of the themes they have used:

> I started working with Farm Bureau Women as a county volunteer when their theme was "If it's to be, it's up to me," and that seemed to fit my situation, too. I've helped choose and develop quite a few themes since then. One was "Hats Off" to Farm Bureau Women. We had meetings where everyone wore a hat and we gave prizes for categories (prettiest, funniest, oldest, etc.), made hat corsages with miniature hats decorated in various ways, used hats as centerpieces, appliqued hats on sweat shirts, etc.
>
> Another year we used butterflies in connection with the theme "the challenge of change," tying changes in rural life and agriculture technology with the metamorphosis of butterflies. We gave inexpensive butterfly pins to all women working in the organizations who attended our state meeting and had a vespers service based on the changes in a butterfly's life.
>
> This year we're using a colorful rooster as a symbol to emphasize the theme "Telling the Ag story—Something to crow about." We're finding many fun ways to use roosters. I received a light-sensitive rooster to put by the door—he crows three times when someone walks by! I've also referred to us sometimes as "Little Red Hens"—you know, the ones who say "I will" when no one else will?

This letter from Beth Lewis, the Senior Vice President of Sales and Marketing for **CRC Press, Inc.**, in Boca Raton, Florida, shares another way a manager used a theme idea:

> Elaine Mathis, the new customer service manager, was so inspired by your presentation last week about good service coming from within that she developed a "theme" for the department. Over the weekend, she came in to the office and put red construction paper hearts around the department, making certain that every person's workspace included a heart. Then, on Monday morning, she had her first departmental meeting. She told them that she thought about your words and when she things of service coming from within each individual, it made her think of "coming from the heart." That led her into "the customer service department is the heart of CRC Press!" The credit and collections department heard about this theme and early this morning, while the customer service people were attending a pre-workday departmental meeting, they came into the department and put helium-filled red balloons on every cubicle and big posters with red hearts that say, "Customer Service is the heart of CRC Press!" The two groups joined together today to have a pot-luck lunch to celebrate Elaine's appointment, too. Only ten days ago, these two departments were focused on "turf" issues and pointing fingers at each other. Now, with your energy and inspiration as the catalyst, they are working together and having fun together!

The Idea: Celebrate Holidays

The Idea in Action

The University of Utah Hospitals and Clinics celebrate each holiday in a special way, according to Wendy Bailey, Coordinator Community Outreach and Volunteer Services, and Sandi Martin.

On Valentine's Day each employee received a See's candy bar that said:

Roses are Red,
So is the "U!"
Our token of Thanks,
For all that *YOU* do!

From the Hospital Administration,
Rick, Dan, Gene, Madeline, Mike, Neil, Pierre, and Ross

To say thank you for bringing your expertise and pride to work each day and for the caring way you attend to our patients, families, and visitors.

Enter to win a $100 Gift Certificate from a list of selected merchants. Complete the information on the backside of the wrapper and drop it off in the Valentine's Box located in the Employee Service Center.

They posted the following "Prescription" for a Happy Valentine's Day:

On St. Patrick's Day each employee received a green flier with shamrocks and an Irish blessing decorating it. It read:

> Dress casual (Might we recommend a red shirt and your best jeans)
>
> Show your appreciation to a coworker, peer, manager/supervisor and/or anyone in our "U" Community by putting an ad in our special Valentine's Classifieds.
>
> Enjoy treats on the house. The Social Activities Committee will be dropping by with some very special Valentine treats.
>
> Buy your sweetheart something he/she has been dreaming of.

TOP O' THE MORNIN' TO YA!
We feel lucky having YOU,
And send our thanks for all YOU DO.
Please join us on this special DAY,
A Breakfast Treat is on its WAY!

Krispy Kreme Donuts and Milk
Friday, March 16, 2001, 9:30–11:30

On Thanksgiving each employee received another See's candy bar that read:

Happy Thanksgiving 2000
Not just at the holidays,
But all year through . . .
Our many thanks,
For all that you do!

They even celebrate Dr. Seuss' Birthday, part of the Read Across America celebration (see below).

Happy Birthday, Dr. Seuss!
Friday, March 2, 2001, birthday cake will be distributed.

You have brains in your head.
You have feet in your shoes.
You can steer yourself
Any direction you choose.

You can sit with a Zead
And decide to read.
Or you can walk with the Nooks
And talk of great books.

March two is the day
That dear Seuss was born.
So it is our goal, we say
To give you such warn.

Our Hospitals and Clinics
Are taking a stand.
Reading is oh, so important
So we'll give you a hand.

Support kids, pets and friends
And make no amends.
The power of reading has no ends.

So you and the kids enter our games
In support of reading
Just think of the brain-power
That you will be feeding!!!

—Written by Melinda Lewis, Human Resources
Show your support. Wear your black shirts and/or
vests and your favorite black pants.

Contests
KIDS: Create a bookmark
ADULTS: Trivial Pursuit Quizzes
Prizes
Preschool–5 years: Dr. Seuss Character Stuffed Animals
6–12 years: Dr. Seuss Book sets
13 years–up: Barnes & Noble gift cards

Employees joined in the celebration and enjoyed birthday cake on the house!

Any babies born on March 2, 2001, will receive their first Dr. Seuss book.

R.E.A.D. (Reading Education Assistance Dogs) will be in Clinic 6 and Hospital waiting rooms.

Children visiting the hospital on March 2, 2001, will receive an age-appropriate book.

Info Fair on Literacy on 1st Floor Bridge 9:00 a.m.– 3:00 p.m.

Pet Sitters International is campaigning to make a Friday in June national "Take Your Dog to Work Day." They feel if employees bring their well-behaved dogs into the workplace for a day, it will encourage others to adopt dogs from animal shelters and humane organizations. If your organization decides to do this, make it a party—have doggie treats and give each pet a name badge!

Netscape Communications Corp. allows employees to bring their dogs every day. Says one employee, "If you get stressed out, you can just walk around and there's a warm, fuzzy dog to pet." According to an article in *The Wall Street Journal,* some rules had to be instituted. Those with allergies can request their work space be in a "dog-free" zone and if a pet has three "accidents" in the office, it cannot return until it has finished doggie obedience school![14]

Rebecca Preston, the Sales Coordinator for the **Perth Convention Bureau in Perth, Australia**, shares ways they make Christmas special in their office: "One Christmas, instead of sending hundreds of Christmas cards to our members and clients, we donated and planted a tree in the city. At the PCN Christmas party, we have a 'Very Red Faces' talent contest, just like the 'Gong Show.' We have done everything from John Revolting ('Saturday Night Fever'), and Dorks of the Dance ('Riverdance'), to synchronized swimming and an army platoon. It is a real team effort and a lot of fun!"

Sesame Place amusement park in Langhorne, Pennsylvania, encourages its student summer employees to bring their parents to work, offering a $25 bonus and donating the equivalents of their parents' daily wages to drug programs. The purpose is to encourage intergenerational understanding and to get extra workers needed in late August when many students are returning to school.[15]

The Idea: Hold Contests

The Idea in Action

Bob Nelson, in an article in *Employee Services Management (ESM) Magazine*, shares several rules for contests:

- ▶ Promote the program and its purpose.
- ▶ Set realistic, achievable, and measurable goals.
- ▶ Limit the contest to a short period of time.
- ▶ Keep the contest rules simple.
- ▶ Ensure that prizes are desirable to employees.
- ▶ Link rewards directly to performance.
- ▶ Give rewards and recognition promptly.

Contests can be used to boost sales, increase product knowledge, build team spirit, and improve morale. Here are some ideas he shares.

People's National Bank in Kewanee, Illinois, has a contest for the marketing of new MasterCard and Visa cards. Employees receive gifts tied to the number of new accounts they open—for the first four they receive a flower; for every five additional accounts, they win the following things in sequence: a $5 gift certificate to Dairy Queen, a waiver of card fees, a $15 restaurant gift certificate, a $50 savings bond, a day off with pay, a riverboat ticket and $25 spending money.

Leadership Synergy in Scottsbluff, Nebraska, created a sales program to send the entire staff to Las Vegas for four days and three nights, all expenses paid, if certain financial goals were met.

Business Incentives in Minneapolis, Minnesota, has foreign and domestic car salespeople call an 800 number and take a product knowledge test over the phone. During the test, a computer randomly chooses 15-20 questions from a pool of about 200. Salespeople who answer 80% correctly win instant merchandise prizes.

 SmithKline Bioscience Laboratories in King of Prussia, Pennsylvania, have a product knowledge competition to learn the company's 1400 types of medical tests. The contest had three qualifying rounds, semifinals, and then finalists from each region faced off at the company's national sales meeting. Participants received a business-card case engraved with their name and the company's logo. Cash prizes were given for the winners.

 Hardee's Food Systems in Rocky Mount, North Carolina, held a Competition for Excellence in which three-person teams from each of more than 2000 restaurants competed against other Hardee's in their districts. They were judged on the three basic qualifications for fast-food employees—service, product makeup, and work area cleanliness—as well as on how well they worked together. The national finalists were treated like VIPs—flown in on the company jet and driven around town in a limo when they came to accept their cash prizes.

 The **Domino Pizza Distribution Company** in Ann Arbor, Michigan, holds an annual company-wide Olympics in which it promotes events ranging from accounting to dough making, vegetable slicing, truck loading, dough catching, and tray scraping. National champions in each of 16 categories receive cash awards, and the team leader who supervises the most "gold medalists" wins a free vacation.

 Blue Cross Blue Shield Association in Chicago, Illinois, held a contest to select employees to appear in the company's commercials.

 Remington Products, Inc., in Bridgeport, Connecticut, held a company contest tied to the theme, "What Makes Remington Good." The winner of a trip to Acapulco wrote a poem about the company.

Great Clips in Medford, Oregon, has a fun contest in which they roll toilet tissues from the front to the back of the salon. Then they ask both customers and employees to guess the number of squares for a free product.

Women, Inc., in Sacramento, California, held a contest asking employees to come dressed as their favorite holiday. Some of the costumes were a turkey, a bunny, Cupid, and an expectant mother.

Other ideas included having a raffle for members of an outstanding workgroup, having a "Crazy Hat Day," and sponsoring a holiday party such as Halloween at an odd time of the year and giving prizes for costumes.[16]

The Idea: Sponsor Product Knowledge Experiences

The Idea in Action

When I was Manager of Quality in Training at **Kaset International** in Tampa, Florida, we invited all the salespeople and trainers for a "Product Knowledge Extravaganza" for a week to help them learn more about the various products we had to offer our customers. The first day was spent getting to know one another, since employees came from all over the U.S. The day included team-building exercises, and each manager in the company gave a short presentation about his/her department. That night we held a party for the group. The second day included professional meetings with their teams and then a brief overview of each product Kaset offered. At the end of the day, each person signed up for three products that interested him or her with a first, second, and third choice. The idea was to choose a product that they knew very little about.

That night I selected teams of three to four people to work on each product, trying to create cross-departmental teams based on one of each person's three choices. The teams were presented the following morning along with the assignment for the rest of the week, which was to research the history and purpose of the product and then to present that information to the rest of the group in some creative way. The idea was to "teach" them about that product so that they could go out and sell or train it with a much more thorough understanding. The teams were also to create handouts to go into a "Product Knowledge Extravaganza" notebook and to submit five questions about their product that the group should learn to answer from their presentation. The rest of the day and the following morning were free for them to work with their team. Since we were a training company, we had many resources available for them to use.

On Thursday afternoon and Friday, each team did a 15- to 20-minute presentation to the rest of the group on their chosen product. Some of them were hilarious—original videotapes, skits that were a spoof of the product and even some of the management team, song lyrics, and a "Jeopardy" game. Each of the presentations was videotaped for future reference. Then each team gave the rest of the group their summary handout, and a Q and A time was held for five to 10 minutes. All senior managers were asked to be present during these presentations.

When all the presentations were finished, a contest was held to determine which team had learned the most from the day and a half of product presentations. I used the questions the teams had submitted, and the CEO and president of the company acted as judges. Each time the team got a right answer they got a silly prize, but the team with the most right answers got gift ceertifi-cates to the nicest restaurant in Tampa. We finished the day with a celebration of the week and our new, educated team!

> Enthusiasm is at the bottom of all progress. With it there is accomplishment. Without it there are only alibis.
>
> —Henry Ford

The Idea: Have Retirement Celebrations

The Idea in Action

Donna Cutting writes:

> I had been the Activities Director at Park Place, a large retirement community for seniors, for two years. It was a wonderful place to work, and I was tremendously close to our residents and the fantastic team I worked with. Nevertheless, I was being led to begin my own speaking and performing business, a dream I'd had for many years.
>
> The night before my last day on the job, my boss asked if I would come in a bit late the next day. I enjoyed "sleeping in" and then headed off to work. When I arrived, over 150 residents, all the department heads, my employees, and other team members were all lining the hallway, greeting me as I came in! The lobby was filled with the many faces I had grown to love over the past two years. They were all applauding ... for me!!!
>
> I could barely stop my tears from flowing as I was escorted down the hallway and into the lobby where I was approached by our newly elected President of the Resident Council who, with tears in *his* eyes, presented me with a framed document, which he read aloud. [Figure 14-1, p. 286.]
>
> It was signed by every member of the Resident Council.
>
> I was presented this beautiful plaque and was the recipient of many wonderful words and warm hugs as I was escorted into our ice cream parlor.
>
> There, the Department Head Team and my own employees had set up a beautiful and scrumptious homemade breakfast in my honor. In addition to all of this, they gave me a gift of some magnificent wind chimes ... a whimsical gift in honor of my new company, "Whimsical Notions." My own staff members, Paul and Noel, also gifted me with a beautiful black bag, which I use to this day.
>
> Throughout the entire day, residents and staff alike would stop me in the hallways, the elevators, and the activities room to say, "We love you, Donna!" Even residents who had *never* attended an activity in the past two years stopped me with hugs and a "We love you, Donna"!

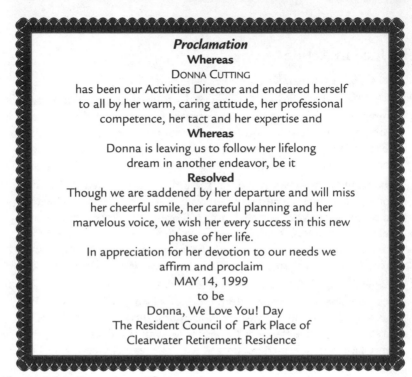

Proclamation
Whereas
DONNA CUTTING
has been our Activities Director and endeared herself
to all by her warm, caring attitude, her professional
competence, her tact and her expertise and
Whereas
Donna is leaving us to follow her lifelong
dream in another endeavor, be it
Resolved
Though we are saddened by her departure and will miss
her cheerful smile, her careful planning and her
marvelous voice, we wish her every success in this new
phase of her life.
In appreciation for her devotion to our needs we
affirm and proclaim
MAY 14, 1999
to be
Donna, We Love You! Day
The Resident Council of Park Place of
Clearwater Retirement Residence

Figure 14-1. Donna's certificate

It truly was "We Love You, Donna" Day!

That plaque is hanging on my wall, the wind chimes sing on my porch, the bag is filled with my business tools, and the memories of the people of Park Place are in my heart. I love them too!

The Idea: Hold "Guerrilla Celebrations"

The Idea in Action

Employee Recruitment & Retention newsletter suggests that we fire up bored employees by having what they call "guerrilla celebration" attacks, which keep employees off balance with what you might be going to do next:

▶ Close the office for one hour on Friday morning to have a "comedy party" where you show funny videos.

▶ Announce on Monday that Friday will be a half day—for no reason.

▶ Have bagels and coffee waiting for employees on a random Tuesday.

▶ Hire temps to answer the phones on a Friday afternoon and show a movie to your staff, complete with popcorn.[17]

The Idea: Share Your Enthusiasm

The Idea in Action

Heidi Sather of Iowa City, Iowa, shares a story about the contagious enthusiasm of one of her college professors:

> Professor Christensen-Szalanski teaches in the College of Business at the University of Iowa. I attended his Business Administration lecture class of about 300 students. Professor C-S is one of the most unique teachers I have ever had! He genuinely cares, motivates, and keeps his lectures interesting. One of the things he does to motivate students is to offer a T-shirt with the class logo on it to every student in the discussion section with the highest average test score. He announces what section won and the teaching assistant of that section to the entire lecture class.

> He always shares his interests in the lectures, giving his students some of his enthusiasm for the task at hand. The most vivid example of this was when, at the end of a lecture, he took a newspaper and ripped it up. He then took the newspaper and made it into several different hats, including a "Robin Hood" style hat and a captain's hat. It is fair to say that he had the attention of every person in that lecture hall! As he did this, he talked about what each hat meant as a manager and how a manager's role is constantly changing. When he finished, the lecture hall erupted in applause! I have never been in a lecture before or after in which a professor was applauded. That speaks volumes about the way the students felt about him and his efforts to make our education the best it could possibly be.

Playfair, Inc., is an organization dedicated to having fun at work. In their newsletter they share some fun ideas to spread enthusiasm and joy in your workplace:

"We've made some revisions in our retirement program. In lieu of a pension, you'll now get one limited-edition Elvis collector's plate per pay period."

Close to Home by John McPherson/Dist by Universal Press Syndicate

> ▸ Hold a limo lottery—the winner gets driven to and from work one day in the company limo or else rent one for the day.
> ▸ Hold an all-employee pizza party with the name of your company spelled out across the tops of the pizzas in mushrooms.
> ▸ Hold a pajama party where your business stays open all night. Encourage your employees and customers to come dressed in their pajamas. Have food, entertainment, and prizes.
> ▸ Send pizza to the home of an employee who has worked overtime so she/he won't have to cook dinner after work.
> ▸ Tape a candy bar to the middle of a long memo.[18]

Paula Easton, **CMS**, wrote about one of the things she does to spread enthusiasm in the company:

> I now have a basket of squeezable critters on my desk. There are 17 different ones such as a lady bug, a butterfly, a seahorse, a pig, a cow, a bear, and a bumble bee. They are wonderful, and everyone who enters just has to touch them! I have already given one away to an administrative employee who just changed jobs from supporting two of our

industry VP's to supporting internal and external PR. She applied for the job, and when I told her she had gotten the position, I gave her the critter she always touched when she was in my office—a rooster—and told her that he could now help her "crow" about getting her new job!

At CMS they also hold a "Spirit Day." On this day they give different colored bandanas to each department to wear. The middle managers wrote a "rap" and sent it by voice mail to everyone, and at lunch the senior managers sang familiar songs with lyrics they made up about the company. Everyone looks forward to the fun of this day!

Ann-Maree Ferguson, the Executive Director of the **Perth Convention Bureau in Perth, Australia**, has selected as their motto: "Boldly go where no Bureau has gone before," and she makes sure her employees get their optimal 10 minutes of laughter every hour. She introduced "spark plug" sessions to their Monday morning staff meetings. A staff member is assigned each week to conduct a 15- to 20-minute session that will motivate and inspire the team for the week. Here are a few of the things they've done:

- ▶ Jill Henry, Convention Marketing Manager, contacted all the parents in advance and asked them to send in a baby photo and a brief description of each of them as a child. Unknown to them, on the next Monday morning, they had to guess who was who. They said they definitely had their quota of laughter that day!
- ▶ Dion Bromilow, Director of Communications and Membership and a PCB golf pro, had a hole-in-one putting competition in the office with an automatic putting machine.
- ▶ Jo-Anne Grist, Executive Assistant, had them playing "Celebrity Heads," where they had to wear a well-known person or character's name on their forehead (which they could not see) and guess who they were by only asking "yes" and "no" questions.
- ▶ Jill Henry introduced the seven dwarves to their office. When someone is happy, they get "Happy" dwarf on their desk for the day. Rebecca Preston, the Sales Coordinator, says, "When you

have 'Dopey' on your desk, you know you will be asked all day what you did to get it, and then we all have a laugh at the silly thing we did!"

Quick Ideas for Enthusiasm

- ▶ Organize a paper airplane flying contest in the midst of a stressful time.
- ▶ Hold a "funeral" for the end of a difficult change effort. Symbolically recognize an ending and then celebrate a new beginning.
- ▶ Design stress support kits filled with things like aspirin, bandages, stress toys, a comedy cassette, Life Savers, etc., to be handed out during a difficult time.
- ▶ Have an ugly tie or ugly hat or ugly shoe contest. Or to bring back memories, try a bubblegum blowing contest!
- ▶ At least once a month spontaneously hand out treats to your staff (ice cream when it's hot, popcorn, bags of red licorice, Cracker Jacks, Bazooka bubblegum, Starbucks coffee, etc.). Have fun with a variety of treats, including those that everyone remembers as kids.
- ▶ Have a "My Favorite Game" week and every day play different childhood games at lunch.
- ▶ Take a walk in a park.
- ▶ Take off your shoes.
- ▶ Each week buy an inexpensive toy and pass it on.
- ▶ Hire a stretch limo for a group outing.
- ▶ Hold a coloring contest and use the best one as this year's Christmas card from the organization.
- ▶ Hold a clean-up day, both inside and outside the organization. Sponsor a picnic lunch and a volleyball game afterwards.
- ▶ Create a collage of all the things that make people happy. Let

everyone contribute and post it in a prominent place, like a cafeteria or breakout room.

▸ Post a trivia question on e-mail every day with a time deadline. Then have a drawing of winners each week for a free lunch.

▸ Have a contest to match pictures of people with pictures of their pets.

▸ Have a group outing to a comedy club on company time.

▸ Have an upper management talent show.

▸ One organization gives a toy Gumby to those who have exhibited outstanding flexibility.

▸ Have a traveling bouquet. Give your co-workers a bouquet of flowers and ask them to keep it for one hour and then pass it on to someone else in the office. Keep it going for several days.

▸ Hire a masseuse to give neck and shoulder massages.

▸ Take joy breaks and teach employees fun things, such as juggling, baton twirling, or Hula Hooping.

▸ Have employees split into groups, create a new product, name it, and write a jingle to present to the other groups—all in 15 minutes.

▸ Sponsor "fun lunches" monthly. Send employee groups for a long lunch on the company once a month. The only rule is *nobody is allowed to talk about work*. If they do, they have to pay for their own lunch.

Notes

1. Harris, Jim, and Brannick, Joan. 1999. *Finding & Keeping Great Employees*. New York, NY: AMACOM.

2. Woodward, Nancy Hatch. 2001. "Discounts Not to Be Discounted." *HR Magazine*, April, p. 91.

3. Cerny, Catrina. 1998. "The Young and the Restless: Serving the New Generation of Employees." *Employee Services Management (ESM) Magazine*, September, p. 15.

4. Ibid., p. 14.

5. Editor. 1997. "Work Week." *The Wall Street Journal*, August 28, p. A1.

6. Nelson, Bob. 1994. *1001 Ways to Reward Employees.* New York, NY: Workman Publishing.

7. Olofson, Cathy. 2000. "Thank God It's Friday." *Fast Company,* April, p. 74.

8. Ardell, Donald B. 1997. "Is Humor a Luxury?" *Employee Services Management (ESM) Magazine,* October, p. 29.

9. Magistro, Nicole. 2000. "Office Fools," *Working Woman,* April, p. 88.

10. 1997. *The Wall Street Journal*, March 4.

11. Price, Bette, and Ritcheske, George. 2001. *True Leaders: How Exceptional CEOs and Presidents Make a Difference by Building People and Profits.* Chicago, IL: Dearborn Trade, pp. 145-146.

12. Gengler, Scott. 2002. "10 Ways to Have FUN at Work." *LaughLines,* Spring/Summer, p. 2.

13. Kleiman, Carol. 2000. "Software Firm's CEO Makes 'Fun' a Priority." *Chicago Tribune,* June 20, Section 3, p.1.

14. Quick, Rebecca. 1999. "They Say Every Dog Has Its Day, So Why Not Make It Nine to Five?" *The Wall Street Journal,* March 18.

15. Editor. 1996. "Work Week." *The Wall Street Journal*, August 26.

16. Nelson, Bob. 1997. "Contests Can Be Great Motivators." *Employee Services Management (ESM) Magazine*, March, pp. 9-12.

17. Editor. *Employee Recruitment & Retention.* Sample Issue, p. 3.

18. Weinstein, Matt. 1999. "Some Fun Ways to Celebrate." *Playfair Newsletter,* April.

Conclusion

If you see people as cost and as a dissolution of profitability, I don't know how you ever reconcile that. The better we treat them, the longer they stay. The less cost of turnover we have, the less cost of training and development that we have. The more experienced workforce we have, the more valuable they are in the marketplace for you, and you can charge for their services.

—James Copeland, Jr., CEO
Deloitte & Touche/
Deloitte Touche Tohmatsu

Someone once said:

You motivate children out of fear.

You motivate adolescents out of peer pressure and appealing to their comfort and pleasure.

You motivate adults out of love and duty to God and themselves.

When I was a child, I mowed the grass because if I did not, I would get punished.

When I was a teenager, I mowed the grass because I was rewarded with money to do it.

As an adult, I mow the grass because it is the right thing to do and is my responsibility.

The less mature will be motivated out of fear of losing their job or reprisals.

The maturing will be motivated out of what they get out of it— monetary compensation, benefits, promotions, etc.

The mature will be motivated out of doing what is best because the job is worth their best effort.

Unfortunately, not all of our employees are mature. According to William J.H. Boetchker, people divide themselves into four classes:

- ▸ Those who will always do less than what they are told.
- ▸ Those who will do what they are told, but no more.
- ▸ Those who will do things without being told.
- ▸ Those who will inspire others to do things.

Which kind of employees would you like to have? Based on all the research that's been done, when we treat employees with CARE, we help them to be the best they can be by meeting those deep underlying needs for self-validation, and we help them have the courage and the desire to perform at their highest level.

Imagine an organization where employees and managers put the interests of others first, where communication is open, and new ideas, truth, and trust abound, where everyone is respected, and managers and employees freely mentor each other. Imagine an organization where employees are encouraged to take risks, and all efforts are appreciated, where everyone feels a sense of meaning and purpose in their work and where they are free to celebrate each small goal accomplished. Just imagine a joyful, spirited workplace—a great place to be an employee and a wonderful place to be a manager!

In their book, *Finding and Keeping Great Employees,* Jim Harris and Joan Brannick suggest eight best practices that impact employee retention:

- ▸ **Engage the soul.** Aligned companies enthusiastically find ways to engage the very hearts and souls of their employees. Great employees naturally search out, join, and stay with organizations that give them compelling reasons to commit their hearts and souls to something beyond quarterly stock reports or annual plans. (**Reason for Being**)

▶ **What gets rewarded gets done.** Employees quickly learn what is and is not important to the company by how they are recognized and rewarded—and reprimanded. (**Appreciation**)

▶ **More than money.** The use of monetary incentives is part (though a relatively small one) of aligned organizations' retention equation. A primary focus is to build an overall retention strategy that deeply connects to something more than an employee's bank account. (**Atmosphere**)

▶ **Learning drives earning.** The first roadblock faced by employees who desire to grow their learning takes the form of an organization that refuses to invest significant dollars in training. The second obstacle is the organization that does not align the learning to core culture. (**Respect**)

▶ **Get a life.** Through blending employees' personal lives into the very fabric of the culture, aligned organizations further loyalty and retention of great employees. It is their burning desire that every employee, from the CEO to the frontline clerk, get a life! (**Empathy**)

▶ **In the loop.** The fastest way to transform a top-performing staff into a group of disgruntled, discouraged, job-seeking workers is to shut them out of the loop of corporate information. (**Creative Communication**)

▶ **Lighten up.** Aligned organizations take their work—but not themselves—very seriously. This subtle distinction often separates the great organizations from the mediocre. (**Enthusiasm**)

▶ **Free at last.** Perhaps the greatest irony in world-class retention practices is that the greater the employee freedom, the greater

the retention. In today's market, anything less than allowing employees a wide range of operational latitude significantly diminishes an organization's ability to be fast, flexible, and responsive where it really counts: on the front line. (**Respect**)
(Reprinted with permission from Joan Brannick and Jim Harris)[1]

This list exemplifies everything that we found in our research and encompasses each of the elements of a CARE-ing workplace. As you truly begin to CARE about your employees, you will find them excited, committed, and willing to do whatever it takes to make your organization world class—and you will all win!

> People are hungry to work in a spirited environment. They are eager to be involved in meaningful work. They want their contribution to be valued and recognized. They want to appreciate others and be appreciated. They want very much to do a good job and find pride in their work. They want to laugh.
> —Rev. Dr. Marie Morgan, President, Morgan Consulting Group

Bill Matthews, the managing partner of Plante & Moran, LLP, says their firm invests a lot in their staff. He sums it up:

We justify it this way—that a happy work force, a motivated staff, will be a more productive staff. Just look at the turnover. Our turnover is half of what the profession is, so it's a tremendous economic advantage for us. And, the fact is, we believe it comes back to the productivity you get from happy people and reduced turnover. Our goal is not to maximize our profitability, our goal is to optimize it.[2]

And finally, Michael McGrath, vice president, executive planning and development with Charles Schwab Companies, sums it up best: "We don't have employees anymore. We have people who choose to spend their time with us. ... We have to re-recruit them every day."[3]

Notes

1. Harris, Jim, and Brannick, Joan. 1999. *Finding & Keeping Great Employees.* New York, NY: AMACOM.

2. Price, Bette, and Ritcheske, George. 2001. *True Leaders: How Exceptional CEOs and Presidents Make a Difference by Building People and Profits.* Chicago, IL: Dearborn Trade, pp. 145-146.

3. Bates, Steve. 2001. "Best Practices Shared During First SHRM Executive Institute Forum." *HR News*, July, p. 7.

Appendix A

Self-Evaluations for Managers

One of the things we know about adult learners (and that is what we all should be) is that new learning needs to constantly be reinforced in practical, easily implementable ways. In this section I will share with you a number of exercises and surveys which you can use to measure your progress in creating a workplace of joy.

All of the following exercises are for you to do yourself as an inventory to help you become a better supervisor or manager. Please use this section of the book as you would a personal journal.

Exercise One: "Best Boss/Worst Boss"

Write down the initials of the worst boss you have ever had:

Now write down what that person did to be such a bad boss:

Write down the initials of the person who was the best boss you've ever had:

Now write what that person did to be such a great boss:

Which kind of a boss are *you*? Look at the specific behaviors you have listed and consider if any of them describe the way you manage your employees:

Exercise Two: "Boss/Leader Exercise"

Think about what the words "boss" and "leader" connote to most people. Now, in two columns, list what each one of them does.

What does a *boss* do?　　　What does a *leader* do?

Compare your two lists. Which one are you with your employees? Where does a *boss* get his or her power? Where does a *leader* get his or her power? Is a boss always a leader? Is a leader always a boss?

Exercise Three: "The Gift of Trust"

Think about a boss you had who trusted you completely. How did that make you feel?

What kind of commitment did you have to that manager?

Do you trust your employees? What are some concrete ways you can demonstrate that trust in actionable, believable ways?

Exercise Four: "Rewards and Recognition"

Create a file folder for each one of your direct reports. In it keep a list of human-level things about that employee, including things like the following:

- ▶ Family information
- ▶ Favorite sports teams
- ▶ Where they grew up
- ▶ Where they went to school
- ▶ What their passion is
- ▶ Their favorite food/restaurant
- ▶ Anything else that makes them unique

Ask each employee to make a list of the things they would really like as rewards (things that cost money) and recognition (things that do not cost money). Then add these lists to each person's folder.

Ask each employee to write on a 3x5 card the reasons that they stay at your organization. Keep these cards in each individual's folder.

On your yearly calendar, write down the name of one employee a week on the first day of that week until you have listed each employee at least once during the year. If you have more than 50 employees who report to you directly or are on your team, you will need to write down more than one name per week. Then *commit* to spending a few minutes that first day going through that employee's folder. Ask yourself what you have done to meet that employee's needs and desires. During the rest of that week, at least twice find ways to appreciate that employee in a special way.

Exercise Five: "Blending Work and Family"

In groups of five or six, ask your employees how you might make their lives at home better. List the ideas they come up with and then brainstorm how you might make some of these happen. Do this exercise at least twice a year.

At least once a year provide an opportunity for the families of your employees to visit your workplace. Make this a celebration!

Exercise Six: "Positive Reinforcement"

In his book, *The Greatest Mentor in the World*, Daniel Bent of Honolulu, Hawaii (**www.danbent.com**), shares an experience the main character has followed by an exercise all of us can do:

A young visitor has come to visit Milo, the founder of the company, to gain wisdom as he rises in his organization. This is Milo's advice:

> Let me give you an example of one of the principles passed on to me. Come look out this window. ... You see that shopping center in the distance? One of its anchor tenants is a department store a lot like the one I worked in as a high school kid two evenings a week and on Saturdays. I was lucky to have that job and even luckier to work for its manager, Mr. Jenkins. Well, one Saturday Mr. Jenkins stopped in

the storeroom I worked in, put his hand on my shoulder, looked me in the eye, and said, "I want to talk to you."

When he said that, I was scared; after all, he was the boss and I wondered what I had done wrong. He then said, "I sure admire how neat you keep the storeroom. Some people think the appearance of a storeroom doesn't matter since our customers never see it. But I know differently. I know it affects how efficiently the work in the storeroom gets done. More importantly, it affects how our salespeople who come in here feel about out operation and themselves. You see, if any part of the place they work in is sloppy, then they'll feel it's okay to be sloppy. Believe me, our customers will have a different experience when they come into contact with any salesperson who feels that way."

So, I went from anticipating condemnation to feeling like I was ten feet tall. You can bet that after that the storeroom was as neat as a pin for as long as I worked there....

Over the years, time and again, I would remember Mr. Jenkins' comment on how neat I kept the storeroom, particularly when things weren't going well for me, say when I had made a costly mistake. It was at times like that I would remember Mr. Jenkins' remark. It would help me realize in the tough times that I was valuable and had a contribution to make. At most, the tough time was just a setback and not my fate. I can't tell you how many times I've recalled what he told me, even his exact words. I could even take you back to my hometown and to that department store and show you exactly where I was standing and where Mr. Jenkins was standing when he spoke to me that day....

Mr. Jenkins' remark was indelibly written on my mind. What's more, I've drawn on that remark—made more than fifty-five years ago— many times throughout my career. It's meant a lot to me. But more important is that it has sometimes directly and always indirectly affected how I felt about myself. So in that way it's helped me accomplish what I've done since then in my career.

Dan uses this story as the opening for a signature exercise he does in his keynote speeches and seminars.

The Exercise:

Recall a positive reinforcement experience of your own. Remember some occasion in your past in which someone, perhaps someone in a position of authority, gave you an "attaboy."

▸ How long ago did it happen?

▸ Tell about how clearly you remember it.

▸ Do you think the person who made the comment remembers it?

▸ Under what circumstances have you remembered this incident?

▸ How valuable has this comment been to you?

Milo's summary:

> Consider its significance from what you have said about it. First, that you have remembered it clearly numerous times over the past twenty years. Second, that you remember it in detail, almost word for word. Third, that it has helped you at times when things weren't going so well. Fourth, that it has significantly contributed to your self-esteem. From this, couldn't you say that the remark has been written indelibly on your memory and has helped you accomplish the great things you've been able to achieve throughout your career?

> *(Reprinted with permission from Dan Bent, Honolulu, Hawaii)*

You have the same power. You can give a similar experience to others. It's what I call the "indelible power of positive reinforcement."

Did you find these things to be true of your experience? Share that story with several others, and ask them about their experiences. Since we know that one of the most important things employees want is appreciation, this exercise can help you see the power of the gift you can give every single day.

Appendix B

Nationwide Insurance Employee Survey

The Human Resources Department of Nationwide Insurance in Portland, Oregon, has been kind enough to let us use the survey they give to employees to measure morale and spirit in their workplace. This survey is based on their core values. Although it is anonymous, they ask for the division or place where each respondent works for general tracking.

Each question is ranked on a four-point scale:
1. Strongly Agree
2. Agree
3. Disagree
4. Strongly Disagree

___1. I enjoy the work I do.

___2. I have the authority I need to make decisions and take reasonable risks.

___3. We have enough people in my work group to get our jobs done on time and to do the work well.

___4. My manager respects me and treats me fairly.

___5. I am satisfied with my opportunities for professional growth and development with Nationwide Insurance.

___6. I am satisfied with my pay and benefits.

___7. Nationwide Insurance managers believe diversity in the workplace strengthens our company.

___8. I have the resources (equipment, software, technical assistance, etc.) I need to do a good job.

___9. Our Sales, Claims, and Underwriting functions work together to achieve our goals.

___10. My manager provides me regular coaching and feedback on my performance.

(Reprinted with permission from the HR Department of Nationwide Insurance, Portland, Oregon)

Appendix C

Hoopla! Rating Test with Starter Ideas

John Pearson, the CEO of the Christian Management Association, has created a "Hoopla!" culture in his organization. He says, "The amount of time and resources you spend on 'Hoopla!' is directly proportional to the morale and spirit of your staff. "Hoopla!' is not what you do, it's a monthly summary of who you are and how much you enjoy working together." "Hoopla!" uses celebration, recreation, parties, food, spontaneity, and lots and lots of fun to mitigate workplace stress and show people they're appreciated. Each month take the "Hoopla!" test for your organization.

Here's a test. Answer "yes" or "no" to each statement below regarding your organization's "Hoopla" culture. (If you're in a larger organization, you may prefer to rate your own department.) Check the box for Yes or No for each question.

Yes **No**

❑ ❑ 1. In the last 30 days our team has celebrated the achievement of a key goal or target with a fun or humorous ceremony, coffee break, or event.

❑ ❑ 2. Supervisors are encouraged to honor team members on their individual employment anniversary dates.

❑ ❑ 3. In the last 90 days we have had a spontaneous party, food break or brief "stress reliever" event that was not on the staff calendar.

❑ ❑ 4. In the last 12 months our team has enjoyed an off-site event (such as a picnic, day at the ball park, etc.) during office hours.

❑ ❑ 5. Our dress code includes year-round "business casual clothes" at least one day a week.

❑ ❑ 6. We have a specific budget for staff fun, events, parties, etc.

❑ ❑ 7. Planning fun events for the staff (formal and informal, scheduled and spontaneous) is on someone's job description—and this person knows it!

❑ ❑ 8. We have a written statement of core values which includes our beliefs on the importance of celebrations, valuing people and their accomplishments, and just plain enjoying work and life!

❑ ❑ 9. In the last 12 months we have invested at least $100 per team member on fun.

❑ ❑ 10. When interviewing prospective team members, it's not uncommon to hear, "Your staff tells me it's fun to work at your organization."

Rate your organization by the number of "Yes" responses:

8-10: Congratulations! Team members are highly valued.

6-7: Sounds fun. Moving in the right direction.

4-5: Better do a Hoopla audit before it's too late.

1-3: It may be too late, but try a "Snack Alert" at 3 p.m. today and empower a Hoopla Team immediately.

(Reprinted with permission from the Christian Management Association)

If you need starter ideas, here are just a few:

▶ Do breakfast followed by a bucket of golf balls at a driving range.

▶ Schedule a staff meeting and, when everyone's assembled, go out for ice cream cones.

▶ Give team members five dollars each to buy a "stress reliever" toy for their desk or cubicle.

▶ Provide free soft drinks and pretzels every Friday afternoon.

▶ Hold an Academy Awards ceremony for the best staff team "home video" on "How We Deal with Stress?"

▶ Install a putting green in the conference room and hold daily "best out of 10 balls" tournaments.

You get the idea. Have fun!

Appendix D

Bibliography

Books and Articles

Allen, Janis, and McCarthy, Michael. 2000. *You Made My Day: Creating Co-Worker Recognition and Relationships.* New York: Lebhar-Friedman Books.

Berrentine, Pat. 1993. *When the Canary Stops Singing: Women's Persepectives on Transforming Business.* San Francisco: Berrett-Koehler.

Block, Peter. 1993. *Stewardship: Choosing Service over Self-Interest.* San Francisco: Berrett-Koehler.

Branham, F. Leigh. 2000. *Keeping the People Who Keep You in Business: 24 Ways to Hang On to Your Most Valuable Talent.* New York: AMACOM.

Briskin, Alan. 1996. *The Stirring of Soul in the Workplace.* San Francisco: Jossey-Bass.

Buckingham, Marcus, and Curt Coffman. 1999. *First, Break All the Rules: What the World's Greatest Managers Do Differently.* New York: Simon & Schuster.

Chappell, Tom. 1993. *The Soul of a Business: Managing for Profit and the Common Good.* New York: Bantam Doubleday Dell Publishing Group.

Cloke, Kenneth, and Goldsmith, Joan. 1996. *Thank God It's Monday,* New York: McGraw-Hill.

Cox, Allan. 1996. *Redefining Corporate Soul: Linking Purpose and People.* New York: McGraw-Hill.

Daniels, Aubrey C. 1994. *Bringing Out the Best in People.* New York: McGraw-Hill.

Emmerich, Roxanne. 1997. *Thank God It's Monday.* Minneapolis: Banner Press.

Glanz, Barbara A. 1996. *CARE Packages for the Workplace: Dozens of Little Things You Can Do to Regenerate Spirit at Work.* New York: McGraw-Hill.

Glanz, Barbara A. 1993, 1998. *The Creative Communicator: 399 Ways to Make Your Business Communications Meaningful and Inspiring.* New York: McGraw-Hill.

Good, Sharon. 1994. *Managing with a Heart: 100+ Ways to Make Your Employees Feel Appreciated.* New York: Excalibur Publishing.

Hansen, Mark Victor, Rogerson, Maida, Rutte, Martin, and Clauss, Tim. 1996. *Chicken Soup for the Soul at Work.* Deerfield Beach, FL: Health Communications.

Harder, David. 2000. *The Truth About Work: Making a Life and a Living.* Deerfield Beach, FL: Health Communications.

Harris, Jim, and Brannick, Joan. 1999. *Finding and Keeping Great Employees.* New York: AMACOM.

Harvey, Eric. 2000. *180 Ways to Walk the Recognition Talk*. Dallas: The WALK THE TALK Company.

Herman, Roger E., and Gioia, Joyce L. 1998. *Lean and Meaningful: A New Culture for Corporate America*. Winchester, VA: Oakhill Press.

Herman, Roger E. 1999. *Keeping Good People*. Winchester, VA: Oakhill Press.

Herman, Roger E., and Gioia, Joyce L. 2000. *How to Become an Employer of Choice*. Winchester, VA: Oakhill Press.

_____, with Andrew T. Perry. 2000. *How to Choose Your Next Employer*. Winchester, VA: Oakhill Press.

Herman, Roger E., and Gioia, Joyce L. 2000. *Workforce Stability: Your Competitive Edge*. Winchester, VA: Oakhill Press.

Herman, Roger E. 2002 *Impending Crisis*. Winchester, VA: Oakhill Press.

Huey, John, Ed. 2001. "The 100 Best Companies to Work For." *Fortune,* January 22.

Jeffries, Rosalind. 1996. *101 Recognition Secrets: Tools for Motivating and Recognizing Today's Workforce*. Chevy Chase, MD: Performance Enhancement Group.

Kaye, Beverly, and Jordan-Evans, Sharon. 1999. *Love 'Em or Lose 'Em—Getting Good People to Stay*. San Francisco: Berrett-Koehler.

Littman, Margaret. 2000. "Best Bosses Tell All." *Working Woman,* October.

Nelson, Bob. 1994. *1001 Ways to Reward Employees*. New York: Workman Publishing.

O'Reilly, Charles A., and Pfeffer, Jeffrey. 2000. *Hidden Value: How Great Companies Achieve Extraordinary Results with Ordinary People*. Boston: Harvard Business School Press.

Peale, Norman Vincent. 1967. *Enthusiasm Makes the Difference*. New York: Prentice Hall.

Price, Bette, and Ritcheske, George. 2001. *True Leaders: How Exceptional CEOs and Presidents Make a Difference by Building People and Profits.* Chicago: Dearborn Trade.

Sheerer, Robin A. 1999. *No More Blue Mondays: Four Keys to Finding Fulfillment at Work.* Palo Alto, CA: Davies-Black Publishing.

Silberman, Mel. 1999. *101 Ways to Make Meetings Active.* San Francisco: Jossey-Bass.

Terez, Tom. MeaningfulWorkplace.com.

Weinstein, Matt. 1996. *Managing to Have Fun.* New York: Simon & Schuster.

Whyte, David. 1994. *The Heart Aroused: Poetry and the Preservation of the Soul in Corporate America.* New York: Currency/Doubleday.

Wingfield, Barb, and Berry, Janice. 2001. *Retaining Your Employees.* Menlo Park, CA: Crisp Learning.

Yager, Jan. 1997. *Friendshifts™—The Power of Friendship and How It Shapes Our Lives,* Stamford, CT: Hannacroix Creek Books, Inc.

Studies

Aon Consulting. 2000. *United States @ Work® Study 2000.* Chicago. 800-438-6487.

Development Dimensions International. February 2001. *Retaining Talent: A Benchmarking Study* by Paul R. Bernthal and Richard Wellings, Bridgeville, PA. 800-334-1514.

Newsletters

Success in Recruiting and Retaining. McLean, VA: National Institute of Business Management, 800-543-2049.

The Motivational Manager. Chicago: Lawrence Ragan Communications, Inc. 800-878-5331.

Employee Recruitment & Retention. Chicago: Lawrence Ragan Communications, Inc. 800-878-5331.

Rewarding Employees. Nelson, Bob, Ed. San Diego: Nelson Motivation, Inc. 800-575-5521.

The Glanz Employee Motivation (GEM) Survey

Behavioral Survey for Employees

This survey is made up of all the specific behaviors that our research showed employees wanted from supervisors or managers. Because these behaviors are observable, are measurable, and can be replicated, supervisors and managers can choose to add these behaviors to their management style or change those specific behaviors that are hindering positive relationships with their employees.

For a per-person fee, supervisors and managers can have each of their direct reports anonymously fill out the survey online, using a secure link. Also managers can complete the survey on themselves to determine their own perception of their management style. Supervisors or managers may then receive an analysis of how their employees perceive their behaviors, a comparison of their own perception with those of others, an analysis of how they score compared with scores of other managers in their organization, if applicable, and an analysis of how their score compares to with scores of other supervisors and managers in their industry.

Options may include a gap analysis report, the report plus a handbook with references to applicable pages in the text that can strengthen specific behaviors, and an individual consulting report with follow-up.

For more information on the GEM Survey, go to **www.barbaraglanz.com/gem** or call 708-246-8594 (before September 2002) or 941-312-9169 (after September 2002).

About the Author

Barbara Glanz, CSP, works with organizations that want to improve morale, retention, and service and with people who want to rediscover the joy in their work and in their lives. She is the author of *CARE Packages for the Workplace: Dozens of Little Things You Can Do to Regenerate Spirit at Work* (McGraw-Hill, 1996), *The Creative Communicator* (McGraw-Hill, 1998), *Building Customer Loyalty* (McGraw-Hill, 1994), and *CARE Packages for the Home: Dozens of Ways to Regenerate Spirit Where You Live* (Andrews McMeel, 1998).

As an internationally known speaker, trainer, and consultant who has a master's degree in adult education, Barbara lives and breathes her personal motto: "Spreading Contagious Enthusiasm."™ Her focus areas are *Regenerating Spirit in the Workplace*, *Building Customer and Employee Loyalty*, *Embracing Change*, and *Blending Work and Family*, and she has presented on four continents and in 48 states.

More than just an exciting speaker, consultant, and author, Barbara has three additional "claims to fame." Her great-grandfather laid the cornerstone where the four states come together (Page, Arizona, is named after him); she played the piano on the TV show "Talent Sprouts"; and she directed David Hasselhof of "Knight Rider" and "Baywatch" fame in his first high school play! Barbara divides her time between her home in Illinois and her writing retreat in Sarasota, Florida, which will soon become her permanent home. She is blessed with three wonderful children and two precious grandchildren, and she has a deep sense of mission about the importance of the work she does.

For more information, contact:
Barbara Glanz Communications, Inc.
E-mail: bglanz@barbaraglanz.com

Web site: www.barbaraglanz.com

(until September 2002)

4047 Howard Avenue
Western Springs, IL 60558
Phone: 708-246-8594
Fax: 708-246-5123

(after September 2002)

6140 Midnight Pass Road, #802
Sarasota, FL 34242
Phone: 941-312-9169
Fax: 941-349-8209